HISPANIAE

Spain and the development of
Roman imperialism,
218–82 BC

HISPANIAE

Spain and the development of
Roman imperialism,
218–82 BC

*

J. S. RICHARDSON
Lecturer in Ancient History,
University of St Andrews

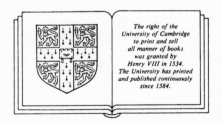

The right of the
University of Cambridge
to print and sell
all manner of books
was granted by
Henry VIII in 1534.
The University has printed
and published continuously
since 1584.

CAMBRIDGE UNIVERSITY PRESS
CAMBRIDGE
LONDON   NEW YORK   NEW ROCHELLE
MELBOURNE   SYDNEY

PUBLISHED BY THE PRESS SYNDICATE OF THE UNIVERSITY OF CAMBRIDGE
The Pitt Building, Trumpington Street, Cambridge, United Kingdom

CAMBRIDGE UNIVERSITY PRESS
The Edinburgh Building, Cambridge CB2 2RU, UK
40 West 20th Street, New York NY 10011–4211, USA
477 Williamstown Road, Port Melbourne, VIC 3207, Australia
Ruiz de Alarcón 13, 28014 Madrid, Spain
Dock House, The Waterfront, Cape Town 8001, South Africa

http://www.cambridge.org

First published 1986
First paperback edition 2004

A catalogue record for this book is available from the British Library

Library of Congress Cataloguing in Publication data
Richardson, J. S. (John S.)
Hispaniae, Spain and the development of
Roman imperialism, 218–82 BC.
1. Spain – History – Roman period, 218 B.C.–A.D. 414
I. Title.
DP94.R53   1986   936.6′03   86-8212

ISBN 0 521 32183 2 hardback
ISBN 0 521 52134 3 paperback

IN MEMORIAM
M. W. F.
R. H. R.
SCRIPTI ET SCRIPTORIS
PATRVM

Contents

Maps

Preface

The collection of the material on which this book is based began as part of the preparation of an Oxford D. Phil. thesis in 1968. The completion of that thesis four years later was, as it turned out, only a stage in a prolonged process of investigation and interpretation, whose results are presented here. In 1968 I proposed to look at all the overseas development of the Roman empire in the second century BC, and it was Sir Ronald Syme, as Camden Professor in Oxford, who suggested that I should begin with Spain, as that might prove the most fruitful area for my purpose. Seventeen years later, I have no reason to contest the wisdom of that advice, and to him and to Martin Frederiksen, who supervised my research with characteristic care and sustaining enthusiasm, I owe even more than I realised at the time.

The extended production of this book could never have been achieved without the help, encouragement and critical good sense of a host of friends, colleagues and pupils too numerous to mention; but I particularly wish to thank Michel Austin, Jill Harries and Geoffrey Rickman, my colleagues in St Andrews; Michael Crawford and Andrew Lintott in England; Professor P. G. Walsh of Glasgow, whose reading of one draft removed many errors; Amanda Pugh, who struggled with a hideous manuscript to produce a legible typescript; and above all my wife, Patricia Richardson, who has lived with Roman Spain for as long as I have. My thanks are also due to the Leverhulme Trust and the British Academy, whose generosity made possible extended visits to Italy and Spain in 1979 and 1983 respectively.

I should also mention that Stephen L. Dyson's book, *The creation of the Roman frontier* (Princeton 1985), appeared too late for me to take full account of his argument in this book.

JOHN RICHARDSON

St Salvator's College
St Andrews
September 1985

Abbreviations

The following works are referred to in abbreviated form.

Astin, A. E. *Scipio Aemilianus* (Oxford 1967) (= *Scipio Aemilianus*) *Cato the Censor* (Oxford 1978) (= *Cato*)

Briscoe, John. *A commentary on Livy, books XXXI–XXXIII* (Oxford 1973) (= *Commentary xxxi–xxxiii*)
A commentary on Livy, books XXXIV–XXXVII (Oxford 1981) (= *Commentary xxxiv–xxxvii*)

Broughton, T. R. S. *The magistrates of the Roman republic*, 2 vols. and supplement (New York 1951, 1952 and 1960) (= *MRR*)

Brunt, P. A. *Italian manpower 225 BC – AD 14* (Oxford 1971) (= *Italian manpower*)

Crawford, M. H. *Roman republican coinage*, 2 vols. (Cambridge 1974) (= *RRC*)

Dahlheim, Werner. *Struktur und Entwicklung des romischen Volkerrechts im dritten und zweiten Jahrhundert v. Christ* (Munich 1968) (= *Struktur und Entwicklung*)
Gewalt und Herrschaft: das provinziale Herrshaftssystem der römischen Republik (Berlin 1977) (= *Gewalt und Herrschaft*)

Galsterer, Hartmut. *Untersuchungen zum römischen Stadtewesen auf der iberischen Halbinsel* (Berlin 1971) (= *Untersuchungen*)

Harris, W. V. *War and imperialism in republican Rome 327–70 BC* (Oxford 1979) (= *War and imperialism*)

Jashemski, W. F. *The origins and history of the proconsular and propraetorian imperium* (Chicago 1950) (= *Proconsular and propraetorian imperium*)

Klotz, A. *Livius und seine Vorgänger* (Berlin/Leipzig, 1940–41) (= *Livius*)

Knapp, R. C. *Aspects of the Roman experience in Iberia 206–100 BC* (Vallodolid 1977) (= *Aspects*)

Lazenby, J. F. *Hannibal's war* (Warminster 1978) (= *Hannibal's war*)

Marquardt, J. *Römische Staatsverwaltung*, 3 vols. (2nd edition, Leipzig 1881–85) (= *Röm. Staatsverwaltung*)

Mommsen, Th. *Römisches Staatsrecht*, 3 vols. (Leipzig 1887–89) (= *StR*)
Römisches Strafrecht (Leipzig 1899) (= *Röm. Strafrecht*)

Abbreviations

Münzer, F. *Römische Adelsparteien und Adelsfamilien* (Stuttgart 1920) (= *Röm. Adelsparteien*)

Nostrand, J. J. van. *Economic survey of ancient Rome* II (Baltimore 1937) 119–224 (= *ESAR* III)

Riccobono, S. *Fontes Iuris Romani Antejustiniani* I (Florence 1941) (= *FIRA*)

Rich, J. W. *Declaring war in the Roman republic in the period of transmarine expansion* (Brussels 1976) (= *Declaring war*)

Sanctis, G. de. *Storia dei romani*, 4 vols. (Turin/Florence 1907–1964) (= *Storia*)

Schulten, A. *Numantia*, 4 vols. (Munich 1914–1929) (= *Numantia*) *Fontes Hispaniae antiquae* vols. III and IV (Barcelona 1935, 1937) (= *FHA*)

Scullard, H. H. *Scipio Africanus in the second Punic war* (Cambridge 1930) (= *Scipio Africanus*)

Roman politics 220–150 BC (2nd edition, Oxford 1973) (= *Roman politics*[2])

Simon, H. *Roms Kriege in Spanien 154–133 v. Chr.* (Frankfurt 1962) (= *Roms Kriege*)

Walbank, F. W. *A historical commentary on Polybius*, 3 vols. (Oxford 1957, 1967, 1979) (= *Commentary*)

Wilson, A. L. N. *Emigration from Italy in the republican age of Rome* (Manchester 1966) (= *Emigration*)

CHAPTER I

Spain and Roman imperialism

The Roman senate first assigned Spain as a *provincia* in 218 BC. According to Livy, the meeting, held probably in March, ordered that *Hispania* should be one of the two areas named for the consuls of the year, the other being 'Africa with Sicily'.[1] Thereafter Spain appeared on the annual list of *provinciae* throughout the period of the republic, usually, after 197 BC, in the form of two areas, *Hispania citerior* and *Hispania ulterior*, nearer and further Spain;[2] and indeed remained under the control of Roman forces and Roman governors at least until the Vandal invasions in the fifth century AD.

The early part of this prolonged involvement of Rome in Spain coincided with the growth of Roman power throughout the Mediterranean basin, beginning in the third century with the wars against Carthage and reaching a climax in the middle of the first century in the wars of the imperial republic in East and West under the command of Pompey and Caesar. It is not surprising therefore that it is on this period in particular that attention has been focussed in the attempt to determine the nature of Roman imperialism.[3] Imperialism is not a static phenomenon, but a process of aggressive acquisition leading to the establishment of some type of domination by one national group over others. None would doubt that by the end of the republic Rome had acquired such domination over most of the peoples of the Mediterranean, and of some, notably in Spain, Gaul and the East, who lived a considerable distance from it. So obvious a growth might be expected to provide material for a straightforward analysis of the empire that it produced and of the factors which produced it. In fact the study of Roman imperialism has been beset by apparent contradictions and anomalies. Some scholars, impressed by the repeated

---

[1] Livy 21.17.1; on the debate and its date, see Rich, *Declaring war* 28–44.

[2] Occasionally, even after 197, the two *provinciae* were amalgamated (Livy 42.28.5–6; 43.15.3). It is probable that the first occasion on which Spain was absent from the senate's annual list of *provinciae* was in 54, following the assignment of Pompey to the peninsula for five years under the lex Trebonia.

[3] Thus, for instance E. Badian, *Roman imperialism in the late republic* (Oxford 1968); Dahlheim, *Gewalt und Herrschaft*; D. Musti, *Polibio e l'imperialismo romano* (Naples 1978); and Harris, *War and imperialism*. Each treats Roman imperialism in this period in a markedly different fashion.

withdrawals of Roman armies from Greece and Asia Minor after the completion of successful wars during the first half of the second century, have argued that Rome's apparent empire-building was the result of a policy of misguided self-defence against largely imaginary threats to her own security.[4] Others, and in particular W. V. Harris, believe that the Roman senate was determined, for motives of greed and the exercise of military power, to annex any territory it could.[5] J. A. Schumpeter saw Rome as a classic case of an aristocratic oligarchy needing to preserve its control of the machinery of the state by continually providing national glory,[6] while Paul Veyne finds the process by which the empire was won so dull and pedestrian as to make him wonder whether there was such a thing as Roman imperialism at all.[7]

Some of these anomalies respond to semantic investigation, both of ancient and of modern usages. Among the latter 'imperialism' itself, with its overtones of late nineteenth-century jingoism and early twentieth-century Leninism, is a notoriously difficult concept,[8] and simply to equate it with military aggression does little to clarify the issues involved. Athens in the fifth century BC, Britain in the nineteenth and Israel in the twentieth century AD may all be said to be militarily aggressive powers, but their imperialisms and their empires are substantially different. In the case of ancient usages, the problems are of another type, but not less daunting. For the age of Cicero and Augustus, there is enough evidence in the Latin authors to show that the extension of Roman power to the edges of the known world was an accepted, almost a commonplace, idea,[9] but, from the third century through to the early first century, it is only Greek sources, and most notably Polybius, which provide any contemporary comment. Such views, valuable though they are, cannot be taken without question to represent the opinions of the men who at this time were creating the Roman empire.[10]

---

[4] So Th. Mommsen, *Römische Geschichte* I[11] (Berlin 1912) 699: 'Nur die stumpfe Unbilligkeit kann es verkennen, dass Rom in dieser Zeit [i.e. after the Hannibalic war] noch keineswegs nach der Herrschaft über die Mittelmeerstaaten griff, sondern nichts weiter begehrte als in Africa und in Griechenland ungefährliche Nachbarn zu haben.' For a history of this concept, see J. Linderski 'Si vis pacem, para bellum: concepts of defensive imperialism', in W. V. Harris (ed.), *The imperialism of mid-republican Rome* (Papers and monographs of the American Academy in Rome, 29, 1984) 133–64.   [5] Harris [n. 3].

[6] In his essay 'The sociology of imperialisms', in *Imperialism and social classes* (Oxford 1951) 68.

[7] P. Veyne, *MEFR* 87 (1975) 795–855, esp. 804ff.

[8] As seen by Musti [n. 3] 13–39, but missed, optimistically, by Harris, *War and imperialism* 4–5.

[9] P. A. Brunt, 'Laus imperii' in eds. P. D. A. Garnsey and C. R. Whittaker, *Imperialism in the ancient world* (Cambridge 1978) 158–91. On the difficulties of *imperium Romanum* as a geographical expression, see A. W. Lintott, *G&R* 28 (1981) 53–67; and in legal terms, D. Kienast, *ZSS* 85 (1968) 330–67.

[10] See my article in *PBSR* 47 (1979) 1–11.

For these reasons the investigation of what the Romans were in fact doing in those areas in which they were present in force is of particular importance. Not only are the patterns which may be discovered in such activity the surest indication of attitudes, both in the senate and in the field, to the growth of the empire; but also the way in which decisions were made and policy laid down in this first period of expansion outside Italy created the background of experience and expectation against which the development of the Roman empire must be seen. For such an investigation, the *provinciae* in Spain yield essential evidence. There the continuity of a Roman military presence allows scope for a comparison of the ways in which Roman aims and methods developed, and the extent of the alteration which that presence brought about in the two centuries which separated the beginning of the Hannibalic war from the subjugation of the north-west under Augustus demonstrates the process whereby such an area became part of the Roman empire.

When Roman forces first landed at the Massiliote colony of Emporion late in 218, the only links they had in the peninsula were with Saguntum, which had been destroyed the year before by Hannibal, and with the string of Massiliote trading posts down the east coast at Rhode (Rosas), Emporion (Ampurias), Hemeroskopeion (Denia) and Alonis (Benidorm). By the time the final conquest of Spain had been completed, with the subjugation of Cantabria and Asturia in the north and north-west two centuries later, and the three *provinciae* of Baetica, Lusitania and Tarraconensis established, the peninsula contained 26 *coloniae*, 24 *municipia civium Romanorum*, 48 communities holding Latin rights, 6 *civitates liberae*, 4 *foederatae* and 291 *stipendariae*. The whole area, with the exception of the newly conquered northern coast, was divided into *conventus* for the purposes of the administration of justice by Roman magistrates.[11] Moreover the regions which had been longest under Roman influence, in Baetica and Tarraconensis, were so far 'Romanised' that the Turdetani in the Baetis valley were said to have lost their own customs and speech in favour of Roman ways and the Latin language, while the Celtiberians in the Ebro valley modelled their life on an Italian pattern and wore the toga.[12] These areas at least had all the administrative apparatus and socio-economic structure that is associated with a fully-fledged, established Roman province. Of course much of this development

[11] For the administrative details, Pliny, *NH* 3.6–17 (Baetica); 3.18–30 (Tarraconensis); 4.113–18 (Lusitania); Marquardt, *Röm. Staatsverwaltung* I², 251–60; M. I. Henderson, *JRS* 32 (1942) 1–13; N. Mackie, *Local administration in Roman Spain AD 14–212* (BAR International Series 172, 1983). It is possible that Pliny overestimated the number of colonies by two (Henderson, *art. cit.*, 2–3).

[12] Strabo 3.2.15 (p. 151); 3.4.20 (p. 167).

took place at the end of the period, particularly in the founding of *coloniae* and the grants of the Latin right by Julius Caesar and Augustus; but the *ius Latii* was itself in part the recognition of a long process which had made certain Spanish communities appropriate recipients of this honourable and very 'Italian' status.[13] The geographer, Artemidorus of Ephesus, writing at the end of the second century BC, remarked on the use of the Roman alphabet among the Spaniards living on the seaboard,[14] and the outlines of the administrative arrangements had been laid down long before. The emergence of the Spanish provinces, as they were known in the late republic and early empire, was an extended and gradual process.

Yet although the Spanish provinces and their institutions were the product of a considerable length of time, the same Roman constitutional mechanism, the *provincia*, underlay the whole period. The *provincia* of Hispania existed from March 218. The next two centuries saw the change from the Roman presence being confined to a tiny enclave on the east coast between the river Ebro and the Pyrenees to its extension to cover the whole of modern Spain and Portugal; and within this Rome's network of alliance and dependence, and with it the fiscal and legal systems that embodied Roman control in the provinces, grew from nothing to cover the communities and peoples which the elder Pliny describes.[15] Throughout this time the formal procedures which set up the commands in Spain remained virtually unaltered: year by year the main, and often the only, business of the senate in Rome connected with the area was the naming of the *provinciae* of Hispania Citerior and Hispania Ulterior to be allotted, usually to praetors, for the exercise of consular *imperium*,[16] or the extension of the commands of such governors already present there. It was not until Pompey was assigned the whole of Spain for five years under the terms of the lex Trebonia in 55 BC that there was any major alteration in the process.[17]

This combination of development and conservatism, so typical of many areas of Roman life, can be seen also in the changing content of the idea of the *provincia*. Throughout the middle and late republic and the early

[13] Henderson [n. 11] 11–12; Sherwin-White, *The Roman Citizenship*[2] (Oxford 1973) 232–5; Galsterer, *Untersuchungen* 7–30.

[14] Artemidorus fr. 22: καὶ ᾽Αρτεμίδωρος ἐν δευτέρῳ τῶν γεωγραφουμένων· γραμματικῇ δὲ χρῶνται τῇ τῶν ᾽Ιταλῶν οἱ παρὰ θάλατταν οἰκοῦντες τῶν ᾽Ιβήρων. Artemidorus' second book dealt with the area covered by the two *provinciae* of his day (fr. 21), excluding Lusitania, which was dealt with in bk 3 (fr. 31). It cannot be argued, however, (as F. Lasserre, *Strabo* II (Coll. Univ. de Rouen, Paris 1966) 193) that this passage shows the complete Romanisation of Turdetania in Artemidorus' time.   [15] Above n. 11.

[16] On this see further pp. 55–7, 75–7, 109–12 below.   [17] Dio Cassius 39.33.

empire one element in the meaning of the word was that of a task or function assigned to a magistrate, in the fulfilment of which he would exercise the *imperium* granted to him by virtue of his election by the people in the *comitia centuriata*.[18] Such a function could comprise a command in a particular geographical area, but need not do so. Livy several times describes an Italian tribe as a consul's *provincia*.[19] During the second Punic war 'the fleet' or 'the war with Hannibal' could be the name of a *provincia*, and later the treasury for a quaestor, or the *urbana provincia* for a praetor marked the allocation of jurisdiction within the city.[20] The meaning is still clearer in the transferred uses of the word. Plautus uses it on ten occasions, always humorously, and usually in a context which makes explicit the comparison between the normal official and military use and the mundane and often underhand activities of the characters in his plays. The same is true of the two occurrences in Terence's comedies.[21] In all these cases the meaning of *provincia* is 'task' or 'undertaking', and in only one, (in which a bailiff's work on a farm is described as his '*provincia*') is there any territorial suggestion.[22] This strand of meaning ('task' or 'function') is still found in Cicero in a humorous context;[23] and in another place he describes the tendencies of falling atoms either to swerve or not to swerve as their '*provinciae*'.[24]

The *provincia* as an allotted task or function appears to be the original use of the word, or at least that usage is the earliest of which we have evidence. During the second half of the first century BC there are clear signs that the word could mean a geographical area equipped with the set of institutions that made up the provincial administration of the late republic: in other words, that *provincia* could also mean 'province'. The sense of a *provincia* being somewhere remote from Rome, where Roman magistrates acted, is found in the second century: both the elder Cato and C. Gracchus, in preserved fragments, spoke of being 'in provincia' in a way which could almost be translated 'on overseas service'.[25] By the time that Caesar was writing his commentaries on his campaigns in Gaul, he

---

[18] Mommsen *StR* I³, 51, 116–36, 468; *Oxford Latin Dictionary*, s.v. provincia 1. The etymology is uncertain (see A. Walde and J. B. Hofmann, *Lateinisches etymologisches Wörterbuch* II (Heidelberg 1954) 377–8).

[19] Livy 3.25.9; 6.30.3; 27.22.2.

[20] Livy 24.9.5. (*classis*) (cf. 44.1.3); 24.44.1, 25.3.3 (*bellum cum Hannibale*); *CIL* I², 583.68 (*aerarium*); Cic. *I Verr.* 1.40.104 (*urbana provincia*).

[21] Plautus, *Capt.* 156, 158, 474; *Cas.* 103; *Mil. Glor.* 1159; *Pseud.* 148, 158; *Stich.* 698–9; *Trin.* 190. Terence, *HT* 516; *Phorm.* 72.

[22] Plaut. *Cas.* 103: 'abi rus, abi dierectus tuam in provinciam.'

[23] Cic. *Cael.* 26.63: 'non dubito quin sint pergraves qui…eam provinciam susceperint ut in balneas contruderentur.'   [24] Cic. *de fin.* 1.20.

[25] Cato fr. 132 (*ORF³*); Gracchus fr. 26 (*ORF³*). Cf. Catullus 10.19.

could refer to the decision of the Roman people in 121 BC not to reduce the conquered Averni and the Ruteni to a province, nor to impose a tax.[26] From then on the phrases 'in formam...' or 'in formulam provinciae redigere' are frequently used of generals turning areas already conquered into provinces,[27] and are used on a series of milestones from Arabia as a description of the official process by which the Arabian province was created.[28] This implies a set of norms, a 'forma provinciae', to which the administration of an area had to conform in order to be a province; but there remains a tension between this usage and the older meaning of 'provincia' which we have already noted. The tribes and peoples which Velleius, for instance, in listing the achievements of the republic in creating the empire, says were each 'redacta in formulam provinciae stipendaria facta',[29] had all of them been assigned as *provinciae* to Roman magistrates before this step was taken. More revealing still is the brief remark made by the epitomator of Livy, who summarises the work of Aemilius Paullus in Macedonia in 167 with the words 'Macedonia in provinciae formam redacta'.[30] Though these words do not appear in the extant passages of Livy book 45 which deal with Paullus' arrangements,[31] they are remarkable both because Macedonia was already the name of the *provincia* of Paullus,[32] and because the result of his work was *not* to turn the area into a province, but into four allegedly independent states. There was no *provincia* decreed by the senate in Macedonia after 167 until 149, when the praetor P. Iuventius went out to oppose Andriscus, the pretender to the Macedonian throne.[33] Here the epitomator must mean that Paullus set up the institutional framework that was to govern the administration and government of the four 'republics', and which indeed was used long after when Macedonia became a Roman province.[34]

The content of the word *provincia* can be seen to develop through the last two centuries BC, so that it came to acquire not only the meaning 'task' or 'function' when used of a magistrate, but also the geographical and institutional significance of a 'province' in the modern English sense. This development coincided with the emergence of those institutions

[26] Caes. *BG* 1.45.2: 'neque in provinciam redigisset neque stipendium imposuisset'.

[27] Livy, *per.* 45; 134; Vell. 2.38.1, 2; 2.97.4; Tac. *Agr.* 14; *Ann.* 2.56; Suet. *Rhet.* 30; *Iul.* 25.1; *Aug.* 18.2; *Tib.* 37.4; *Cal.* 1.2; *Nero* 18; *Vesp.* 8.4.

[28] *CIL*, III, 14149.19, 21, 30, 39, 42, 50; 14150.11 all from 111 AD.

[29] Vell. 2.38.1.   [30] Livy, *per.* 45.

[31] It is possible that the epitomator was influenced by the words 'Macedoniae formula dicta' (Livy 45.31.1).   [32] Livy 45.16.2, cf. 44.19.1.

[33] Arrangements for Macedonia: Livy 45.29.4–30.8. For Iuventius, see Broughton, *MRR* I, 458.

[34] Livy's note that his laws stood the test of a long period of use must mean that they continued in use after the 30-year life of the four 'republics' (Livy 45.32.7).

which made up the provinces of the late republic and early empire. Moreover this is a change the importance of which is not simply semantic and philological. By the time of Augustus, at least, the provinces were seen as the central component of the empire; the gradual shift in the idea of the *provincia* marks the emergence of the Romans' own view of what their empire was.[35] For the study of this pattern of ideas and their development, the study of the early years of Roman Spain is of particular significance and fascination.

At the time of the first allotment of Hispania as a *provincia*, the institutions of 'provincial' rule in the later sense had scarcely begun to appear. The treaty drawn up in 241 between the Romans and the Carthaginians at the end of the first Punic war had laid down that the Carthaginians should evacuate Sicily and the islands between Sicily and Italy, and a similar clause ensured a Carthaginian withdrawal from Sardinia, following the Roman descent upon the island in 238/7.[36] In Sicily we have no evidence of a Roman presence for some 14 years. It is inconceivable that the Romans took no immediate steps to ensure at least the military security of the western part of the island following a war lasting for 24 years which had been fought specifically in order to wrest control from Carthage. There is no sign, however, that it was assigned as a *provincia* during this period. If a *provincia* was at this time a task given to a magistrate, the question which must be answered is 'Which magistrate?' Though our sources are scanty in the extreme, we know that for most of the 230s the consuls were occupied elsewhere, while the two praetors were primarily concerned with jurisdiction in Rome itself, and although they occasionally undertook additional responsibilities outside Italy[37] at this time, they can hardly have had a regular oversight of what must have been a sensitive area. It is possible that a non-magistrate was voted *imperium*, a method certainly used in Spain between 210 and 197, but there is nothing to suggest such a procedure in Sicily, nor any indication of the activity of the fairly substantial body of troops which, if the Spanish parallel were to be pressed, would be expected.[38] A more plausible guess is that the Romans relied on their ally, Hiero of Syracuse, supported at most by a naval squadron which may have been stationed at Lilybaeum; but there is no trace of such a force, nor of its commander,

[35] See my 'Polybius' view of the Roman empire', *PBSR* 47 (1979).
[36] Polybius 3.27.2 and 8.
[37] Thus P. Cornelius, said by Zonaras (8.18) to have died on service in Sardinia in 234.
[38] On the situation in Spain between 210 and 197 see below p. 66. These men certainly had *provinciae* and *imperium consulare* and commanded at least one legion.

who would presumably have been a *duovir navalis*.[39] Under such circumstances Sicily would not have been a *provincia*.[40]

In Sardinia, things were very different. After the first occupation of the island by Ti. Sempronius Gracchus, the consul of 238, we hear of campaigns fought there and in Corsica each year down to and including 231, always under the command of a consul.[41] On each of these occasions at least, Corsica and/or Sardinia must have formed a *provincia*, probably, if later practice may be taken as indicative, consisting of the two islands together.[42] Our record of military involvement only ceases with the outbreak of the Illyrian war in 230.

In 227 Rome took what proved to be the momentous step of increasing the number of praetors elected annually to four, two to continue as previously with primary responsibility for urban jurisdiction, two to be sent abroad, to Sicily and Sardinia.[43] This meant that thereafter the responsibility for these areas would be assigned as *provinciae* to magistrates of the city of Rome. It is interesting to note that Solinus, writing in the third century AD, regards this as the date at which each of the two islands (Sicily *and* Sardinia) became a *provincia*.[44]

It is impossible to be certain why this change was made at this point, but it is likely that it was in some way connected with the disruption caused by the war with Teuta and the Illyrian dynasts. Seen with hindsight, the Illyrian expedition of 229 looks like a relatively small-scale punitive raid, a natural stage in the development of Roman aggressive imperialism.[45] At the time the perspective will have been different. Polybius, writing in the next century, preserves something of the sense of surprise that must have been felt by the Greek world at this 'first crossing under arms of the Romans into Illyria and this part of Europe'.[46] For the Romans themselves, this was the first venture overseas since they

---

[39] On the *duoviri navales* see Mommsen, *StR* II³, 579–81; J. H. Thiel, *A history of Roman sea-power before the second Punic war* (Amsterdam 1954), 9–28, argues for the disappearance of the institution between 282 and 181.

[40] Cicero's remark that Sicily 'prima omnium, id quod ornamentum imperi est, provincia est appellata' (*II Verr.* 2.1.2) was not intended as a precise observation on the administrative machinery of the years 241–227, and should not be understood as such.

[41] For references, see Broughton, *MRR* I, 221–6.

[42] Though the joint administration is only referred to in a remarkably unreliable passage of Festus (*Brev.* 4), the fact is confirmed by the practice of the early second century – cf. Livy 40.18.3, 19.6, 34.12; 42.1.3, 7.2; Marquardt *Röm. Staatsverwaltung* I², 248.

[43] The increase in numbers is reported by Livy, *per.* 20, and connected explicitly with the government of the two provinces by Pomponius (D. 1.2.2.32) and Solinus (5.1).

[44] Solinus 5.1: 'utraque insula in Romanum arbitratum redacta iisdem temporibus facta provincia est, cum eodem anno Sardiniam M. Valerius, alteram C. Flaminius praetor sortiti sint.'

[45] This is the view, for instance, of Harris, *War and imperialism*, ch. 5, esp. pp. 195–7.

[46] Pol. 2.12.7.

had driven the Carthaginians from Sicily and invaded Sardinia. In particular, it was an amphibious operation which involved both consuls, whose predecessors from 238 down to 231 had been largely involved with Sardinia; and, more importantly, it also required a fleet.[47] The consul, Cn. Fulvius Centumalus, commanded a fleet of 200 ships, a number only just short of the entire Roman fleet at the Aegates Islands in the battle that ended the first Punic war.[48] This must have emphasised the precarious nature of Roman control of Sicily, Sardinia and Corsica, which depended directly on the maintenance of a naval presence in the seas west and south of Italy, at least so long as their *military* presence was not continuous but consisted of troops sent to fight specific campaigns. If, as is probable, Roman ships stationed at Lilybaeum were withdrawn to fight in the Adriatic in 229, this might well have drawn attention to the need for a regular succession of magistrates with *imperium*, and thus led to the regular appearance of the two areas on the annual list of *provinciae*.

Whatever the reason, it was not until 227 that praetors were sent to Sicily and Sardinia. It was not until that date that the presence of Roman troops and a Roman commander, which is always essential to the notion of a *provincia*, was established on a permanent basis. The renewal of the war with Carthage, and the first assignment of Hispania occurred less than ten years later.

The *imperium* of a Roman magistrate is not a vague abstraction. Even though *imperium* itself is a word of uncertain origin, indefinable in content and at times almost magical in its connotations, it is always attached to particular individuals, holding particular offices or commissions within the state;[49] its application, that is to say, is usually precisely defined, and always in principle susceptible of definition. Central to this definition of application is the *provincia*. From the beginning of the emergence of the idea of Roman power, of the Roman empire, on a world-wide scale, the *provincia* described and defined the particular task given to a holder of *imperium*. The process by which the *provincia* became a province, with all that that word implies of legal, fiscal and administrative responsibilities, was not only the redefinition of the task of the holder of *imperium*, but also the formulation of what the empire was perceived to be.

The examination of this process as it took place in Spain between 218 and 81 BC requires an analysis of the activity of the men who commanded

---

[47] Already by 231, negotiations showed clearly the likelihood of war in Illyria (so Harris, *War and imperialism* 195).

[48] Polybius 2.11.1, cf. 1.59.8; Walbank, *Commentary* I, 124; Thiel [n. 39] 93, 305 n. 786.

[49] On *imperium*, see the classic account of Mommsen, *StR* I³, 22–4, 116–36; also E. Meyer, *Römischer Staat und Staatsgedanke*³ (Zurich 1964) 117ff.

there in that period, and to whom the *provinciae Hispaniae* were allotted by the senate. For this reason, after an account of the state of Spain before the arrival of the Romans, this book consists of an investigation of the magistrates and pro-magistrates sent out by the senate to employ the power and authority given them by the senate and people of Rome within the confines of the Iberian peninsula. What they did there, and how they related to the peoples and conditions they found, as well as to the city which they had left and to which they would return, is a complex and interesting story in its own right; but it is also more than that. What happened in Spain reveals, in a way which is not true for any other part of the Mediterranean world at that time, the way in which Roman military aggression became, at the hands of the men who practised it, the source of the Roman empire, and how the institutions created by a city-state to wage war provided the structures of the provinces of the imperial republic.

CHAPTER 2

Spain before the Romans

To understand the actions of the Romans in Spain in the 140 years which followed the declaration of war against Hannibal in 218 it is essential to be aware of the context in which those actions took place. The peoples they found there and, perhaps even more importantly, the structure of the land in which they fought were more than a mere back-drop to the events of the period. They, more than anything else, determined what it was possible for a Roman commander to do, and so shaped the activity and policy of the men who were to create Roman Spain.

The land

In no part of the Roman world is the connection between physical geography and political and military control closer or more important for the understanding of their methods and ideas than in Spain.[1] The dominant feature of the geography of the peninsula is the great central tablelands, the *mesetas*, which cover about one-half of the total land area. To the north these are bounded by the range of the Cantabrian mountains, which extends eastwards to form the Pyrenees; before this, however, the edge of the *meseta* has turned south-eastwards along the line of the Sierra de la Demanda, which, after a gap created by the valley of the River Jalón, continues in a broadening cluster of *sierras* to reach the sea just north of Sagunto, at the northern end of the coastal plain of Valencia. The eastern edge is formed by the watershed which runs parallel with the Mediterranean coastline behind the plain of Valencia, and divides the relatively short rivers, such as the Turia, the Júcar and the Segura, which run eastwards into the Mediterranean, from the Tajo and the Guadiana, which run across the *mesetas* to the Atlantic coast. In

---

[1] In general A. Schulten, *Iberische Landeskunde* I (Strasbourg 1955), and M. Cary, *The geographic background of Greek and Roman history* (Oxford 1949) 231–43, on the historical significance of the geography of the peninsula; and, for a general account, Ruth Way and Margaret Simmons, *A geography of Spain and Portugal* (London 1962).

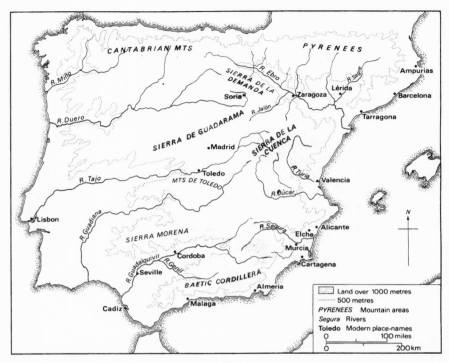

1   Spain

the west, the hills which form the modern frontier between Spain and
Portugal rejuvenate these rivers, so that after a sluggish course across the
tablelands they gain momentum as they approach the ocean. At the
southern edge, the Sierra Morena rises gently from the *meseta* to drop
sharply into the valley of the Guadalquivir (the ancient Baetis). The
whole of this high plateau is intersected by two ranges of mountains, one
relatively high but broken, dividing the course of the Duero (Roman
Durius) from the Tajo (Roman Tagus), the other the smaller Montes de
Toledo, standing between the Tajo and the Guadiana (Roman Anas).

Today the whole of this area is arid and very difficult to cultivate and,
outside the towns and cities, sparsely populated, especially in the north.
In part this is due to deforestation, which has taken place in modern
times: Strabo talks of most of Spain as inhospitable, with mountains,
woods, and plains covered with a light soil with an uneven distribution
of water.[2] The forests of Castile, which covered the central *meseta* area,

[2] Strabo 3.1.2. (p. 137).

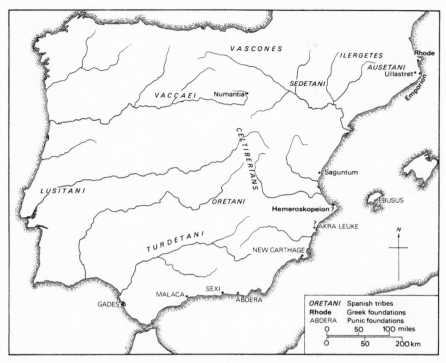

2 Pre-Roman Spain

flourished at least down to the early sixteenth century, and their
destruction was due to the need for ship-timber in the era of Spanish
expansion into the Americas, and to the damage brought about by the
privileges granted to the sheep-rearing industry.[3] The lack of water, away
from the rivers, must have been a constant factor, however, and is due
to the mountain barriers which on all sides cut off the *meseta* from the
sea, and give it a continental, rather than a mediterranean climate, with
sparse, irregular rainfall, and a far greater range of temperature than the
coast-lands.[4] The broken mountain ranges and the rivers which cross the
tablelands from east to west may have hindered communications, but
certainly never prevented penetration. Castile in the sixteenth century
was covered by a network of roads carrying goods of all sorts, north and
south, and the great herds of sheep that annually passed to and from the
summer pastures of the southern *meseta* from the towns of Old Castile

[3] J. Klein, *The mesta: a study in Spanish economic history 1273–1836* (Cambridge, Mass. 1920)
306–8, 320–2.   [4] Way and Simmons [n. 1] 44–59.

in the north confirm the picture.[5] However, the harsh climate and low fertility of the whole area will have made it seem, as Strabo's description suggests, desolate and unattractive.[6]

Of the two river basins which flank the *mesetas*, that of the Ebro to the north-east shows similar climatic conditions to the central tablelands, from which it is separated by the Sierra de la Demanda and the hills which run down from the valley of the Jalón, a southern tributary of the Ebro, to the Mediterranean coast. The northern side of the basin is formed by the Pyrenees. Though the valley broadens from the upper reaches of the river as it flows towards the Mediterranean, the end of the basin is closed off by the Catalan hills, through which the river flows in a steep gorge before it reaches the sea across the mud-flats created by its own delta. The result is that although the Ebro rises in an easterly extension of the Cantabrian mountains, a mere 45 kilometres south of the Atlantic coast, and flows into the Mediterranean, the basin itself is barely affected by these stretches of sea. Although lower than the *mesetas* it has the same 'continental' extremes of climate, with the same aridity, and presents the same difficulties for agriculture.[7]

The valley to the south of the southern *meseta*, that of the Guadalquivir, or Baetis as the Romans knew it, is very different. This area, Andalusia, enclosed between the Sierra Morena at the edge of the *meseta* to the north, and the mountains of the Baetic Cordillera, the highest in Spain, cutting it off from the Mediterranean, lies open to the Atlantic to the south-west. As a result, though the summers are extremely hot, the winters are mild. Already in antiquity, the soil was renowned for its richness and fertility,[8] and remained so despite conquest and reconquest by Vandals, Moslems and Christians from the fifth to the thirteenth centuries AD.[9] Although the mouth of the river was surrounded with salt marshes, which now form the famous salt-flats known as Las Marismas, the estuary was broad, and, unlike the Ebro, allowed access for large vessels well inland.[10]

Finally, on the fringe of the peninsula, there are the coastal plains. The Atlantic coasts of the north and west are not of immediate concern. The Romans only reached these areas relatively late in the second century BC, both because of their geographical remoteness from the first parts to receive their attention in the east and south, and because of the barriers presented by mountains and *meseta*, which made them relatively inaccess-

---

[5] F. Braudel, *The Mediterranean and the Mediterranean world in the age of Philip II*[2] (London 1972) I, 52–5, 91–4; Klein [n. 3] 17–29; G. Menendez Pidal, *Los caminos en la historia de España* (Madrid 1951). [6] Strabo 3.1.2. (p. 137).
[7] Way and Simmons [n. 1] 24–7, 289–95. [8] Strabo 3.2.4 (p. 142); Pliny, *NH* 3.3.7.
[9] Braudel [n. 5] I, 82–3. [10] Strabo 3.1.9. (p. 140); 3.2.4. (p. 142).

ible. The plains of the east coast, however, were, for the same reasons, of prime importance. The Catalonian plain, enclosed on the west by the eastern extremity of the Pyrenees and by the Catalonian hills, which box in the Ebro valley; the plains of Valencia and Murcia, forming the Spanish Levant; and the smaller coastal plains of Almeria and Malaga, closed in by the high mountains of the Baetic Cordillera, all share a fertility largely due to the alluvial deposits brought down by the mountains which separate them from the interior. Though the rainfall varies from a moderate but fairly regular amount in Catalonia to a low precipitation in the south, especially around Murcia and Cartagena (Roman Nova Carthago) and though temperatures are of course higher in the south than in the north, the whole coastline avoids the extremes of temperature and aridity of the central *mesetas*.

The mountain barrier, here as elsewhere in Spain, also presents a major obstacle to communications. There were ways into the hinterland, especially into the Ebro valley from Tarraco to Ilerda; from Saguntum, through the mountains to the Jalón valley; from the southern end of the plain of Valencia along the route later followed by the *via Augusta* to Castulo at the head of the Baetis valley; and from Nova Carthago over to the valley of the Genil (Roman Singilis) and thence to the lower Baetis. Roads also ran across the high mountains of the Baetic Cordillera from Urci (in the bay of Almeria) to Castulo, and from Malaga (ancient Malaca) to Cordoba. None of the ways was an easy route and the main traffic here in the early Roman period must have been along the coast, from the Pyrenees to Nova Carthago.[11] One major effect of the geography of the peninsula has always been to separate the coastal fringes from the centre, and an indication of this can be seen in the continued existence within the peninsular unit of four identifiable languages even down to the present day: Catalan in the north-west corner; Basque in the western Pyrenees and the eastern end of the north coast; Portuguese on the major part of the western coast and its hinterland; and Castilian in the centre, spreading, because of long political supremacy, into the rest of the country.

[11] On the coastal road, and the route over to the Baetis valley, see Strabo 3.4.9 (p. 160); on the problems of crossing the mountains behind the coast, note his remark that they were περατός πεζῇ (passable on foot) (3.4.6. (p. 159)).

The inhabitants

(a) Celts and Iberians

The pattern of ethnic and political distribution in the peninsula, so far as it can be determined for the moment of Rome's first interest in the late third century, was largely determined by the geographical factors outlined above. Precision in locating and identifying the tribal units is impossible. Strabo, writing early in Tiberius' reign, complained not only of the prolixity and ignorance of Greek writers on the subject, and of the slavish copying of the Greeks and lack of intellectual curiosity in the Romans, but also of the difficulty of writing with exactness of peoples who were broken up into small political and geographical elements, always likely to extend or contract, to combine together, or to move to another area.[12] Despite the work of ethnographers, philologists and archaeologists over the past hundred years, much still remains obscure.[13]

It is possible, however, to distinguish two general areas. On the *mesetas*, and the north and west coasts lived peoples who were semi-nomadic with a basically pastoral economy and who seem to have impinged on their more settled and prosperous neighbours, especially to the south, in the Baetis valley, chiefly through their raiding parties.[14] That at least is the mark that they have left in the classical sources. To this group belonged the Lusitanians, who were to cause such problems to the Romans in the third quarter of the second century, under their leader Viriathus. These peoples were for the most part Celtic in origin, one section, which lived in the north-eastern corner of the *mesetas* being known as the Celtiberians, presumably either through mixture between the Celts with the earlier Iberian population, or simply because of their proximity to the Iberians. The Celtiberians seem to have lived largely in scattered villages, though excavations at such centres as Numantia and Termantia show that they also used larger, well-fortified towns.[15]

The inhabitants of the coastal strip (Catalonia and the Spanish Levant), and the Baetis valley, seem to have been more urbanised. They

[12] Strabo 3.4.19 (pp. 165–6).
[13] For general accounts of the peoples of Spain in this period, see P. Bosch-Gimpera, *El poblamento antiguo y la formacion de los pueblos de España* (Mexico 1944); ed. R. Menendez Pidal, *Historia de España* 1.3 (*Etnologia de los pueblos de Hispania*) (Madrid 1954); M. Almagro, *Origen y formacion del pueblo hispano* (Barcelona 1958) 91–111.
[14] J. Malaquer de Motes, 'Los pueblos de la España celtica', in Menendez Pidal [n. 13] 1.3, 5–194.
[15] Strabo 3.4.12–13 (pp. 162–3); B. Taracena, 'Los pueblos celtibericos', in Menendez Pidal [n. 13] 1.3, 197–299. On their towns see Strabo 3.4.13 (p. 162) for Poseidonius' criticisms of Polybius, who, according to Poseidonius, described even fortified towers as cities; also Taracena, *op. cit.* 224–7.

are generally referred to by modern scholars as the Iberians, although to what extent this represents a true ethnic and/or cultural unity is uncertain. Even the name 'Iberia' was used by the ancients to cover different areas, as Strabo observed.[16] Certainly the Iberian alphabet, a mixture of alphabetic and syllabic signs, was common to both, though it is likely that the language these signs expressed was different in the Baetis valley from that of the east coast. Indeed the Baetis valley was, as its geography would lead one to expect, a separate unit, known as Turdetania, and almost certainly the site of the legendary Tartessos, of whose mineral wealth Greek poets and Hebrew prophets knew at least from the sixth century BC.[17] Archaeological remains from both the east coast and from the Baetis valley show that settlement sites were generally small, easily-defensible hill-tops; exceptions to this are the wealthy sites in the Tartessos region, and in particular Carmona and El Carambolo; and towns on or near the east coast, either founded by Greek colonists or heavily influenced by nearby Greek settlements. An example of this is the large town at Ullastret, just south of the Phocaean/Massiliote colony of Emporion (modern Ampurias).[18]

(b) Greeks, Phoenicians and Carthaginians

To the extent that there was a more advanced state of urbanisation in some 'Iberian' areas, this seems to have been due to the influence of Phoenician, Greek and Carthaginian colonists, or in the case of the 'Tartessian' towns, perhaps also to the mineral wealth which first attracted the attention of those colonists. However, seen from the Roman point of view, these colonies are of more significance in their own right than for their effect on the Iberian population, since it was because of them that Rome was drawn into the affairs of the peninsula.

The Greeks had had settlements down the east coast at least since the sixth century BC; Rhode (modern Rosas), the most northerly, was said to have been founded by the Rhodians, but an alternative story made it a

[16] Strabo 3.4.19 (p. 166); cf. A. Arribas, *The Iberians* (London, n.d.).

[17] Strabo 3.1.4–2.15 (pp. 137–51). On Tartessos/Tarshish in ancient sources, see for instance Stesichoros fr. 4 (Diehl); Isaiah 2.12ff.; 1 Kings 10.22. The sources are discussed by A. Schulten, *Tartessos*[2] (Hamburg 1950) 27–30, 55–71. For a review of the state of Tartessian studies, see *Tartessos y sus problemas* (v Symposium internacional de Prehistoria Peninsular) (Barcelona 1969).

[18] In general, see A. Arribas [n. 16] 97–115. On towns in the Baetis valley, M. Bendala Galán, *La necropolis romana de Carmona (Sevilla)* (Seville 1976); J. de Mata Carriazo, *Tartessos y El Carambolo* (Madrid 1973); for Ullastret, Arribas [n. 16] 102–4 and M. Oliva Prat, *Ullastret: Guia de las excavaciones y su museo* (Gerona 1967), and *id.*, 'Las fortificaciones de la cuidad prerromana de Ullastret, Gerona, España' in *Atti de VI Congresso Int. delle Scienze preistoriche e protoistoriche* (Roma 1966) III, 23–8.

Massiliote colony.[19] The Massiliotes, or the Phocaeans who had originally been responsible for the founding of Massilia itself, and had largely transferred their population there after the destruction of Phocaea by the Persians in *c.* 546, were certainly responsible for other settlements in this area. Apart from Rhode, that nearest to Massilia itself is Emporion (modern Ampurias), on the coast some 25 kilometres north-east of Gerona.[20] Further south, between the mouth of the Sucro (modern Júcar), south of Valentia, and Nova Carthago (modern Cartagena), Strabo records the presence of three Massiliote settlements, of which he names one, Hemeroskopeion, which he says was called Dianium (Διάνιον) in his day.[21] The other two are probably to be identified with Alonis, mentioned by Pomponius Mela and Ptolemy, and placed by the latter just south of Benidorm;[22] and Akra Leuke, the Roman Lucentum and modern Alicante, first known as the site of a Carthaginian foundation by Hamilcar Barca in 231, but probably, from the name, originally a Greek settlement.[23] One other colony, placed nearer to the Straits of Gibraltar than any other, is also recorded by Strabo. Its name was Mainake, and Strabo says that by his time only the ruins of it remained, but that it had been a colony of the Phocaeans, between the Phoenician settlements at Malaca and Sexi.[24] It is likely that Mainake had disappeared long before the third century BC, perhaps following the naval defeat of the Phocaeans by the Carthaginians and Etruscans at Alalia off Corsica in *c.* 539.[25]

The Carthaginians, and their predecessors the Phoenicians, who founded Carthage itself in the late ninth or eighth century BC, also had long-standing settlements in Spain, placed to exploit the riches of southern Spain, and especially the mineral resources won from the Sierra Morena by the Tartessians. Seventh-century material has been found in tombs from Gades (modern Cadiz) and Sexi (modern Almunecar), and it is likely that Abdera and Malaca, also Phoenician settlements on the

[19] Strabo 3.4.8 (p. 160) says some say it was an Emporitan, others a Rhodian foundation. Emporion itself was, of course, Massiliote (cf. A. García y Bellido, *Hispania Graeca* (Barcelona 1948) II, 55–8).

[20] Strabo 3.4.8 (p. 160); García y Bellido [n. 19] II, 19–50, M. Almagro, *Ampurias*² (Barcelona 1951) gives a brief outline of its significance.

[21] Strabo 3.4.6 (p. 159). Cf. Artemidorus fr. 19; Avienus 476. Despite the earlier view of García y Bellido [n. 19] II, 51–5, there is no trace of such a Greek colony at modern Denia (G. Martín, *La supuesta colonia griega de Hemeroskopeion* (Valencia 1968).

[22] Pomponius Mela 2.93 (Allonis); Ptolem. 2.6.14 (Ἀλωναί). Artemidorus described Ἀλωνίς as νῆσος καὶ πόλις Μασσιλιάς (Steph. Byz. *s.v.*).

[23] Diod. Sic. 25.10.3–4; García y Bellido [n. 19] II, 58–60.

[24] Strabo 3.4.2 (p. 156); García y Bellido [n. 19] II, 3–19.

[25] Herodotus 1.166; cf. García y Bellido [n. 19] I, 200–5; J. Boardman, *The Greeks overseas*² (Harmondsworth 1973) 202–12.

south coast, were made in the seventh or sixth centuries.[26] After Carthage's defeat by Rome in the first Punic war (264–241), the problems caused by the merciless war against her own mercenaries in Libya (241–238) and the loss of Sardinia to the Romans (238–237), the leaders of the Carthaginian state seem once again to have turned their thoughts to Spain. In 237, Hamilcar Barca was sent to Spain, where, accompanied by his young son Hannibal, he 'recovered', according to Polybius, 'Carthaginian possessions in Iberia', by a combination of war and diplomacy.[27] Later sources ascribe to him a policy of ruthless plundering of the helpless Spaniards, and of torturing to death their leaders while enrolling the soldiery in his own army. While a general who had just seen the horrors of the 'mercenary war' cannot be expected to have been squeamish, it is probable that Roman hatred of his son Hannibal, to whom similar traits are attributed, is responsible for this emphasis.[28] During the nine years he commanded the Carthaginian forces in Spain, he succeeded in bringing Turdetania (i.e. the Baetis valley) under his control and in extending his power up the eastern seaboard as far as the settlement known to the Greeks as Akra Leuke, modern Alicante, which he founded and established as a fortified post on the coast nearest to Carthage.[29] It was here, or just outside it at Helike (probably modern Elche) that he died in battle, showing, according to Polybius, exemplary courage.[30]

Hamilcar was succeeded by his son-in-law Hasdrubal, who continued the policy of extending Carthaginian control in southern Spain. The sources indicate that he relied on diplomacy as well as on warfare; Diodorus states that he married the daughter of an Iberian king and was acknowledged as supreme general by 'all the Iberians'.[31] This last must be an exaggeration, but it seems to have been the practice of Spanish tribes to recognise a victorious general in this way, even if he was a foreigner. After the battle of Baecula, Polybius records, Scipio was acclaimed as king, though he refused the title.[32] Hasdrubal further

---

[26] Strabo 3.4.2–3 (p. 156); A. García y Bellido, *Fenicos y Carthaginenses en occidente* (Madrid 1942) 119–24; B. H. Warmington, *Carthage*² (London 1969) 32–3.

[27] Polybius 2.1.5–9.

[28] Diod. Sic. 25.10; Appian 5.17–21; cf. Livy 21.4.9 on Hannibal.

[29] Turdetania: Strabo 3.2.14 (p. 151). Akra Leuke: Diod. Sic. 25.10; Livy 24.41.3–4.

[30] Polybius 2.1.8. On the site of the battle, Livy 24.41.3 and Diod. Sic. 25.10. Tzetzes, *Hist.* 1.27, who says he drowned in the Ebro, and Nepos, *Hamilcar* 4, who describes him as fighting the Vettones, who lived in the Duero valley, seem hopelessly confused. On Hamilcar in Spain, see O. Meltzer, *Geschichte der Karthager* II (Berlin 1896) 392–405; S. Gsell, *Histoire Ancienne de l'Afrique du Nord* III (Paris 1918), 126–31; B. H. Warmington [n. 26] 192.

[31] Diod. Sic. 25.12; Livy 21.2.3–7.   [32] Polybius 10.40.2–9; Livy 27.19.3–6.

strengthened the Carthaginian position on the Mediterranean coast by the foundation of a town called Carthage, the 'new town', known to the Romans as Nova Carthago, and now called Cartagena. This is sited even more advantageously than Akra Leuke for contact with African Carthage, and has a magnificent harbour. Here he built a strongly fortified city, including a 'royal palace', which may have lent further credence to the view, elaborated by the near-contemporary Roman historian, Fabius Pictor, that he was aiming at the establishment of a dynasty in Spain.[33] Certainly the Barcid family were intimately connected with Carthaginian rule in the peninsula. When Hasdrubal was murdered by a Celtic slave, whose master the Carthaginian is said to have killed, he was replaced by Hannibal, who also married a Spanish princess.[34] The link was continued after Hannibal's departure for Italy in 218, for he left his brother Hasdrubal in command in Spain, and subsequently sent a third brother, Mago, to reinforce him. Mago was indeed the last Carthaginian commander to withdraw from Spain in 206, following the victories of Scipio at Baecula and Ilipa.[35] Without going so far as Fabius Pictor, and imagining a private kingdom being set up by Hamilcar Barca and his family, there is no doubt both that the Carthaginians established control of at least the Baetis valley and the east coast south of Cabo de la Nao by military and diplomatic means, and that the main executants of this policy were the Barcids.[36]

The first Roman contacts: the Ebro treaty and Saguntum

It is in this context of an expanding Carthaginian domination of southern Spain that there appear the first signs of Roman interest in the peninsula in the political sphere. Finds of Italian pottery of the third century BC in the eastern coastal area indicate some earlier commercial contact, and this indeed may be presupposed by the obscure clause in the second treaty between Carthage and Rome recorded by Polybius in his description of diplomatic relations between the two states before the outbreak of the Hannibalic war. The Romans were prohibited by the treaty from

[33] On the foundation of Cartagena: Polybius 2.13.1, 10.10; Diod. Sic. 25.12. On Hasdrubal's alleged intentions: Polybius 3.8.2. (quoting Fabius); 10.10.9, cf. Walbank, *Commentary* I, 310–11.
[34] Death of Hasdrubal: Polybius 2.36.1; Livy 21.2.6; Diod. Sic. 25.12; Appian, *Ib.* 8; Val. Max. 3.3 ext. 7; Justin 44.5.5; Zonaras 8.21. Hannibal's wife: Livy 24.41.7; Sil. Ital. 3.97–107.
[35] Hannibal's brothers: Polybius 3.33.6; 9.22.2–3. Mago's withdrawal: Livy 28.36.1–37.10.
[36] Thus Polybius describes Hamilcar as πολλοὺς μὲν πολέμῳ, πολλοὺς δὲ πειθοῖ ποιήσας Ἰβήρων ὑπηκόους Καρχηδόνι (2.1.7). The only major Carthaginian commander in Spain not related to Hamilcar, was Hasdrubal son of Gisgo, on whom see S. Gsell [n. 30] II (1918) 267–8.

plundering, trading or founding a city beyond 'Mastia Tarseiou', which is plausibly identified with a Tartessian settlement on the site, later occupied by New Carthage.[37] The first positive intervention recorded in the sources is an embassy mentioned in a fragment of Cassius Dio. If Boissevain has restored the passage correctly, the embassy took place in 231 BC, when envoys were sent to investigate the expansionary activities of Hamilcar Barca, even though, as Dio says, the Romans had as yet no interests in Iberia. Hamilcar responded to their enquiries by saying that he had to fight the Iberians in order to pay the Romans the money still owed by the Carthaginians, and the Roman envoys withdrew, apparently in some confusion. Though the historicity of this account has been debated, there would seem to be no substantial reason for discrediting it. It reveals a lack of Roman interest, at least at the political level, before the Barcid expansion, and indeed the embassy itself seems to have had no results. All that can be deduced from the story is that Rome was by 231 aware that Carthaginian power was growing in Spain, which is likely to be true, irrespective of the accuracy of Dio's report.[38]

It may be the insignificance of this meeting which led Polybius to ignore it when describing the events in Spain which preceded the outbreak of the second Punic war. He does, however, describe in some detail the negotiations between Hasdrubal and a Roman embassy which came to him in 226 or 225, and which concluded the so-called Ebro treaty. The Romans, according to Polybius, saw the power of Carthage in Spain expanding and becoming more threatening to themselves under Hasdrubal's direction, and so began their interference in the affairs of Iberia. They could not at that time undertake a war against the Carthaginians, because they were themselves under threat of an attack from the Gauls, so they decided to conciliate Hasdrubal, and therefore agreed with him that the Carthaginians should not cross the river Ebro under arms.[39] This agreement was next mentioned, in Polybius' account, by an embassy sent by the Romans to Hannibal in the winter of 220–219 in response to repeated appeals from the people of Saguntum. When Hannibal entered winter-quarters at his base at Cartagena, he found the embassy awaiting him, warning him both to leave Saguntum alone, as it was under Roman protection, and not to cross the Ebro, contrary to the agreement with Hasdrubal.[40] Polybius explains later that Saguntum had

---

[37] Polybius 3.24.4; Walbank, *Commentary* I, 347; Knapp, *Aspects* 205–8.

[38] Dio fr. 48 (Boiss.). The arguments for and against authenticity are well discussed by G. V. Sumner, *HSCP* 72 (1968) 205–15 and *Latomus* 31 (1972) 474–5, who overestimates the importance of the event. See also Walbank, *Commentary* I, 168.

[39] Polybius 2.13.3–7.   [40] Polybius 3.15.1–5.

established a relationship with Rome before the time of Hannibal. He describes the beginning of their dealings with Rome in language which implies a formal surrender (*deditio in fidem*) by the Saguntines, and cites as evidence of this having happened an occasion (presumably subsequent to the *deditio*) when they called in the Romans as arbitrators at a time when Saguntum was in a state of internal political turmoil.[41] There has been much argument in recent discussion about whether Polybius is correct either in his statement, or in his use of evidence and, more particularly, about whether there was a formal agreement between Rome and Saguntum.[42] The question is probably incapable of resolution, but Polybius makes it clear that the connection between the two was close enough for not only the Saguntines but also Hannibal to believe that an attack on Saguntum would bring Roman retribution.[43]

Although there is some uncertainty about the previous nature of the links between Rome and Saguntum, the view that Polybius takes seems thus far to be clear and plausible: that Rome's intervention in Spanish affairs before the second Punic war consisted of two occurrences, the treaty with Hasdrubal prohibiting the Carthaginians from crossing the Ebro under arms, concluded just before the war against the Gauls of 225; and the connection with Saguntum, arranged at some date between the signing of the Ebro treaty and the murder of Hasdrubal in 221.[44] In the passage discussed so far, Polybius seems to treat these two events as quite separate, as well he might, considering that Saguntum lies inland from the Mediterranean coast some 150 kilometres south of the Ebro delta. In two places, however, he brings the two together, and has been suspected of presenting the attack on Saguntum as a violation of the Ebro treaty.[45] The first of these is the warning given by the Roman ambassadors to Hannibal at Cartagena in the winter of 220/219 neither to attack Saguntum nor to cross the Ebro. Although the combination of the Ebro and Saguntum has made scholars suspicious of Polybius' meaning, a

[41] Polybius 3.30.1–2.

[42] Against a treaty: J. S. Reid, '*Problems of the second Punic War*' in *JRS* 3 (1913) 179–90; E. Badian, *Foreign clientelae (264–70 BC)* (Oxford 1958) 48–52; A. E. Astin, *Latomus* 26 (1967) 589–93. *Contra*: T. A. Dorey, *Humanitas* 11–12 (1959–60) 1–10; Harris, *War and imperialism* 201.

[43] Hannibal: Polybius 3.14.9–10. Note that although the Saguntines could have surrendered themselves to the Romans, as some Illyrians and Corcyraeans had done in 228 (Polybius 2.11.5ff.), this need only have resulted in a loose relationship of *amicitia* (Dahlheim, *Struktur und Entwicklung* 53–6 and 69–73).

[44] On the chronology, see Polybius 2.13.3 (no action in Spain before the Ebro treaty); 3.30.1. (Romano-Saguntine agreement πλείοσιν ἔτεσιν ἤδη πρότερον τῶν κατ' Ἀννίβαν καιρῶν); and the discussions by Walbank, *Commentary* I, 170 and Sumner [n. 38] 213 n. 27.

[45] Thus Walbank, *Commentary* I, 171–2; for further discussion, and for the view adopted here, see P. Gauthier, *RPhil* 42 (1968) 91–100; P. J. Cuff, *Riv. stor. dell'ant.* 3 (1973) 163–70.

Roman warning of this sort makes perfectly good sense. The need to capture Saguntum shows that Hannibal had not as yet the control of the coastal plain which would facilitate movement from his base at Cartagena along the route to the Pyrenees. However, his campaign the previous summer against the Vaccaei had brought him into the valley of the Duero, and if Polybius' claim that none south of the Ebro dared to face him except the Saguntines sounds exaggerated, none the less he had for the first time brought a Carthaginian army within striking distance of the line of the Ebro valley.[46] A reminder of his brother-in-law's contract with the Romans will not have seemed out of place.

The second passage is part of Polybius' summary of the arguments about responsibility for the outbreak of war in 218. If anyone posits the destruction of Saguntum as the cause of the war, he argues, it must be agreed that the Carthaginians were in the wrong in bringing the war about, through violation both of the treaty of Lutatius, which preserved the immunity of allies on both sides from attack, and of that concluded with Hasdrubal, which prohibited the Carthaginians from crossing the Ebro under arms.[47] There is clearly something awry here. The Carthaginians did not agree with Polybius' interpretation of the Lutatius treaty,[48] but that is immaterial to the argument. What is important is that he here appears to state that the attack on Saguntum involved a breaking of the Ebro treaty, which is clearly absurd. Either Polybius is wrong about the location of Saguntum, which would cast doubt on his whole account of the Ebro treaty; or he is guilty of some other error or unclarity. It is extremely improbable that Polybius is here guilty of a geographical howler. Not only does he show clearly elsewhere that he knew well enough the correct relationship between Saguntum and the Ebro,[49] but in one place in the context of this very discussion of the outbreak of the war, the position of Saguntum south of the Ebro is essential to his exposition of the actions of Hannibal in 220–219. Hannibal knew, says Polybius, of the special relationship between Rome and Saguntum, and was unwilling to provoke the Romans before he was ready; therefore he first conquered all that area within the Ebro, except for Saguntum, before assaulting the town itself.[50] Clearly Polybius knew that Saguntum was south of the Ebro.

The explanation of Polybius' error is not, however, hard to find. It is clear from his argument that the position he is putting forward, that the

---

[46] Polybius 3.14, esp. § 9. For the location of the Vaccaei, see Ptolemy, *Geogr.* 2.6.49.

[47] Polybius 3.30.3.

[48] Thus Polybius 3.21.5.

[49] Polybius 3.97.5–6, 98.6–7.

[50] Polybius 3.14.9–10.

sack of Saguntum was the cause of the war, is not Polybius' own. Indeed he has specifically rejected this view earlier in the discussion.[51] At that point, the opinion, which he ascribes to some of those who had written histories of Hannibal, is formulated in terms of two causes of the war: the first was the siege of Saguntum, the second the crossing of the Ebro. As it stands there is no internal contradiction in this. The only difficulty which Polybius raises is the description of these events as causes (αἰτίαι); he himself would rather describe them as the first acts of the war (ἀρχαὶ τοῦ πολέμου). It is probable therefore that in summarising briefly a position that he in any case did not himself hold he carelessly telescoped the violations of the two treatises which he had described together earlier in the same book.[52]

Polybius' account of the Ebro treaty seems then to be consistent, and, with the one exception just mentioned, clearly expressed: the agreement was that the Carthaginians would not cross the Ebro under arms, and made no reference to anything else, so far as Polybius knew. Later writers had other ideas. Livy describes the event as the renewing of a formal treaty (*foedus*) to the effect that the Ebro should be the boundary between the empires of the Carthaginians and the Romans, and that Saguntum was specifically exempted from the provisions of the treaty.[53] Appian, writing in the middle of the second century AD, makes the simple compact described by Polybius even more formal and complex. The agreement is concluded at Carthage between the Carthaginians and Roman ambassadors; the Ebro was to be the boundary of the Carthaginian empire in Spain; the Romans were not to wage war against those within that boundary, who were subject to the Carthaginians, nor the Carthaginians to cross the river for warlike purposes; and the Saguntines and the other Greeks in Spain were to be free and autonomous.[54] The language is certainly that of a formal Hellenistic treaty, but the circumstances and the content of Appian's account make it difficult to allow him much credit. Not only does he explicitly place Saguntum between the Ebro and the Pyrenees (a mistake which he compounds elsewhere by identifying Saguntum and Cartagena[55]), but he assumes the Greek origin of Saguntum; and, more importantly, he transfers the site of the making of the agreement to Carthage, and seems to envisage a transaction at a far

---

[51] Polybius 3.6.1–3. [52] So Gauthier and Cuff [n. 45].

[53] Livy 21.2.7, cf. 21.18.9. The idea of the Ebro as the boundary of the empire may come from Cato, whom Livy makes refer to the treaty in these terms in a speech in Spain in 195 BC (34.13.7.).

[54] Appian, *Ib.* 7.25–7.

[55] Appian, *Ib.* 12.46–47; 19.24; 75.320. He attributes the foundation of Cartagena to Hannibal rather than Hasdrubal. See above pp. 19–20.

higher diplomatic level than either Polybius or Livy. Indeed the increased formality of the proceedings and the geographical waywardness of Appian's story seem to take one stage further the discrepancies between Livy and Polybius. While Livy at least knew that geographically Saguntum was south of the Ebro,[56] none the less he describes the Saguntines as preserving their freedom under the treaty with Hasdrubal, being in the midst of the empires of the two peoples.[57] Though this need not be a *geographical* statement, a false geography could easily have been drawn from it.

It is not difficult to see why the Roman annalists, whom Livy is presumably using, should differ from Polybius in this way. No doubt it was hard, if the sack of Saguntum was taken as the cause of the war,[58] to explain the relevance of the Ebro treaty, unless Saguntum were in a special position with regard to the content of the treaty, or north of the Ebro, or (as Appian has it) both. Equally, as Polybius stresses that the Carthaginians, during the debate at Carthage in 218 before the outbreak of the war, denied the validity of the treaty because it had not been formally agreed to by the government of Carthage,[59] it is not surprising that later pro-Roman sources should enhance the importance and formality of the negotiations which led to the treaty's signing.

Modern writers have generally, and rightly, preferred Polybius to Livy or Appian.[60] In one particular, however, many have wished to add to his account a clause which would place similar restrictions on the Romans to those which Polybius records as binding the Carthaginians; that is, that the Romans recognised Carthaginian dominion *south* of the Ebro, and agreed not to interfere there.[61] Although it is impossible to settle this matter before deciding the intention of the Romans and of Hasdrubal in making the agreement, two points should be noted. First, not only did Polybius not know of such a clause, but he states specifically that, apart from the mention of the Ebro as a line the Carthaginians should not cross under arms, the Romans made no stipulation whatsoever about the rest of Spain.[62] This certainly implies that they neither claimed for themselves

---

[56] As is clear from Hannibal's expostulations, Livy 21.44.6.

[57] Livy 21.2.7: 'foedus renovaverat populus Romanus ut finis utriusque imperii esset amnis Hiberus, Saguntinisque mediis inter imperia duorum populorum libertas servaretur.'

[58] Polybius 3.6.1., and Walbank, *Commentary* I, 305; Klotz, *Livius* 122–4.

[59] Polybius 3.21.1.

[60] See survey and bibliography in H. H. Schmitt, *Die Staatsverträge des Altertums* III (Munich 1969) 205–7.

[61] Thus, for instance, Walbank, *Commentary* I, 168–72. G. Chic Garcia (*Habis* 9 (1978) 233 and 236) goes so far as to assume a similar bilateral recognition in the treaty of 346 (Polybius 3.24.1–13).

[62] Polybius 2.13.7 τὴν μὲν ἄλλην Ἰβηρίαν παρασιώπων, τὸν δὲ καλούμενον Ἴβηρα ποταμὸν οὐκ ἔδει Καρχηδονίους ἐπὶ πολέμῳ διαβαίνειν.

the area north of the Ebro, nor acknowledged Carthaginian control of all parts south of the river. Secondly, the two substantial accounts of the final negotiations between the Roman ambassadors and the Carthaginian senate which immediately preceded the declaration of the Hannibalic war in 218 (those of Polybius himself and of Livy[63]) are also silent about any such provision. Both writers provide considerable detail of the Carthaginian response to Roman charges about the sack of Saguntum, and it is remarkable that if the Ebro treaty contained a recognition of Carthaginian domination in the area of Saguntum, and a Roman undertaking not to interfere there, there is no mention whatever of the fact. This implies that the treaty did not contain such a clause, or at least that neither historian knew of it.[64]

The literary tradition can readily be explained as originating with an account on which Polybius drew, and of another, deriving probably from the pro-Roman version of Fabius Pictor. The first described an agreement between Hasdrubal and the Roman ambassadors sent to him, that the Carthaginians would not cross the river Ebro under arms; the second, under the influence of the events which immediately preceded the Hannibalic war, exalted the status of the 'treaty', inserted a reference to the Ebro as a boundary between Roman and Carthaginian territory, and, by means of a diplomatic or geographical fiction, included Saguntum within its terms. If these are the origins of the versions which survive, it is to the Polybian account that we should look first to see whether it can yield a coherent explanation of Roman and Carthaginian attitudes and actions in 226/225.

The first question to ask is what an Ebro treaty of the Polybian variety could have been for, and in particular why the line which the Carthaginians were not to cross under arms should have been the Ebro. The distance of the Ebro from the known areas of Carthaginian activity in the time of Hasdrubal is great, and has led several modern scholars to surmise that the river referred to was not the Ebro at all, but some other river further south.[65] There is one respect, however, in which the Ebro, and only the Ebro among those Spanish rivers which flow into the Mediterranean, would perform the function described by Polybius. Unlike the other smaller rivers, which rise in the mountains bordering

---

63 Polybius 3.20.6–21.8; Livy 21.18.

64 On these negotiations see most recently Rich, *Declaring war* 56–118, esp. 109–18.

65 Thus J. Carcopino, *Les Etapes de l'impérialisme romaine*[2] (Paris 1961) 19–40, postulates the river Júcar, which reaches the sea south of Valencia. Sumner [n. 38] 222–32 rejects Carcopino's arguments as ill-founded, and proposes either the Gorgos or the Ebo, two small rivers which debouch into the Mediterranean slightly to the north of Cabo de la Nao.

the eastern edge of the plateau of the *meseta*, the Ebro forms a line almost right across the peninsula, rising some 40 kilometres south of Santander, where the mountains drop down steeply to the Atlantic coast, and running in a remarkably direct course until it reaches the Catalonian hills, through which it breaks to reach the Mediterranean.[66] It is thus ideally suited to act as a line preventing movement north towards the Pyrenees. Indeed it is perfectly possible for an attack to be made into northern Spain as far as the Ebro valley without crossing any of the rivers which flow into the Mediterranean south of the Ebro, by climbing up out of the valley of the Guadalquivir (the Roman Baetis) through the Sierra Morena, by the Peñarroya pass to the westward or by the Valdepeñas pass, which connects the upper part of the valley with the headwaters of the Guadiana. This is particularly important, as the valley of the Baetis was the main base of the Carthaginian empire in Spain even before its extension to the east and the foundation of Cartagena.[67] The point is neatly illustrated by the campaigns of Hannibal in 220. In the course of a series of attacks on the Vaccaei, who inhabited the middle stretch of the Duero, and the Carpetani in the vicinity of Toledo, he appears to have crossed and recrossed the Sierra Morena by each of these passes in turn. If so, he will have 'subdued all those within the line of the river Ebro' (to use Polybius' description) without travelling down the Mediterranean coastline at all.[68]

If the primary function of the Ebro in the treaty was to act as a line cutting across the peninsula, then it is clear what the intention of the treaty was. Polybius mentions it as a preliminary to the war conducted between Rome and the Gauls in 225. The Romans became aware of Carthaginian expansion, and were worried by it, but as they had the Gauls to deal with, they concluded the treaty with Hasdrubal for the time being.[69] If, as has often been suggested, the Romans heard of the possibility of a Carthaginian move into northern Spain from the Massiliotes who, through their colonies and trading stations at Emporion, Hemeroskopeion, Alonis and Akra Leuke, might be expected to have an interest in the progress of Hamilcar and Hasdrubal, as well as some knowledge of the peninsula, then the understanding of the geography of Spain which is implied by the choice of the Ebro need cause no surprise.[70]

The Ebro treaty then should be seen as an attempt by the Roman senate to separate the Gauls from the Carthaginians, and in this respect

[66] See the description in Way and Simmons [n. 1] 24–7.
[67] See above p. 19.
[68] Polybius 3.14; Walbank, *Commentary* I, 317.
[69] Polybius 2.13.3–7.
[70] Cf. F. J. Kramer *AJP* 69 (1948) 1–26; G. V. Sumner [n. 38] 208 n. 10.

it has features in common with the peace terms imposed on the Illyrian queen Teuta in 228. In the latter case, the queen was not permitted to sail south of Lissos with more than two light ships.[71] As Badian has shown, this provision was strictly concerned with the movement of naval vessels as such, and was not, as some have supposed, a clause about territorial boundaries, either Roman or Illyrian.[72] Equally, there is no reason to believe that the Ebro treaty, which Polybius describes in the chapter immediately following the passage on the settlement with Teuta, was anything other than a limit on the movement of Carthaginian armed forces.

In this case, it is most unlikely that the agreement made with Hasdrubal in 226 had any effect at all, either at the time or later, on the status of Saguntum, and its relationship with Rome and Carthage. The Romans were making no acknowledgement of Carthaginian sovereignty south of the Ebro, nor, therefore, would they need to make a special exception for Saguntum. Equally, if relations between Rome and the Saguntines began or developed further after the conclusion of the negotiations with Hasdrubal, there would have been no reason within the terms of the agreement for the Carthaginians to have entertained a grievance or the Romans guilty consciences.[73] No doubt the Romans used Saguntum as a forward position from which to maintain a watch over Carthaginian expansion in southern and eastern Spain. This is consistent with the fears which Polybius describes as giving rise to the Ebro treaty, and with the visit of Roman ambassadors to Hamilcar in 231.[74] Hannibal is said by Polybius to have regarded Saguntum in this light, and, for that reason, to have carefully avoided interfering with it while expanding his control of the central areas of Spain south of the Ebro.[75] Saguntum was far more of a danger to a Carthaginian general intending to extend his territories in Spain than was the Ebro treaty, and it must be assumed that, when Hannibal attacked Saguntum, he knew full well what the consequences were likely to be.

Roman interest in the Iberian peninsula before the outbreak of the war with Hannibal in 218 was solely concerned, so far as our sources allow us to see, with the activity of the Carthaginians there. With one exception,

---

[71] Polybius 2.12.3, cf. 3.16.3; Appian, *Illyr.* 7.21.

[72] E. Badian, *PBSR* 20 (1952) 78–9 = *Studies in Greek and Roman history* (Oxford 1964) 6–9.

[73] Walbank, *Commentary* I, 170–1, formulates neatly the arguments that there must have been a violation of the Ebro treaty in Roman relations with Saguntum; but this arises from his view that the treaty must have been a mutual non-intervention pact, thus implicitly defining spheres of influence (pp. 169–70).

[74] Polybius 2.13.3–4; Dio fr. 48 (Boiss.).   [75] Polybius 3.14.9–10.

all the contacts between Rome and Spain at the diplomatic level were with Carthaginian commanders there. The exception, of course, is Saguntum; but here too the Romans seem to have been concerned only with the relationship between Saguntum and the Carthaginians, not with Saguntum itself. Although there has been much discussion about the chronology of the assault on and sack of the town by Hannibal, and the Roman response to these events, it is clear both that the siege took eight months to complete, and that the declaration of war against Carthage was not made until after the town had been captured.[76] This surely indicates that it was the success of Hannibal and the growth of Carthaginian power which motivated the Romans, not a desire to preserve a friendly ally on the coast of Spain. The Ebro treaty also shows Roman distrust of Carthaginian expansion in Spain under the ambitious direction of the Barcid family, rather than any immediate intention by the senate to establish a Roman presence south of the Pyrenees.[77] The specific fear was of a Carthaginian–Gallic combination which would have been a very serious threat in the mid- and late 220s.

Subsequent events were to prove Roman suspicions well founded. No sooner had Hannibal heard the news of the Roman declaration of war, than he sent messengers to the chief of the Gallic tribes inhabiting the Alpine region and the Po valley, reckoning, according to Polybius, that it was only if he received their co-operation that he would be able to reach Italy, and conduct the war there.[78] The Gauls were to prove unreliable allies, but neither Hannibal nor the Romans could know that before 218, and it is easy to see how important their geographical location in northern Italy must have seemed, especially given the weakness of the Carthaginian navy following the treaty of 241.[79] Moreover, once the link between the Gauls and the Carthaginians had been made, it proved surprisingly durable. The last Carthaginian known to have fought against the Romans on Italian soil, one Hamilcar, 'dux Poenorum', was led in triumph by C. Cornelius Cethegus, when he celebrated his victory over the Insubres and Cenomani in Cisalpine Gaul as late as 197. Though he was no doubt an abandoned straggler from one of the Carthaginian armies which had been in Italy ten years previously, the Romans were sufficiently impressed

[76] Polybius 3.17.9; 3.20.1; cf. A. E. Astin, 'Saguntum and the origins of the Second Punic War', *Latomus* 26 (1967) 579ff.; F. Hampl, *Aufstieg und Niedergang* 1. 1, 430–4; J. W. Rich, *Declaring war* 38–44.
[77] This is specifically mentioned by Polybius (2.13.3) as the reason for the agreement with Hasdrubal.
[78] Polybius 3.34, esp. 4–5. (See Walbank, *Commentary*, ad loc. on the correct translation of this section.)
[79] J. H. Thiel, *A history of Roman sea-power before the second Punic war* (Amsterdam 1954) 319.

by his presence and his authority to identify him as the reason for the outbreak which Cornelius put down.[80]

It has recently been argued that Roman relations with Spain before the Hannibalic war were simply a further instance of Roman aggressive greed, and that 'Spain in particular was probably regarded by Roman senators as a rich prize that could be won in a war against Carthage'.[81] There is no doubt that such attitudes were a major factor in Roman foreign policy through the third and second centuries, to an extent that has been underrated by many modern writers. In the particular case of Spain, however, there is little sign that they were of much weight in shaping the actions of the senate. The possibility of rich prizes will not have been ignored, but on all the occasions when the Romans took any action, and especially over the Ebro treaty with Hasdrubal in 226, the major consideration seems to have been the possibility of war, and the importance of ensuring that when hostilities broke out, they did so at a time and in circumstances that were most favourable to the Romans. Spain as an area of exploitation, political or economic, seems to have been a secondary concern, compared with the presence of an expanding and potentially hostile Carthaginian dominion.

[80] Livy 32.30.12; 33.23.5.   [81] Harris, *War and imperialism* 205

CHAPTER 3

The war zone: 218–206

Roman involvement in Spain: the original motives

To the Roman senate immediately before the outbreak of the war with Hannibal in 218, Spain was an area of Carthaginian activity, and thus of Roman interest when war was declared. *Hispania* had already been decided upon by the senators as one of the two regions in which the war was to be fought; according to Livy, their first action on hearing of the sack of Saguntum was to assign that *provincia* to the consul P. Cornelius Scipio.[1] The context of this assignment and the normal usage of the period[2] make the senate's intention clear. Spain, along with Africa-with-Sicily, the other *provincia* named at this time, were to be the places within which the consuls were meant to exercise their *imperium*. The naming of these *provinciae* was an essential step in the prosecution of the war, not a territorial claim.

It is not difficult to see why Spain seemed important to the senate. First, and most importantly, it was where Hannibal and his army were, and therefore where it was expected that the war would actually take place, when the embassy bearing the final ultimatum left for Carthage once the consular commands had been assigned.[3] In the event, the delay to Scipio's recruitment plans (caused by the need to divert at least a part of his troops to deal with the attack by Gauls in the north of Italy on the newly planted Latin colonies of Placentia and Cremona),[4] and still more the speed of Hannibal's advance across the Pyrenees and through southern France thwarted the senate's expectation. Scipio sailed from Pisa, and after a journey of five days round the coast of the Italian and French riviera, arrived at one of the mouths of the river Rhône. There

---

[1] Livy 21.17.1; cf. Polybius 3.40.2.   [2] See above Ch. 1.

[3] Livy 21.18.1; Polybius 3.20.6 On Roman thoughts as to the probable theatre of the war, see Polybius 3.14.13: οὐ μὴν ἐν Ἰταλίᾳ γε πολεμήσειν ἤλπισαν, ἀλλ' ἐν Ἰβηρίᾳ. De Sanctis (*Storia* III.2², 4–5) argues on grounds of probability that the Roman intention was to meet Hannibal in southern Gaul, but the sources do not support him.

[4] Polybius 3.40; Livy 21.25.1–26.4.

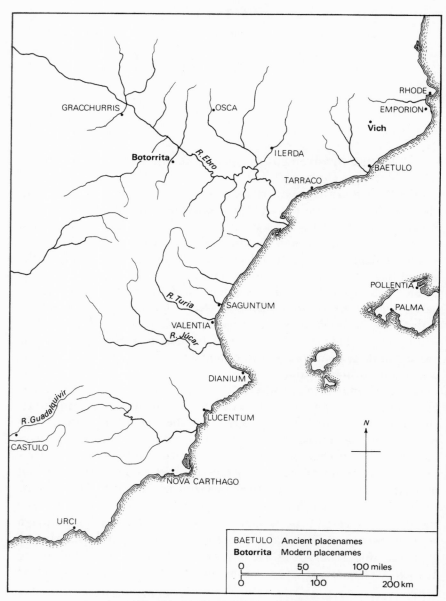

3   The Spanish Levant and the Ebro Valley

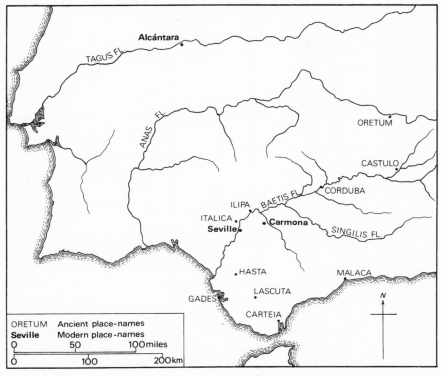

4   South-western Spain

he heard that Hannibal was crossing or, if Livy is right, had already crossed the Pyrenees. Sending scouts ahead (which included certain Gallic mercenaries in the pay of Massilia), he marched up the Rhône, to arrive at the crossing place three days after the Carthaginian army had gone over. Scipio promptly returned to the coast, where he decided to divide his forces, returning himself with a small number of men in order to join those already in northern Italy in facing Hannibal. The greater part of his army, however, he sent under the command of his brother Cnaeus to Spain.[5]

This decision was clearly taken by P. Scipio without consulting the senate. As often, the circumstances required a rapid response.[6] In this

[5] Polybius 3.41.4–8, 49.1–4; Livy 21.26.3–5, 32.1–5.

[6] Both Polybius (3.64.10) and Livy (21.40.3–4), in the speeches they give to Scipio before the battle of the Ticinus, explicitly state that this decision was Scipio's own. Note especially, in the Livian passage, Scipio's remark that 'ille exercitus, Hispaniae provinciae scriptus, ibi cum fratre Cn. Scipione meis auspiciis rem gerit ubi eum gerere senatus populusque Romanus voluit'; though this is almost certainly Livy's own expansion of the Polybian passage.

33

case, however, there is every reason to suspect that had the senate been consulted, their advice would have coincided with Scipio's opinion. Not only had Spain been named as a *provincia*, and the army conscripted for the purpose of fighting there, but throughout the period of the war, when Hannibal was in Italy, not in Spain, the senate continued to provide for the fighting in the Iberian peninsula. Spain was still significant even after Hannibal's departure. It was the base from which Hannibal had set out, and, given the superiority of Roman sea-power, it is probable that he expected such supplies and reinforcements as might reach him from outside Italy to come from there. When Cn. Scipio first landed in north-eastern Spain, he quickly captured the town of Cissa (at or near modern Tarragona), together with a large supply of equipment and money left there by Hannibal before he had set out to cross the Pyrenees earlier the same year.[7] The quantities of arms and other supplies captured by the younger Scipio at New Carthage in 209 also emphasise the potential importance of Spain to the Carthaginian army in Italy.[8]

Apart from supplies, Hannibal might have expected reinforcements of troops from Spain. The army with which he arrived in northern Italy late in 218 included 20,000 infantry of which 8,000 were Iberians.[9] Before he had left Spain, not only had he sent 13,850 Spanish infantry and 1,200 cavalry to protect Libya, but also left 10,000 foot and 1,000 horse with Hanno, sending others back to their homes to preserve local goodwill and to act as a pool from which he might draw reinforcements.[10] In addition to manpower, Spain also provided the Carthaginians with finance, which might well be crucial for the payment of the army, which, like all such Carthaginian forces, was largely mercenary.[11] The silver mines which the Carthaginians exploited in Spain provided wages for these soldiers.[12]

A Roman presence in Spain would be a major blow to Hannibal's plans for the invasion of Italy, especially if the supply lines between the invasion force and its Spanish bases could be severed. Such must have been P. Scipio's reasoning, when he made his decision at the mouth of the Rhône. It is important to note that, although his thinking seems to have coincided

[7] Polybius 3.76.1–7; Livy 21.60. On the site of Cissa, see E. Hübner, *Hermes* 1 (1866) 83ff; J. Vallejo, *Tita Livio libro XXI* (Madrid 1946) xlviii–lv. Iberian coins from the area of Tarraco are marked 'Cese'; but Livy and Polybius mention both 'Cissis'/Κίσσα and Tarraco in the same passages, which indicates that they at least thought the two were distinct. (Polybius 3.76.5,12; Livy 21.60.7, 61.2,3,11).

[8] Polybius 10.19.1–2 on the money captured there. Livy 26.47.5–10 adds details of military equipment. Note also the fears of the senate in 217 which, according to Polybius, encouraged them to send the elder P. Scipio to Spain (Polybius 3.97.3).

[9] Polybius 3.56.4.

[10] Polybius 3.33.10, 35.5–6.   [11] Polybius 6.52.4ff.

[12] So Diodorus 5.38.3. On Carthaginian exploitation of Spanish mines see *JRS* 66 (1976) 140.

with the intentions of the senate, the way in which his policy was put into action was entirely Scipio's own. Cnaeus Scipio, who commanded the Roman forces in Spain from his arrival in autumn 218 until Publius himself at last reached his *provincia* in the summer of 217, held no commission from the senate nor had he been elected to any magistracy by the people. Livy and Polybius, describing his being sent to Spain by Publius, call him simply the brother of the consul, while later sources suggest that he was his brother's *legatus*.[13] It is probable that his authority to command stemmed from *imperium* delegated to him by Publius, because the latter was unable to undertake his *provincia* himself. Such delegation had occurred before, and indeed during the Hannibalic war and the decade which followed it the senate made use of a similar device, appointing men to the *imperium pro praetore* through the agency of the urban praetor, in order to add flexibility to the rigid structure of magisterial and pro-magisterial commands.[14] On this occasion, however, it was P. Scipio and not the senate who took the initiative, for he had in any case no time to consult them, eager as he was to confront Hannibal in northern Italy.[15] Although the decision to send his troops on to Spain no doubt coincided with the senate's own opinion on the importance of Spain to the war effort, that decision was made and implemented by P. Scipio himself.[16] It was to prove crucial both to the course of the war and to the history of Roman Spain.

Publius and Cnaeus Scipio 218–211

In the autumn of 218, the first Roman army to set foot south of the Pyrenees landed at the Massiliote colony of Emporion (modern Ampurias, about 150 kilometres north of Barcelona by the coastal road).[17] It consisted of the greater part of P. Scipio's consular army of two legions, the usual contingent of Roman citizen cavalry, with 14,000 allied foot and

[13] Polybius 3.49.4; Livy 21.32.3. Cf. Appian, *Ib.* 14.54; Zonaras 8.23. Mommsen (*StR* II³, 652 n. 2) believes that Gnaeus may have been sent out by vote of the people because Livy refers to him later as *imperator* (25.32.1; 26.2.5). For another explanation of these passages, see below p. 41.

[14] Cf. the appointment of L. Scipio by Q. Fabius Maximus in 295 (Livy 10.25.11): of M. Livius Denter by P. Decius Mus in the same year (Livy 10.29.3); and of A. Postumius Albinus by his brother Sp. Albinus in 110 (Sall. *Jug.* 36.4, 37.3, 38.1). On propraetors appointed through the *praetor urbanus*, see Mommsen, *StR* I³, 680–6, esp. 681 n. 6.

[15] Polybius 3.49.1–4; Livy 21.32.1–5.

[16] That the decision was Scipio's is made explicit in the speeches given to him by both Polybius (3.64.10) and Livy (21.40.3–4). These, particularly Livy's, are, however, certainly compositions of the historians themselves.

[17] Polybius 3.76.1; Livy 21.60.1–2.

1,600 allied horse.[18] Publius himself took only a small section of this army back with him;[19] Cnaeus, acting no doubt under the authority delegated to him by his brother (probably *imperium pro praetore*) commanded the remainder until Publius arrived in Spain in mid-217.

Initially, the Roman commander could expect little local support. He could rely to some extent on the Massiliotes, whose settlements stretched down the coast as far as the Cabo de la Nao, even if some of those further south had now been absorbed by the Carthaginians. They not only provided a base at Emporion, but also a certain amount of naval assistance.[20] Massilia was almost certainly by this time a 'friend and ally of the Roman people',[21] but her influence in Spain, though helpful, was no substitute for establishing relations with the local peoples themselves. This Cnaeus proceeded to do by a combination of force of arms and diplomacy, and having made inroads into the hinterland with the aid of his new allies, succeeded in capturing the town of Cissa, with the supplies which Hannibal had left there, as well as the Carthaginian general Hanno and the Spanish leader Indibilis. Hasdrubal, Hannibal's brother, responded with a sudden and successful raid north of the Ebro, before retiring to winter-quarters in New Carthage, leaving garrisons on the south bank of the Ebro.[22] Scipio established himself for the winter at Tarraco, which was to become the main centre of operations for himself and his brother, and remained the northern base even after the capture of New Carthage by the younger Scipio in 209.[23]

Early in the summer of the following year (217) Cnaeus moved south to meet the forces of Hasdrubal which were then moving northward by land and sea towards the Ebro. Having abandoned his first idea of launching a simultaneous attack on both army and navy because of the size of the Carthaginian forces, he sent out his fleet of 35 ships to meet Hasdrubal's contingent of 40 ships at the mouth of the Ebro. After a short

[18] Livy 21.17.8.

[19] Livy 21.32.3–5.

[20] Polybius and Livy, following him, describe two Massiliote spy-ships as involved in the battle at the mouth of the Ebro in early summer 217 (Polybius 3.95.6–7; Livy 22.19.5). Whether or not there were more Massiliote vessels present at the battle, there may well have been other naval assistance at other times.

[21] An inscription from Lampsacus from 196 BC or shortly after mentions the attendance of a Lampsacene embassy at the renewing of the already existing alliance between Rome and Massilia (*SIG*³ 591, 11.27 and 52–4).

[22] Polybius 3.76; Livy 21.60.1–61.4. On the site of Cissa, see above n. 7. Indibilis ('Ανδοβάλης) is not mentioned here by Livy, whose account also includes a passage (21.61.5–11) which seems to be a doublet of 61.1–4 (de Sanctis, *Storia* III.2², 230 n. 59).

[23] Pliny, *NH* 3.3.21 describes it as 'colonia Tarracon, opus Scipionum, sicut Carthago Poenorum'. In 210, the younger Scipio used it as his first base of operations (Livy 26.19.12); for Tarraco and New Carthage as the two centres, see Livy 28.17.11.

struggle, the Romans were successful, and even captured 25 of the Carthaginian ships, after they had been beached by their crews.[24]

News of this success stiffened the resolve of the senate to carry out their original intentions with regard to Spain, and Publius Scipio, whose *imperium* had been prorogued after his consulship the previous year, was dispatched to join his brother with substantial reinforcements, consisting of 30 warships, 8,000 soldiers and a large quantity of supplies.[25] The senate's decision was no doubt influenced by the attempt of a Carthaginian fleet, immediately after the defeat at the Ebro, to establish a naval presence in the waters of the western Mediterranean. After attacks on Sardinia and on the Italian coast at Pisa, however, they were frightened by the approach of the Roman fleet under Cn. Servilius Geminus. Even though this attempt was unsuccessful, it must have emphasised the importance to the Carthaginians of keeping Hannibal supplied, and thus the importance also of Spain, the closest Carthaginian base, whether by land or sea.[26]

Although the ancient sources vary in their estimate of Cnaeus' achievements before his brother's arrival in the peninsula,[27] his establishment of a base at Tarraco, his push south to the Ebro and his links with the local tribes all provided a good foundation on which to base the Roman campaign against the Carthaginians. There is no sign that he was in any way inhibited by any thoughts that his position or his policy needed further ratification from Rome. Certainly Publius is said to have followed up his brother's initiative later in the same year, when the two together advanced 160 kilometres south of the Ebro along the coast to Saguntum. There they were presented with a number of Iberian hostages, sons of leading men, through the treachery of an Iberian named Abilyx, foolishly trusted by the Carthaginian commander, Bostar, who had been sent north by Hasdrubal to check the Roman advance. Publius is said to have returned these to their families, and gained great goodwill as a result.[28]

---

[24] Polybius 3.95.1–96.6; Livy 22.19.1–20.2. The famous fragment of Sosylus (Jacoby, *FGH* 176 F.1) is thought to refer to this battle, although the conflict described is clearly longer and more complex than that in Polybius and Livy, and involved crucial participation by a Massiliote contingent not mentioned elsewhere (U. Wilcken, *Hermes* 41 (1906) 103–41, and 42 (1907) 510–11; G. A. Lehmann, *Fondation Hardt Entretiens* 20 (1973) 175–82. [25] Polybius 3.97.1–4; Livy 22.22.1.

[26] Polybius 3.96.7–14; for the senate's fears, Polybius 3.97.3.

[27] Polybius adds nothing to his account of the naval victory while Livy describes an extraordinary series of military adventures throughout Spain; (Livy 22.20.3–21.8). Those on land are certainly fictitious (see de Sanctis, *Storia* III.2², 184; Klotz, *Livius* 143; J. Lazenby, *Hannibal's war* 127). *Appian, Ib.* 15.57, says that Cnaeus achieved nothing to speak of; and Polybius in passing mentioned that there had been no move south of the Ebro before Publius arrived (Polybius 3.97.5).

[28] Polybius 3.97.5–99.9; Livy 22.22.1–21; Zonaras 9.1. K. J. Beloch (*Hermes* 50 (1915) 361) thought the hostage story a doublet with the younger Scipio's action at New Carthage in 209 (Polybius 10.18.3ff); but cf. Lazenby, *Hannibal's war* 128.

This seems to be a natural continuation of the policy established by Cnaeus the previous year.

Of the activities of the two brothers over the next five years, little can be said with certainty. In 216 Hasdrubal received reinforcements, and was planning an attack by land and sea, presumably up the east coast, and against the Balearic Islands, which Cnaeus is said to have raided and from which ambassadors had come the previous summer. He was distracted, however, by a revolt among the tribes of the south, which was only put down with difficulty.[29] Further disaffection was caused by the news that Hasdrubal had been ordered to march to Italy as soon as possible, on instructions that had reached him from Carthage. Hasdrubal replied pointing out that much damage had been caused by the mere rumour of his departure, and that if he were to carry out his orders, Spain would be in Roman hands before he had crossed the Ebro. The response to this letter was the dispatch of Himilco with an army and an increased fleet to watch Spain in Hasdrubal's absence. As a result, in early 215 rather than in 216, where Livy places it, Hasdrubal set out, bringing with him adequate supplies of money to bribe the Gallic tribes who guarded the Alpine passes.[30]

However, before he could reach the Alps, he had to pass the Ebro, and it was on the south bank of the river, at a town which Livy calls Hibera, that he met the forces of P. and Cn. Scipio. Hasdrubal was defeated in the set-piece battle which followed, and much of his army destroyed. It is not surprising that the Scipios should write back to the senate, delighted 'not so much at the victory, as in having prevented Hasdrubal's crossing into Italy'. Coming in the aftermath of the great Roman defeat at Cannae, this was good news indeed.

The letter did not only contain good news. The Scipios also had to draw to the attention of the senate the fact that they had neither money to pay wages, nor clothing nor food for their army or for the allies who served with the fleet.[31] Money could if necessary be levied from local sources; but the other supplies were crucial if either the army or the *provincia* was to be maintained. In fact the last shipment of supplies for Spain recorded by the sources had left Italy shortly after P. Scipio in the winter of 217/216.[32] Certainly, as Livy records, the senate did not question the truth or the justice of the request, but observed that at a time

---

[29] Livy 23.26.1–27.8 cf. 22.20.7–9, for Gnaeus in 217. The 'Tartesii' of Livy (26.5ff) are probably identical with the Turdetani, whose main territory was in the Baetic valley; and Ascua (27.3), captured by Hasdrubal, is probably Pliny's Oscua (*NH* 3.1.10) near to Corduba (cf. Ptolem. *Geogr.* 2.11).

[30] Livy 23.27.9–28.3. On the date, see de Sanctis, *Storia* III.2², 235 n. 71.

[31] Livy 23.48.4ff.   [32] Polybius 3.106.7.

when they had vast forces deployed on land and sea, war threatening in Macedonia, the *vectigal* from Sardinia and Sicily substantially cut by the need to maintain forces there, and the number of soldiers reduced by the slaughter of Lake Trasimene and Cannae, resources were simply not available. Their only recourse was to credit from the *societates publicanorum* which undertook the provisioning of the Roman armies. In response to an appeal from the praetor, three companies agreed to undertake the work, postponing payment until there was money available in the *aerarium*, in return for exemption from military service for the duration of the contest, and for state insurance against damage to their goods by enemy action or bad weather while these were being shipped. The fact that the senate was prepared to go to such lengths to supply the Spanish army, despite the evident possibility of fraud,[33] shows the importance that it attached to the Spanish campaign.

The events of 215–212 are very unclear, as a result of Livy's confused use of what seem to be inferior sources.[34] It is possible that shortly after the defeat of Hasdrubal at the Ebro in 215, the Romans captured from the Carthaginians the small towns called Iliturgi and Intibili, both lying a short distance south of the mouth of the river.[35] It is likely that Saguntum was recaptured in 212 (Livy says that his took place in the eighth year of its possession by the enemy, but records the event under 214.)[36] The details of these events, however, and the occurrence of the others which Livy records are at least extremely doubtful. He represents the two Scipios as having the ability to range far and wide across the peninsula (in particular down into the Baetis valley), which is belied by their inability to capture Saguntum until 212, an essential prerequisite for movement down the Mediterranean coastline, and thence into the Baetis valley. It is likely that whatever they were doing in 215–212 was confined to the eastern coastal strip, and probably that section of the coast north of Saguntum. Probably some of this period was spent strengthening their hold north of the Ebro, where we are told they devoted much attention to Tarraco.[37] It is possible, too, that they made contact with the Numidian King Syphax, a story told by both Livy and Appian. Though their accounts are contradictory in detail, and the whole story is

[33] Such fraud was actually committed by two of the nineteen *publicani*, and was discovered three years later (Livy 25.3.9–11).

[34] Livy 23.49.5–14; 24.41.1–42.11. On these passages see de Sanctis *Storia* III.2², 236 n. 73 and 237 n. 76; Lazenby, *Hannibal's war* 129.

[35] Livy 23.49.5–14. On the site of Iliturgi in this passage, see K. Gotzfried, *Annalen der römischen Provinzen beider Spanien 218–154* (Erlangen 1907) 9; and A. Schulten, *Hermes* 63 (1928) 288–301.

[36] Livy 24.42.9–10. On the date (212), see Klotz, *Livius* 162.

[37] Above, n. 23.

suspiciously like that of the younger Scipio's encounter with Syphax in 206, there may have been (as Livy suggests) an attempt in this period to build up an anti-Carthaginian alliance, and the proximity of eastern Spain to the north African coastline, combined with their dominance at sea, might have encouraged the Scipios to look in that direction. In any case, Syphax is reported as being defeated by his neighbour, Gala, and Gala's son, the young Massinissa.[38]

Although it would be rash to be too certain about the position in Spain at this time, it is likely that by the end of 212, Publius and Cnaeus Scipio were in control of the eastern seaboard from Emporion to Saguntum, and had successfully prevented the establishment of Carthaginian contacts between Spain and Italy. Their policy, so far as it can be identified, seems to have been one of steadily building up good relations with local tribal leaders; of confining Hasdrubal as far as possible to southern Spain, and certainly south of the Ebro; and of avoiding (if we ignore the confused accounts which have found their way into Livy's narrative) unnecessary extension of their forces which might have placed at risk the separation of Hannibal from his base and his supplies which was the fundamental reason for their presence in Spain at all.

There are reasons to believe that a change of policy took place during 212. At the beginning of his confused account of events in Spain under the year 214, which seems to contain some events at least which belong to 212,[39] Livy for the first time describes Publius and Cnaeus as dividing the land forces between them. Previously, he has always shown them acting together.[40] It is likely that this division took place in 212. Certainly Appian stresses that at the end of that year their forces were in winter–quarters some distance from one another.[41] Moreover it is in this year for the first time that there is mention of two *provinciae* in Spain, albeit in a very cursory manner. Hitherto *Hispania* had been allotted to P. Scipio in his consulship in 218, and there is one record of his *imperium* being prorogued in that *provincia* for 217.[42] As for Cn. Scipio, if we assume that *imperium* (probably *pro praetore*) was delegated to him by his brother in 218, there is no reason to believe that he held the *imperium*

---

[38] Livy 24.48.1–49.6; Appian, *Ib.* 15.58–16.60. Appian states that Hasdrubal was withdrawn from Spain to deal with Syphax, while Livy has both Hasdrubal Barca and Hasdrubal, son of Gisgo, in Spain at this time (Livy 25.32.2 and 4), and emphasises the absence of Carthaginian help in Massinissa's victory over Syphax (Livy 24.49.6).

[39] Livy 24.41.1–42.8; cf. above n. 37.

[40] Livy 22.22.3; 23.29.17; 23.49.6. He mentions, under 216, a division between land and sea forces (Gnaeus taking the former, Publius the latter), but this is not confirmed by his subsequent account (Livy 23.26.2).

[41] Appian, *Ib.* 16.61.   [42] Livy 21.17.1; 22.22.1.

at all once Publius had rejoined him in 217.[43] In the provincial allocations for 212, however, Livy records that the Spains (in the plural) were allotted to Publius and Cnaeus Scipio.[44] This should imply that both were now holding *imperium*, and that they were, at least formally, independent of one another, each with his own *provincia*. Cnaeus' position as a holder of *imperium* is confirmed by the description of him as *imperator* by Livy on three occasions after this (two in the context of senatorial debates) although the word has not previously been applied to him. Though the precise significance of this word is far from clear at this time, it must at least imply the holding of *imperium*.[45]

The decision to operate separate commands seems to imply the undertaking of new military initiatives on a wider front than previously. Such a development could only take place once Saguntum had been recaptured and, while it is uncertain whether the new command structure was introduced just before or immediately following the taking of Saguntum, it is part of the same policy. Indeed if Appian is correct, Publius had reached Castulo, which lies at the head of the valley of the Baetis, in time to set up winter-quarters there, in the winter of 212/211.[46] Appian names Cnaeus' winter-quarters as 'Orso', which should be Urso (modern Osuna). This, however, is too far west, and it is more likely that he spent the winter not far from Ilorci on the R. Segura (the ancient Tader) where Pliny locates the site of his pyre.[47]

The immediate causes of the disaster which followed in 211 are not hard to establish. Publius, with two-thirds of the available forces, moved against two of the three Carthaginian armies in Spain, commanded by Hasdrubal, son of Gisgo, and Mago, while Cnaeus, with the remaining third and the Celtiberian mercenaries who had been fighting with the Romans at least since 213, faced Hasdrubal Barca.[48] Barca, knowing the

---

[43] Above pp. 35–7.

[44] Livy 25.3.6: Hispaniae P. et Cn. Corneliis.

[45] Livy 25.32.1; 26.2.5; 27.4.6. Mommsen (*StR* II³, 652 n. 2), Jashemski, *Proconsular and propraetorian imperium* 22–3, Broughton (*MRR sub annis* 217–211), G. V. Sumner (*Arethusa* 3 (1970) 85–7) and R. Develin, *Klio* 62 (1980) 356–7 all note this usage, though they have not observed its chronological significance and have argued for a uniform pattern between 217 and 211. On the meaning of *imperator* see Cic. *Phil.* 11.8.20; Mommsen, *StR* I³, 123ff; R. Combès, *Imperator* (Paris 1966), 9–38.

[46] Appian, *Ib.* 16.61. Livy places the deaths of the Scipios in 212 (25.32.1ff), but says this was 'anno octavo postquam in Hispaniam venerat Cn. Scipio' (25.36.14), i.e. in 211. The sending of C. Nero in the autumn of 211 also suggests that the disaster had taken place earlier the same year (Livy 26.17.1–3). (See de Sanctis, *Storia* III.2², 432 n. 4; Lazenby, *Hannibal's war* 130.)

[47] Pliny, *NH* 3.1.9. It has been suggested that Appian's text should be emended to read Λόρκωνι rather than 'Ορσῶνι (Schulten, *FHA* 3.92; Scullard, *Scipio Africanus* 50 n. 1; A. Klotz, *Appians Darstellung des zweiten punischen Krieges* (Paderborn 1936) 71 n. 2, but this does not follow from the description of the final battle, as Gnaeus had moved some way from his camp when he was trapped and killed (Appian, *Ib.* 16.63; Livy 25.33.8–9). [48] Livy 25.32.1ff; cf. 24.49.7.

fickleness of the Celtiberians and being adept at their language, persuaded them to desert, and Cnaeus was forced to retreat from his previous position. In the mean time, P. Scipio under pressure from the Numidian cavalry, commanded by Massinissa, heard that further reinforcements for the Carthaginians were about to arrive, in the person of Indibilis and 7,500 Suessetani from north of the Ebro. Leaving his legate, Ti. Fonteius, in charge of the camp, Publius set off to intercept Indibilis. This manoeuvre was successful until the Numidian cavalry realised what had happened, and, advancing against P. Scipio, overwhelmed his forces and killed Scipio himself. Cnaeus, in the meantime, decided if possible to join up with his brother, and managed to slip away by night. He was, however, pursued and trapped on a small hillock, where his forces were defeated and he himself was killed. A number of his soldiers, however, escaped to join up with Fonteius and the remnants of Publius' army.[49]

The senate and the commanders in Spain 218–211

The successes and the eventual failure of the campaign of the Scipio brothers seem to have their origin in the planning and policy of the two men who were actually in the field. The senate in Rome is, throughout the period, involved only in two capacities. First it was they who originally allocated *Hispania* to P. Scipio as consular *provincia* for 218, and prorogued his *imperium* within the same area in 217.[50] Similarly, when the change in the conditions in Spain required, so the Scipios thought, a division of forces, so that each commanded his own, it was in the senate that the necessary redistribution of *provinciae* took place.[51] Secondly the senate was responsible for the provisioning of the forces in Spain with food, equipment and money. The sources mention large-scale supplies being sent with P. Scipio and the reinforcements that went with him to Spain in mid-217.[52] Earlier that year there had already been an attempt to send a shipment to Spain from Ostia, but it had been captured by a Punic naval squadron in the vicinity of Cosa on the Etruscan coast.[53] Polybius mentions a further shipment of supplies in the winter of 217/216; and in 215, in response to the Scipios' written request for

---

[49] The account given is from Livy. Appian, *Ib.* 16.61–3 differs in detail, omitting mention of Celtiberian treachery. Livy's account is supported by the remarks given by Polybius (10.6.1–7.2) to young Scipio, saying that this earlier defeat had resulted from the division of the armies and the treachery of the Celtiberians.

[50] Livy 21.17.1; 22.22.1.
[51] Livy 25.3.6.
[52] Livy 22.22.1.
[53] Livy 22.11.6.

provision of at least food and clothing, goods were obtained on credit from the *publicani*.[54]

The senate, then, can be seen to be providing the essential underlay, in terms of command-structure and supplies, to enable P. Scipio to carry out the task assigned to him. However, beyond that it would seem that the formulation of policy in Spain was the responsibility of the men on the spot. Two major changes of direction can be identified, despite the weakness of the sources: the decision to send Cnaeus on to Spain in 218 and his appointment as a delegated holder of *imperium*; and the division of forces in 212, in order to pursue a more active offensive against the Carthaginians. There can be no doubt that the first of these was a decision made without consulting the senate, and it is probable that the second also resulted from the judgement of the Scipios in Spain, rather than from a senatorial decree.[55] This is hardly surprising. The senate had the war in Italy to manage, and although we hear of letters being sent from Spain to Rome to announce progress and to request aid,[56] the Spanish campaign was the most remote of any conducted during the struggle against Hannibal, and therefore inevitably that most distant from senatorial supervision and control. So far as the sources allow us to see, it was in any case not felt necessary to exercise such control, and the decisions of the Scipios were supported by the requisite senatorial action, and their demand for supplies was met promptly. It was not a lack of interest on the part of the senate which left the conduct of the war in Spain in the hands of the Scipios, for they recognised the significance of the war there even during those difficult times when Rome itself was under threat.[57] Rather it was the inevitable result of the remoteness of Spain and the conditions of war.

Recovery and victory: 211–206

The defeat of the Scipios in 211 seems from the sources to have been almost total, with both the armies' commanders dead, both armies in disarray far from their base, and their Spanish allies abandoning them.

[54] Polybius 3.106.7; Livy 23.48.4ff.

[55] Note that the description put by Polybius into the mouth of Scipio Aemilianus of the reasons for the catastrophe of 211 ('the treachery of the Celtiberians and the division of their own forces' – τὸν διαʒευγμὸν τῶν ἰδίων στρατοπέδων 10.7.1) suggests that the Scipios were responsible for the division.

[56] Livy 23.29.17 (probably the same letter as that whose reception is described by Livy 23.48.4).

[57] So Val. Max. 3.7.10.

That the Romans were not driven completely from the peninsula is in itself remarkable, and a credit to the *eques Romanus*, L. Marcius, whom the sources describe as having rallied the remnants of Cn. Scipio's forces, joined up with those of P. Scipio which had been left in camp when he himself had made his last disastrous foray, and led the combined group back up the coast to their base north of the Ebro. It is perhaps not surprising that the Roman annalists, on whom both Livy and later retailers of myths and anecdotes drew, succumbed to the temptation to heroise Marcius, and invest him with a semi-divine aura. They also provided him with a successful counter-attack against the Carthaginians.[58] The fact that he, together with Ti. Fonteius, P. Scipio's legate, managed to prevent the complete destruction of Roman interests in Spain by falling back into a position blocking Hasdrubal's path to Italy, is praiseworthy enough, and was only possible because of the slowness of the Carthaginians in following up their advantage.[59]

Marcius' valour was, we are told, acknowledged by the senate when they received a letter from him, though they were angered by his use of the title 'propraetor'. It is likely enough that Marcius, in command in Spain, should think it appropriate to give himself this style, especially if he had, as Livy reports, been selected as their leader by his troops. The senate, however, were disturbed by the possibility that the *imperium* might be granted merely by vote of an army and took steps to provide a properly appointed *imperium*-bearer.[60] In fact, it was not until after the capture of Capua later in the year that a commander was found. C. Claudius Nero who had been commanding forces with *imperium pro praetore* at Capua, was ordered by the senate to sail from Puteoli with a force of 6,000 infantry and 300 cavalry, together with 6,000 infantry and 800 cavalry from the allies.[61]

The details of Livy's account of Nero's period in Spain have been doubted and he must surely be wrong to suggest that Nero was replaced before the end of the year.[62] Indeed it seems that his chronology of the years 211 to 208 for the events in Spain has moved them backwards by

[58] Livy 25.37.1–39.18; Val. Max. 1.6.2, 2.7.5, 7.15.11; Frontinus 2.6.2, 2.10.2; Silius Italicus 13.696–703; Pliny, *NH.* 2.111.241; cf. Ed. Meyer, *Kleine Schriften* II (Halle 1924) 446 n.

[59] Polybius (9.11) ascribes this to mutual rivalry. Scipio the younger was to observe a similar lack of co-operation two years later (Polybius 10.6.5).

[60] Livy 26.2.1–6; cf. 25.37.5–6. The use of the term *propraetor* indicates a late annalistic source, but the story itself is probable enough (A. Klotz, *Hermes* 50 (1915) 484–520; U. Kahrstedt, *Die Annalistik von Livius B. XXXI–XLV* (Berlin 1913) 2ff; A. H. McDonald, *T. Livi ab urbe condita* V (Oxford Classical Text 1965) xlii.

[61] Livy 26.17.1–3.

[62] Livy 26.17.4–20.4. On the stories of Nero's successes in Spain, see Scullard, *Scipio Africanus* 55 n. l.

one year, with the result that, for instance, he dates Scipio's successful attack on New Carthage to 210 when it is certain that Polybius placed it in 209. Livy himself notes the discrepancy between the different sources he used for this event, but cannot believe that Scipio spent a whole year in Spain doing nothing. The most economical hypothesis would seem to be that Scipio did not leave Rome for Spain in order to replace Nero until 210, and that the attack on New Carthage occurred in the spring of the following year.[63]

C. Nero had been in the peninsula for less than a year when he was replaced by the young P. Cornelius Scipio, son of the P. Scipio who had died in the disaster of 211. The appointment itself was extraordinary. Scipio was only 25 years old, and had held no higher office than that of aedile. Moreover the means of his appointment were, so far as we know, unprecedented. Although the story as it appears in Livy shows signs of the conflation of several sources, and may very well have been influenced in its details by the story of Scipio Aemilianus' volunteering for Spain in 151, there can be little doubt that Scipio was voted the *imperium pro consule* by a popular assembly, either by the *comitia centuriata*, as Livy has it, or possibly by the *comitia tributa*, as was done on subsequent occasions.[64] The reasons for replacing Nero are not stated by Livy, nor is the use of such unprecedented procedure adequately explained. He describes a fruitless discussion of who should be sent, taking place presumably in the senate; this was concluded by instructions to the consuls to call an assembly to decide the matter.[65] The intrinsic improbability of this suggests some political moves behind the scenes, and the eventual choice of Scipio makes it likely that the supporters of his family were instrumental in whatever was happening.[66] The family connections must have been important, though the details of the manoeuvre must remain obscure, especially if, as seems to be the case, Livy is here combining disparate sources.

The senate does, however, seem to have taken some care to ensure that Scipio was supported in his task, and that they had some control at least over his progress. M. Iunius Silanus was sent out with Scipio as

[63] Livy 27.7.5–6. The account in Polybius (10.6.20) comes from book 10 according to the *codex Urbinas*, and thus from either 210/209 or 209/208 (Walbank, *Commentary* II, 14–15); if Livy's dating to '*principio veris*' is retained, the earliest date would be spring 209 (de Sanctis, *Storia* III.2², 453 n. 38; A. Klotz, *Hermes* 80 (1952) 340).

[64] Livy 26.18.1–11. On the parallel with 151 (Polybius 35.4), see de Sanctis, *Storia* III.2², 440 n. 18. On the role of the two assemblies, Mommsen, *StR* II, 311 n. 1; W. Liebenam, *RE* IV, 694; G. W. Botsford, *The Roman assemblies* (New York 1909) 188 n. 2. On Scipio's age, Polybius 10.6.10, Livy 26.1.18.7; cf. Walbank, *Commentary* II, 199.

[65] Livy 26.18.2–4.   [66] Scullard; *Roman politics*² 66–7.

propraetor to assist in the conduct of the campaign.[67] He had been, as praetor, sent to Etruria in 212, and his *imperium* had been prorogued there for 211, and though scarcely likely to be an old man, as one late source suggests, will certainly have been Scipio's senior. His being sent to assist with lesser *imperium* was a sensible provision, given the size of the task and Scipio's lack of experience, but emphasises the unusual nature of the latter's appointment.[68] The senate does seem to have had some doubts about the wisdom of the measure, however. When the *provinciae* were being allotted in the following year, the *imperium* of Scipio and Silanus was not extended for the whole year, as was normal, but until such time as the senate should recall them. This has been seen as an expression of trust in the two commanders, but it is far more likely that their tenure was being made precarious, so that they could be brought back from Spain as soon as the senate had reason to suspect their competence.[69]

When, towards the end of the campaigning season of 210, Scipio, with Silanus and a force of 10,000 infantry and 1,000 cavalry, landed at Emporion and marched thence to Tarraco, he first congratulated the army (and in particular Marcius) for holding on to the *provincia* successfully despite the double defeat of the previous year.[70] The area still under Roman control seems to have been the old 'Scipionic' area north of the Ebro. It is possible that Saguntum was still in friendly hands, though the only reason for thinking so is that the sources do not mention any subsequent recapture.[71] Nero seems to have achieved nothing beyond consolidating and reinforcing the remnants of the two armies which had been brought north by Marcius and Fonteius.[72] That in itself is hardly

---

[67] Livy 26.19.10: 'propraetor adiutor ad res gerendas'.

[68] On Silanus' previous career, Livy 25.20.1–3; 26.1.5. On his age, Zonaras 9.7.4. The suggestion (Jashemski, *Proconsular and propraetorian imperium* 25–6; Broughton, *MRR* I, 284 n. 4) that he was 'propraetor with imperium pro consule' depends on an overliteral interpretation of Polybius 10.6.7 and Livy 28.28.14, and on a confusion of office ad *imperium*. *Praetor pro consule*, the office of praetor with the *imperium* of a consul, was certainly used later (see below pp. 75–7) but *propraetor pro consule*, the *imperium* of praetor and consul combined, would be anomalous or impossible (cf. Mommsen, *StR* II, 650 n. 2). Despite G. V. Sumner, *Arethusa* 3 (1970) 88 and R. Develin, *Klio* 69 (1980) 358–60 there is no reason to credit Silanus with *imperium pro consule*, either in the literary sources, or in the accounts of the Spanish campaigns.

[69] Livy 27.7.17. Jashemski, *Proconsular and propraetorian imperium* 29–30. Develin [n. 68] 359–60 suggests that this was intended to be an extension of *imperium* for more than a year because of the distance from Spain. However, this does not explain why their *imperium* was in fact renewed in 208 (Livy 27.22.7).

[70] Livy 26.19.11–20.3. This passage probably also belongs to the annalistic heroising of Marcius; hence the geographical understanding of *provincia* (see above Ch. 1 and above n. 58).

[71] So Ed. Meyer [n. 58] 451; *contra* Scullard, *Scipio Africanus* 52.

[72] Appian, *Ib.* 17.65–6 seems correct in his assessment of Nero as having achieved nothing remarkable (cf. his similar judgement on Cn. Scipio in 217, *Ib.* 15.57; above p. 37 n. 27). He does, however, somewhat remarkably transfer Marcellus to Spain from Sicily at this time.

surprising, and indeed Scipio himself, probably for lack of time, did no more that year then lead his troops away into winter-quarters.

Early the following year, Scipio successfully carried out a plan which was to alter not only the complexion of the war in Spain, but in the long run the progress of the war as a whole. The three Carthaginian generals Hasdrubal Barca, Hasdrubal son of Gisgo and Mago, had divided their forces into three, and were occupied in operations against various groups of Iberians, two of them in the far west and the nearest (Hasdrubal Barca) among the Carpetani, in the Toledo region. The reasons for this disposition of forces was partly the quarrelling between them and partly the unrest caused by their harsh treatment of their allies. The result was that none was less than ten days' march away from their base on the Mediterranean coast at New Carthage.[73] Scipio therefore seized the initiative, and, leaving Silanus at the Ebro with 3,000 foot and either 300 or 500 horse, crossed the river with 25,000 foot and 2,500 horse, and perhaps an additional 5,000 troops from his Spanish allies.[74] Laelius, his close friend and legate, was given secret instructions to meet him at New Carthage with the fleet, while he himself marched rapidly southwards down the coast towards the Carthaginian base. Both Polybius and Livy say he reached New Carthage on the seventh day after he had left the Ebro, a rate of progress which is quite incredible; but the march must have been rapid, and certainly caught the garrison there off their guard.[75] A brilliant two-part assault, frontally against the main entrance to the town, and then by a wading-party across the lagoon on its north side, was completely successful, and Mago, the Carthaginian commander, surrendered the citadel shortly after.[76]

The strategic effects of this capture were immense. Not only had Scipio succeeded in breaking out of the restricted area within which his father and uncle had remained for most of their time in Spain; not only had he carried the war into enemy territory, as he was to do again when in 205 he embarked upon the invasion of Africa while Hannibal was still in Italy; but he had also, by a single move, pushed the seat of the war back from the eastern coastal strip across the Sierra de Segura and into the valley of the Baetis. At no point after this did the Romans have to fight the

---

[73] Polybius 10.7.3–5; cf. Walbank, *Commentary* II, 202.

[74] Polybius 10.6.7; Livy 26.42.1; Scullard, *Scipio Africanus* 66 n. 2.

[75] Polybius 10.9.7; Livy 26.42.6. On the speed of march, see H. Droysen, *RhMus* 30 (1875) 67; U. Kahrstedt, *Geschichte der Karthage* III (Berlin 1913) 509 n. 1; de Sanctis, *Storia* III.2², 450 n. 35; Scullard, *Scipio Africanus* 67 n. 1; Walbank, *Commentary* II, 204.

[76] Polybius 10.9.8–15.11; Livy 26.42.6–46.10. See especially the discussions by Scullard, *Scipio Africanus* 69–92; Walbank, *Commentary* II, 205–20, and bibliography listed there. Add now J. Lovejoy, *CP* 67 (1972) 110–11; Lazenby, *Hannibal's war* 134–40.

Carthaginians on the eastern coastal strip, which hitherto had seen all the fighting.

This shift in the theatre of war and the spectacular nature of Scipio's achievement also brought new support from the leaders of Spanish tribes. The first recorded as having joined him was Edesco, who came to him at Tarraco after his return thither from New Carthage. Although it is not certain which area he controlled, he clearly was an important leader.[77] Other leaders who came over at this time included Indibilis and Mandonius of the Ilergetes, an important tribe in the lower Ebro valley.[78] In both cases Scipio handed over to his new allies their womenfolk, whom he had captured, and it was probably during this winter also that these three chieftains acknowledged their submission to him by addressing him as king.[79]

It was with this increased support from the Spanish tribes, and encouraged by the worries of the senate about the danger of Hasdrubal crossing the Alps and joining Hannibal in Italy that Scipio planned his action for 208. Laelius had been sent to announce the capture of New Carthage, and had heard the fears expressed by the *patres*. It was not until after he returned to Tarraco that Scipio set out, but the aggressive policy he pursued in 208 was in any case the natural complement to the events of 209. He must, moreover, have made provision for his move south before Laelius rejoined him.[80] A full-scale confrontation of the two armies seems to have been inevitable, as Hasdrubal on his side needed a victory to prevent further Spanish defections. Should he fail, he could always make a last attempt to take his troops out of Spain to join his brother. Such at least is the picture of Hasdrubal's thoughts given by Polybius, and although it is hard to imagine where he can have found the information, it is likely enough.[81]

The clash when it came was at Baecula, placed by both Polybius and Livy in the high mountain region at the head of the Baetis valley, the 'saltus Castulonensis'.[82] Scipio's superior tactics routed the Carthaginians but Hasdrubal Barca was able, by withdrawing in time, to extract a large

[77] Polybius 10.34.1–35.3; Livy 27.17.1–2. The description of Edesco as τὸν ᾽Εδετανῶν δυνάστην at Polybius 10.34.2 originated from an emendation of Schweighaeuser's for τὸν δυνατόν δυνάστην of the text, and was originally given simply *exempli gratia* (J. Schweighaeuser, *Polybii Historiae* III (Leipzig 1790) 267); Walbank, *Commentary* II, 246.

[78] Polybius 10.35.6–8; Livy 27.17.3. On the Ilergetes, A. Schulten, *RE* IX, 999.

[79] Before, at least, the battle of Baecula in summer 208 (Polybius 10.38.3, 40.3).

[80] Livy 27.7.1–4, 17.8.

[81] Polybius 10.37.3–5. cf. Walbank, *Commentary* II, 247.

[82] Polybius 10.38.7; Livy 27.20.3. On the site of the 'saltus', see P. P. Spranger, *Historia* 7 (1958) 95–112. On the site of the battle, Scullard, *Scipio Africanus* 300ff; for doubts on the traditional siting at Bailen, R. Corzo Sanchez, *Habis* 6 (1975) 231–4.

proportion of his troops, his treasure and his elephants, and to move away northwards.[83] Scipio did not pursue him, though he did send a small force to watch the transit of the Pyrenees, which is strange if one of his main concerns had been to prevent Hasdrubal from leading reinforcements into Italy. It is possible that he had left Silanus north of the Ebro when he himself had come south. Though the sources do not mention this, it was the pattern he had adopted in the previous year: moreover Livy's description of the allotment of armies and provinces for Spain in 208 suggest that the senate at least envisaged them working separately, with an army and a *provincia* each. It may have been intended that Silanus would block any Carthaginian movement northwards from the Roman base at Tarraco. If so, the plan failed, for there is no mention of any encounter between Hasdrubal and Silanus, and the Carthaginian forces seem to have evaded confrontation as they followed Hannibal to Italy.[84]

Despite this, Baecula was an important success, especially for the war in Spain. Further tribes, now from the south in the vicinity of the battle, came over to the Roman side, and, as Edesco and Indibilis had done, acclaimed Scipio as their king. This time, however, Scipio refused their acclamation, and while hoping that he would be kingly in character, preferred to be hailed as commander (*imperator*). The significance of this event in the history of the acclamation of a successful general as *imperator* is great, even if its immediate meaning is unclear. At least it confirms the picture seen already of the effect of Scipio's campaigns on the indigenous peoples, and the high regard they had for him as an individual.[85] Once again, as with the case of Edesco and Indibilis, Scipio responded by freeing Iberian captives, and also, according to Livy, Massiva, Massinissa's nephew, who had been captured with the Numidian cavalry.[86]

The remainder of 208 and 207 seems to have been spent by both sides in consolidating their positions, and waiting, perhaps, to see how Hasdrubal Barca might fare in Italy. A conference of the three Carthaginian generals after the defeat at Baecula is recorded by Livy.[87] After Hasdrubal Barca's withdrawal to Italy, Hasdrubal son of Gisgo was to be given all the remaining troops, and to withdraw into a part of the

[83] Polybius 10.39.7–8; Livy 27.19.1.

[84] Livy 27.22.7: suae Hispaniae suique exercitus. Cf. the arrangements made for P. and Cn. Scipio in 212, Livy 25.3.6. On Scipio's action after Baecula, Polybius 10.40.11; Livy 27.20.2. It is not clear which route Hasdrubal took across the Pyrenees (despite, for instance, B. Caven, *The Punic wars* (London 1980) 206–7). On the absence of Silanus, note the criticism, attributed by Livy to Silanus, of Scipio's negligence, Livy 28.42.14.

[85] Polybius 10.40.2–9; Livy 27.19.3–6. See A. Aymard, *Revue du Nord* 36 (1954) 121–8; R. Combès [n. 45] 51–68.

[86] Polybius 10.40.10–11; Livy 27.19.8–12.   [87] Livy 27.20.3–8.

country as yet untouched by the disaffection. Mago meanwhile was to try to recruit further forces in the Balearic Islands.

It is indeed while recruiting in the following year (207) that Mago is next mentioned, though in the central region. He was there with the newly arrived Carthaginian commander Hanno, rapidly building up a considerable force. Against them Scipio sent out Silanus with 10,000 infantry and 500 cavalry, about half the total of Roman forces then in Spain.[88] The Carthaginians were defeated, and Hanno captured, although Mago succeeded in escaping with the cavalry. The site of the clash seems to be in the southern part of the *meseta*, probably the region near the headwaters of the Baetis.[89]

Scipio himself apparently hoped that there might be a chance of concluding the war by a final confrontation with Mago. He therefore advanced into the Baetis valley. Mago, however, fell back toward Gades, and strengthened the cities of the lower Baetis by distributing his forces among them.[90] Scipio had to content himself with sending his brother, Lucius, with 10,000 foot and 1,000 horse, against a town which Livy calls Orongis, and which was probably on the north side of the Baetis valley, in the Sierra Morena.[91] At the end of the campaigning season, Lucius was sent back to Rome to report, just as Laelius had been in 209, taking with him several notable captives, including the Carthaginian general Hanno.[92]

The last great battle of the Romano-Punic war in Spain, usually known as the battle of Ilipa, is now extremely difficult to locate, and some doubt also has been placed on the dating Livy gives it, in early 206. Though the latter may well be correct,[93] the normal (and largely unchallenged) identification of the site with Ilipa, a town situated at Alcala del Rio, some 14 kilometres north of Seville on the north side of the Guadalquivir, the ancient Baetis, is problematic. No source gives the battle-site this name, and, as has been recently pointed out, the Carthaginian general, Hasdrubal son of Gisgo, could not have made directly for the sea from the northern side of the river, after the battle, since he would have been separated from

[88] Livy 28.1.1–5. For the Roman forces in Spain, see Livy 27.36.12; Brunt, *Italian manpower* 420.

[89] Livy 28.1.6–2.12. The battle is said to take place ten days' ride from the 'Gaditana provincia' (cf. A. Schulten, *FHA* III, 129–30. This cannot be Celtiberia properly so-called (i.e. the north-eastern *meseta*), and probably 'Celtiberia' is used here, as elsewhere, to describe the whole *meseta* (cf. A. Schulten, *Numantia* I (Munich 1914) 222).

[90] Livy 28.2.14–16.

[91] Livy 28.3.1–16. Orongis is probably the same as Auringis, placed by Livy, in a garbled passage (24.42.5), in eastern Baetica. On its position, near to silver mines, see O. Davies, *Roman mines in Europe* (Oxford 1935) 111ff; Schulten, *FHA* III, 84–5.

[92] Livy 28.4.1–4.

[93] Scullard, *Scipio Africanus* 304–9, *contra* M. Jumpertz, *Der römisch-karthagische Krieg in Spanien* 211–206 (Berlin 1892) 28ff, de Sanctis, *Storia* III.2², 481–5.

it by the swamps of the *marismas*, covering a large area to the north of the mouth of the Guadalquivir.[94] Though unsatisfactory, it is perhaps safer to say no more than that the battle must have occurred not far from the Baetis and in the western part of the river valley.

There is no doubt, however, that when the opposing forces met they were fighting for supremacy in Spain. Hasdrubal, son of Gisgo, and Mago commanded the remaining Carthaginians; Scipio was joined by Silanus and a Spanish chieftain called Culchas. Although the Carthaginians had been driven back almost to the Atlantic, Scipio had the majority of his forces with him, and all of his officers, with the exception of his brother Lucius, who was left at base, either in New Carthage, or, as Livy has it, in Tarraco.[95] Despite this, Scipio was outnumbered[96] and, had he been decisively defeated, there can be little doubt that the Carthaginians would have rapidly regained the territory they had lost, and the allegiance of the notoriously fickle Spanish leaders.

In the event, the great set-piece battle proved a success for the Romans, though the intervention of a thunderstorm prevented them pushing their advantage to a final conclusion.[97] Hasdrubal was prepared to attempt the defence of his camp on the following day, but the desertion of many of his Spanish allies, including especially the chief of the Turdetani, one of the most important tribes of southern Spain, persuaded him to retreat towards the coast during the following night. Scipio pursued him hard, and in the end he escaped from the coast with a mere 6,000 men, who were picked up by a naval squadron from Gades. Mago also embarked in ships sent back for him by Hasdrubal. Scipio and Silanus meanwhile marched back separately to Tarraco, whence Lucius Scipio was sent with news to the senate that Spain had been recaptured.[98] Scipio's message has been described as exaggerated and premature.[99] Exaggerated certainly, since there were vast areas of the peninsula in which the Romans had not even set foot; and the announcement of the 'recapture'[100] is also odd, as

---

[94] Livy calls the place 'Silpia' (28.12.14); Polybius, Ἰλίπα (11.20.1); while Appian puts the Carthaginian camp at Καρμώνη (25.96). On Ilipa see Strabo 3.142 and *CIL* II, p. 141ff esp. no. 1085. For discussion, see Ed. Meyer [n. 58] 406ff; Scullard, *Scipio Africanus* 126–8; R. Corzo Sanchez [n. 82] 234–40.

[95] Polybius 11.20.3–5, 23.1; Livy 28.13.5, 14.15, 16.15; Appian, *Ib.* 26.104, 28.112.

[96] Carthaginian numbers were 70,000 foot and 4,000 horse (Polybius 11.20.2; cf. Livy 28.12.14) or 50,000 foot and 4,500 horse (Livy 28.12.13). Roman numbers were 45,000 infantry and 3,000 cavalry (Polybius 11.20.8) or 45,000 *in toto* (Livy 28.13.5) (see Walbank, *Commentary* II, 296–7; J. Lazenby, *Hannibal's war* 135).

[97] Polybius 11.21.1–24.9; Livy 28.13.6–15.11. See Scullard, *Scipio Africanus* 128–40; Lazenby, *Hannibal's war* 145–50.

[98] Livy 28.15.12–17.1.   [99] So Lazenoy, *Hannibal's war* 151.

[100] L. Scipio...nuntius receptae Hispaniae Roman est missus (Livy 28.17.1).

no Roman had yet made any claim to hold as much of Spain as Scipio now controlled. Yet seen in terms of the war between Rome and Carthage the final victory had been won. Later in the year Mago, still clinging on in Gades, was recalled by Carthage, and ordered to take his fleet, collecting what forces he could in Gaul and Liguria, and to join up with Hannibal. Before he left, he could not resist one last sortie against New Carthage, trying to accomplish by sea what Scipio himself had achieved by his lightning raid in 209. He was, however, repulsed by the inhabitants with heavy losses, and on his return to Gades, found himself shut out there too. Though he captured, and, according to Livy, tortured to death the chief magistrate of the town and his *quaestor*, he was compelled to withdraw to the Balearic Islands, whereupon the Gaditanes surrendered to the Romans. The last Carthaginian commander had thus withdrawn, and the last Punic stronghold surrendered without further Roman military action. The task which had been entrusted to the elder P. Scipio in 218 had at last been accomplished.[101]

Before the final departure of Mago, however, Scipio had already shown the way in which he saw future developments once the primary task of denying the Carthaginians access to the resources of Spain had been completed. So far as the war was concerned, he made contact with Syphax, and even visited him is Africa, leaving his own *provincia* in the hands of L. Marcius at Tarraco and M. Silanus in New Carthage.[102] As it happened, so the story goes, Scipio was just approaching port with two quinqueremes when Hasdrubal son of Gisgo, who was also coming to visit Syphax, caught sight of the Roman ships and pursued them with seven triremes into the neutral harbour. Syphax invited the two to dinner, whereupon Scipio not only impressed both with his personality but concluded a formal agreement with Syphax.[103] This displays Scipio's belief that, now the Spanish campaign was over, the next centre of Roman activity should be in Africa. In the event, however, his contact with Syphax was not very useful, as Hasdrubal subsequently won him over by giving him his daughter Sophoniba in marriage.[104]

---

[101] Livy 28.36.1–37.10.

[102] Livy 28.17.11. Scullard, *Scipio Africanus* 308, believes Livy has them the wrong way round, as Marcius is at New Carthage when Scipio returns. Livy does say, however, that Marcius had to be summoned from Tarraco (28.19.4).

[103] Polybius 11.24a.4, Livy 28.17.3–18.12;Appian, *Ib*. 29.114–30.119. The status of this formal agreement ('foedere icto', Livy 28.18.12) is difficult, as Scipio does not seem to be an official emissary, and Syphax cannot be renewing the *amicitia* from 213 (Livy 24.48.1–49.6; above p. 39) which had been confirmed in 210 (Livy 27.4.5–6). Cf. M. Holleaux, *Rome, la Grèce et les monarchies hellénistiques* (Paris 1921) 171 n. 2; A. Heuss, *Die volkerrechlichen Grundlagen der röm. Aussenpolitik* (Klio Beiheft 31, 1933) 29–30.

[104] Polybius 14.1.4, 7.6; Livy 29.23.1–5; 30.12.11.

Less romantic, but more significant for the subsequent development of Roman Spain, were Scipio's other activities before his departure for Italy. First, he and Marcius attacked two recalcitrant native towns, named Castulo and Iliturgi by Livy.[105] The usual problems of identification of Iberian place names make it hard to be certain about these locations but they cannot be too far from New Carthage, since Scipio marched thence to Iliturgi in five days.[106] These were the first attacks on Iberian towns since the defeat of the Carthaginians. The reason given was that they had participated in the massacre of P. and Cn. Scipio in 211, but if there is any original material in the speech Livy gives to Scipio before the assault on 'Iliturgi' it would seem that his troops needed some additional encouragement to persuade them to fight the Spaniards, which they had not needed while they opposed the Carthaginians.[107] Certainly there are signs of a policy not merely of fighting the Carthaginians but also of establishing Roman control and a Roman presence on a long-term basis. Once the two towns had succumbed, Marcius and Laelius were sent on further westwards, down into the Baetis valley, against another town, said to have been of pro-Carthaginian sympathies,[108] and from there westwards again towards Gades.[109] It was by a natural extension of this part of his policy that Scipio established the settlement of Italica, the modern Santiponce, some 8 kilometres north of Seville. Though Appian, the only source to mention its foundation, describes it as intended for the wounded, there can be little doubt that a Roman settlement so far west was meant to establish a permanent Roman presence.[110]

If these events foreshadowed future developments, there were also signs of future difficulties. On Scipio's return from his expedition with Marcius he celebrated with gladiatorial games in New Carthage.[111] Shortly after, however, he fell ill, and the news spread rapidly. His recently acquired allies, Mandonius and Indibilis, encouraged by reports of his death, began to ravage the territory of two Roman allies on the coast, in the area of the Ebro mouth, the Suessetani and the Sedetani. Roman troops stationed nearby at Sucro, probably on the river of the same name, the modern Júcar, mutinied, complaining that they were still

---

[105] Livy 28.19.1–20.12; Appian, *Ib.* 32.127–31; cf. Polybius 11.24.10.

[106] Livy 28.19.4 (Walbank, *Commentary* II, 305).   [107] Livy 28.19.6–8.

[108] Astapa, not far from modern Osuna: Livy 28.22.1–23.5; Appian, *Ib.* 33.132–6. Cf. E. Hübner, *CIL* II, p. 196.

[109] Livy 28.23.6–8.

[110] Appian, *Ib.* 38.115; Hübner and Schulten, *RE* IX, 2283–4. On the status of Italica, see below n. 127. Recent excavation reveals that there was pre-Roman settlement (M. Pellicer, V. Hurtado and M. La Bandera, 'Corte estratigrafico de la Casa de Venus', in *Italica* (Excavaciones arqueologicas en España 121, 1982) 29–73.   [111] Livy 28.21.1–10.

being kept far from home, despite the fact that the enemy had been conquered. However, by the time it was learnt that Scipio was fit and well, their demands had lessened to prompt payment of their *stipendia*, and that vengeance for the deaths of P. and Cn. Scipio be taken against the 'Iliturgitani'. By this name is meant, it seems, the Ilergetes, with whose chieftains, Mandonius and Indibilis, the ringleaders of the mutiny were alleged to be in consultation. The complaint about *stipendia* was met by raising money from Roman allies, and the sedition put down by a stiff talk from Scipio, followed by the public execution of 35 leaders.[112]

Scipio had then to deal with the threat from Mandonius and Indibilis, still in revolt.[113] The two sides met in battle four days' march from the Ebro mouth, and if this was the seat of the rebellion, it is easy to understand the importance which Scipio attached to it. A strong and hostile force in this position could easily disrupt the communications along the coastal strip which the two Scipios had been at pains to establish. Scipio once again produced a harangue which implied the importance of making clear the Roman predominance in Spain, over both Carthaginians and Celtiberians. In the event the native forces were defeated, and the two leaders were quick to ask for terms, which were granted. The cash which Mandonius and the Ilergetes handed over provided pay for the troops; and doubtless Scipio was happy enough to have established Roman military superiority with such speed, the more so as Laelius in a surprise attack on a Carthaginian squadron from the port of Carteia, in the extreme south, had displayed Roman command of the waters round Spain.[114] Scipio was in any case anxious to return to Rome for the consular elections.

The Scipios and the beginnings of Roman Spain

The period of over twelve years between the allotment of the *provincia Hispania* to the consul P. Scipio in 218, and the departure of his son from Spain in 206 was of fundamental importance for the shaping of the Roman involvement in the peninsula. As an investigation of the background to the war in Spain has shown, there is no sign of Roman interest in Spain as such before the fall of Saguntum, which preceded the declaration of war against Carthage in 218. Roman concern with Iberia,

---

112 Polybius 11.25–30, Livy 28.24.1–29.12; Appian, *Ib.* 34.137–36.146.
113 Polybius 11.31.1–33.6; Livy 28.31.5–34.12; Appian, *Ib.* 37.147–8.
114 Livy 28.30.3–31.1.

where it can be traced, is related solely to the maintenance of a watch over the growth of Barcid power and influence there, and the treaties made between Rome and Hasdrubal in 226 and between Rome and Saguntum at some point in the 220s make most sense when seen as an institutional form of this surveillance.[115] The next 12 years saw the extension of the same policy, under the conditions of war between Rome and Carthage. Spain became, from the Roman point of view, a battlefield in the struggle against the Carthaginians.

Yet before Scipio left in 206, he had already shown that the end of the fight against Carthage there did not mean the end of Roman interest in Spain. It is important to note that the experience and the ideas which underlay the earliest Roman experience in Spain, and thus the development of their earliest administrative practice, was an experience of warfare. Although there were inevitably substantial modifications to the patterns established by the three Scipios and in some cases reversals of the methods they had employed, the work of subsequent governors is best seen in terms of what they had established. Roughly speaking, this may be categorised in three ways: the pattern of command; administrative arrangements; and relations with indigenous peoples.

(a) The pattern of command[116]

The structure of command in Spain was determined at two levels. In constitutional terms, the determination of areas of responsibility (*provinciae*) and of power (*imperium*) was decided by the senate and people of Rome, in various combinations; in practice, questions as to who should command which troops, and where and how they should fight were decided on the spot.

If Livy is accurate in his record of senatorial decisions (and there is perhaps more likelihood of precision in such a case than in most others)[117], there was considerable variation and experiment on the constitutional plane. As argued above, it is probable that the Spanish war was seen as a single *provincia* under a single commander with consular *imperium* from 218 to 212, and that the position of Cn. Scipio during this time was that of a temporary stand-in, appointed by his brother during his absence from his *provincia* in 218–217. The alteration of this pattern

---

[115] See above pp. 20–30.

[116] Two recent writers, G. V. Sumner (*Arethusa* 3 (1970) 85–102) and R. Develin (*Klio* 62 (1980) 355–67) have discussed the Spanish command-structure during this period. I have refrained from the prolonged discussion which would be necessary to make clear my disagreements with them, and refer the reader to them for an alternative view.

[117] See the remarks of F. W. Walbank in *Livy* (ed. T. A. Dorey) (London 1971) 56–9.

to produce two commanders *pro consule* and two *provinciae* emerged from the changed situation in Spain, and was partly responsible for the disaster of 211. After the sending of C. Nero, probably still *pro praetore*, as a stop-gap measure, the younger P. Scipio was dispatched *pro consule* to Spain, again a single *provincia*, with M. Iunius Silanus as his assistant with *imperium pro praetore*. This pattern probably remained the same throughout Scipio's period in Spain, though there is one slight indication that in 208 the senate may have been thinking again of two separate commands.[118]

The point which emerges most strikingly from this survey is that the senate clearly was interested in what was going on in Spain, at least from the point of view of the allocation of *provinciae* and *imperium*, a task which they must have undertaken annually. Indeed it seems that on one occasion at least, in 209, just after the young and previously untried Scipio had gone out, they were prepared to consider withdrawing him and his *adiutor* Silanus before the end of the year, should it prove necessary. The commanders took pains to keep the senate informed about their progress and, as in the case of the letter from the two Scipios in 215, of their needs.[119] It is noticeable that more is heard of such contacts after the arrival of the younger Scipio in 210. This may simply be due to the chance of some letters having been recorded and others not, but may reflect the uncertainty about the sending of Scipio already noted, and of course the fact that he had more good news to announce than had his father and uncle.

Despite this interest and apparent willingness to experiment, the advice and the decisions of the senate appear to have had almost no effect on the conduct of the war. Thus the change of policy in 212, if such there was, seems to have come from the Scipio brothers themselves rather than from the senate; and the fears of the senate, expressed to Laelius in 209, of the danger of Hasdrubal Barca breaking out of Spain and joining Hannibal in Italy, seem almost to have been disregarded by Scipio.[120] Furthermore the major decisions which shaped the progress of the Roman campaigns were taken not in Rome but wherever the armies and their commanders happened to be. P. Scipio at Massilia in 218; the division of forces in 212; the rallying of the shattered Roman forces north of the Ebro in 211; the attack on New Carthage in 209; the settling of

---

[118] Livy 27.22.7.
[119] Thus from Cn. Scipio in 217 (Polybius 3.97.1; Livy 22.22.1); from the two Scipios in 215 (Livy 23.29.17, 48.4); from Marcius in 211 (Livy 26.2.1–6); from the younger Scipio in 209 (via Laelius, Livy 27.7.1–4) and in 207 and 206 (via L. Scipio, Livy 28.4.1–4 and 17.1).
[120] Livy 27.7.1–4.

Italica in 206:[121] all these were outside the control of the senate, which, once it had made the essential 'provincial' allocation, could only express its applause or disapproval or grief from a distance. The necessities of a war conducted so far from Italy made this inevitable.

(b) Administrative arrangements

Because Spain at this time was seen as little more than a battleground, administration meant provisioning, paying and maintaining the Roman army. Initially this was a matter of supplies from Rome. Manpower, the first essential, was of course sent from Italy in 218 and 217, and then again with C. Nero in 211 and with the younger P. Scipio in 210. Scipio had at his disposal some 28,000 foot and 2,800 horse (presumably Roman and Italian allies combined) by the time he launched his attack on New Carthage in 209.[122] As for provisions, when P. Scipio arrived in Spain in 217 he brought with him a large quantity of supplies, and more were sent in the winter of 217/6. In 215, when the Scipios wrote to the senate, they asked for money for the *stipendium* of their troops, as well as food and clothing, and the younger Scipio is said to have brought 400 talents with him in 210.[123]

Despite this dependence on Rome, and thus on the senate and the *societates publicanorum* who undertook the provisioning, there are clear signs that as Roman power grew in Spain, the commanders there became at least self-sufficient. Already in 218, Cn. Scipio was conducting campaigns against the Ilergetes and Ausetani, at that time allies of the Carthaginians, for the specific purpose of raising finance, and by 215, though desperate for food and clothing, the Scipios reckoned that they could find money for *stipendium* for the troops from the Spaniards themselves.[124] A clear instance of this process can be seen in 206, when P. Scipio met the demand for *stipendium* from his troops by levying from his allies and then by a requisition from the defeated chieftain of the Ilergetes, Mandonius.[125] It is certain that a large part of the money which the younger Scipio raised by various means during his time in Spain was

---

[121] It is probable that Italica had no legal status as a community until it became a *municipium* either under Julius Caesar or Augustus. This lack of formal recognition suggests strongly that the senate had no part in the settlement (Galsterer, *Untersuchungen* R. Knapp, *Aspects* 111–16; J. Gonzalez Fernandez, 'Italica, municipium iuris Latini', *Mélanges de la Casa de Velasquez* 20 (1984) 17–44.

[122] Polybius 10.6.7, 9.6; Livy 26.42.1. See Brunt, *Italian manpower* 679–80.

[123] 217: Livy 22.22.1; 217/16: Polybius 3.106.7; 215: Livy 23.48.4ff; 210: Polybius 10.19.2.

[124] Livy 21.61.6–11; 23.48.5.

[125] Livy 28.25.9ff; 29.12; 34.11. R. Bernhardt, *Historia* 24 (1975) 418, believes that this *stipendium* is tribute, but does not note the context of military supply.

spent there. At the capture of New Carthage he is said to have taken 18,300 pounds of silver not counting dishes, ornaments and other miscellaneous pieces of gold and silver plate. Despite more years of successful campaigning, and the *stipendium* raised from Mandonius, he returned with 14,342 pounds of silver, and a large number of silver coins.[126] A substantial sum must have been expended in Spain, either by himself or by his troops.

It is likely that, in addition to money, Scipio, and perhaps his predecessors, were able to raise levies of foodstuffs and equipment from allies and from defeated foes. There are no more requests for provisions after the letter of 215, and, as will be seen, both grain and clothing were being drawn from Spain by Scipio's immediate successors. It is these exactions of provisions and pay for the Roman troops serving in Spain which became, over the next decades, the taxes which the Romans levied in coin and in produce from the Spanish tribes.[127]

(c) Relations with native tribes

Of all the various fields of activity of the Roman commanders in Spain, that of their relations with the indigenous peoples is the most difficult to assess. Not only are the reports of such relations peculiarly susceptible to reworking by Roman historians wishing to give a more favourable, or sometimes merely more romantic appearance to the events; but even were it possible to be certain what had happened, the interpretation of such relations must depend on an understanding of the immediate background of political and personal interplay between the protagonists which we have no hope of obtaining for Spain in the late third century BC.

Despite these uncertainties, a development of policy is observable. It is clear that the two major traditions on which Livy drew for his account of the Scipio brothers both represented them as determined to win over local support from the Carthaginians, from Cn. Scipio's first approaches to the Iberian tribes north of the Ebro in 218, through the reception and return of the hostages held by the Carthaginians at Saguntum in 217 to the use of Celtiberian mercenaries in the later stages of their campaign.[128] The younger Scipio similarly freed the citizens of New Carthage after its capture, and (although there are traces here of idealisation both in

---

[126] Livy 26.47.7; 28.38.5. See van Nostrand, *ESAR* III, 123–5.

[127] See below pp. 114–17. On the development of taxation, see my article in *JRS* 66 (1976) 147–9.

[128] Cn. Scipio in 218: Polybius 3.76.2, Livy 21.60.3; and in 217; Livy (A) 22.20.10–12, 21.1–8 (cf. Klotz, *Livius* 143); at Saguntum in 217: Polybius 3.97.2, Livy 22.22.4–21; in 215 (?) Livy (A) 23.49.14, cf. de Sanctis, *Storia* III.2², 236 n. 73; Celtiberian mercenaries: Livy (A) 24.49.7–9. It was these last whom Hasdrubal Barca won over before his attack on Cn. Scipio in 211 (Livy 25.33.1–9).

Polybius and still more in Livy) took great care over the well-being of the Iberian hostages he found there, especially the relatives of Indibilis, an important chieftain from northern Spain, and one most closely associated with the Carthaginians.[129] The large number of Iberian defections from the Carthaginian to the Roman side which followed the capture of New Carthage and the battle of Baecula has already been mentioned, and the fruits of this were evident in the support Scipio received from at least one Iberian chieftain in his last major encounter with the Carthaginians in 206.[130]

It is interesting to compare this policy of the Scipios with that of the Barcid family, who had for so long dominated Carthaginian policy in Spain. By 210, the younger Scipio was receiving news of widespread dissatisfaction with their treatment of their allies, or so, at least, he told his troops before setting out for New Carthage.[131] Although there are several such accusations of harshness by the Carthaginians to the Spaniards, it is clear that this is not the whole story. Hamilcar Barca is said to have been ruthless and cruel, torturing to death Iberian leaders while enrolling their soldiery in his own army, but his son-in-law, Hasdrubal, not only married an Iberian princess, but was, according to Diodorus, acknowledged as 'supreme general' by all the Iberians, and built himself a royal palace at New Carthage.[132] Hannibal also married an Iberian, and this adds to the picture of strong family ties between the Barcids and the Spanish nobility.[133] This must be set against Roman accounts of harshness, and though there was no doubt much dissatisfaction at the conscription of troops by Hannibal, it must be remembered that the Scipio brothers gained their Celtiberian mercenaries by offering the same pay as had the Carthaginians.[134] Moreover, even when the Carthaginian cause was all but lost in Spain, in mid-206, the Carthaginians still had support in some Iberian settlements in the Baetis valley.[135]

[129] Polybius 10.17.6–8, 18.3–15, 19.3.–7; Livy 26.47.1–50.7. On Livy's misunderstanding of Polybius, and his romanticizing of parts of this account, see Walbank, *Commentary* II, 216–19.

[130] Note also the defection of the chief of the Turdetani 'cum magna popularium manu' in the closing stages of that battle (Livy 28.15.14).

[131] Polybius 10.6.3, 7.3; Livy 26.41.20.

[132] Above pp. 19–20. On Hasdrubal, Diodorus 25.12, Polybius 10.10.9. The observations of N. Feliciani, *Boll. de la real acad. de la hist.* 46 (1905) 366–71 are excessively severe on the Barcids, in comparison with the Scipios.   [133] Livy 24.41.7.

[134] Livy 21.11.13; 24.49.7–8. Some Iberian mercenaries in Italy in 215 are said to have deserted Hannibal for Marcellus (Livy 23.46.6) and others at the capture of Arpi in Apulia in 213 (Livy 24.47.8); similarly a Spanish chieftain, Moericus, came over to the Romans during the siege of Syracuse (Livy 25.30). To encourage further defections, P. and Cn. Scipio sent 300 young Celtiberian nobles to Italy in 212 (Livy 24.49.5).

[135] Notably Astapa (Livy 28.22.1–23.5: Appian, *Ib.* 33.132–6). Compare also the attack on Orongis in 207, Livy 28.3.1–16.

It is tempting to draw a parallel between the personal, family-based, almost dynastic power of the Barcids within the Carthaginian regions of Spain, and that of the Scipios. In both cases the continuity within the family is striking. A further similarity may be seen in the desire of the Iberians to recognise Scipio as their king. This first appears as early as 209, when the citizens of New Carthage, unexpectedly sent back to their own homes, salute Scipio with the ritual of *proskynesis* (prostration) in thanks for their salvation.[136] More significant is the similar *proskynesis* of the tribal rulers Edesco, Indibilis and Mandonius before the battle of Baecula,[137] and Scipio's acclamation as king by a number of Iberian chieftains after the battle.[138] It may have been Scipio's modesty and, as Livy hints, his political sense which made him prefer to be called 'general', but this acclamation too, as has not always been recognised, places him in the Spanish context in the line of the Barcids. The personal nature of the bond between Scipio and his Spanish allies is further emphasised by the provisions of the agreement made between him and Indibilis and his associates immediately after the acclamation-incident. The main clause, according to Polybius, was that they should follow the Roman commanders, and obey their orders.[139]

It would be easy to overemphasise such a parallel. Whatever might be said of the Barcids,[140] it would be wrong to accuse the Scipios of aiming at a Spanish monarchy. Unlike the Barcids, they had more to gain at home than in Spain. Nevertheless the attitude of the Spaniards to a leader who offered prospects of reward was similar in both cases and there seems to have been a similarity also in the decline of such good relations. As already noted, it may well have been Hannibal's need for troops which caused disenchantment, and Polybius notes that it was after the Roman threat had apparently been destroyed with the defeat of Publius and Cnaeus Scipio that the Carthaginians began to ill-treat their allies.[141] In the same way it was after the final defeat of the Carthaginians that P. Scipio the younger had to turn his attention to the disciplining of towns whose offence had been against Romans through previous support of the Carthaginians, and to putting down revolts among Roman allies.

The reason given by Livy for the revolt of Mandonius and Indibilis

---

136 Polybius 10.17.8.
137 Polybius 10.34.1–35.8, 40.3.
138 Polybius 10.40.1–9; Livy 27.19.3–7.
139 Polybius 10.38.5. See the discussions by A. Aymard [n. 85] 121–8; R. Etienne, *La culte impériale dans la péninsule ibérique d'Auguste à Dioclétien* (Bibl. des écoles françaises d'Athènes et de Rome, 191 (1958) 81–93; R. Combès [n. 45] 55–68.
140 Thus Polybius 3.8.2 (quoting Fabius Pictor) that Hasdrubal wanted a monarchy in Spain (above p. 20 n. 33).   141 Polybius 10.36.3–4.

is that they had nothing to hope for from the Romans once the Carthaginians had been driven out of Spain.[142] This implies that they understood Scipio's intentions to be for a long-term Roman presence in Spain. This must have been confirmed by the founding of Italica and by the establishing of a Roman *praefectus*, and presumably a garrison, at Gades, under the terms of the agreement reached with Marcius, who received their surrender of Gades after Mago had departed.[143] The sending of a *praefectus* was not a particularly severe imposition, for during the Hannibalic war allied communities in Italy requested that *praefecti* be sent to them for their own protection. Indeed one of the first such to be sent was M. Iunius Silanus, who at this time was serving in Spain as Scipio's *adiutor*, and who in 216 had gone to Naples as *praefectus*.[144] However, this does certainly imply the presence of Roman troops.

When Scipio left Spain after four years of highly successful fighting, he had not only driven the Carthaginians out of a potentially vital base for the war in Italy, he had also laid the foundations for a continuing Roman control at least of the eastern coastal strip and the valuable Baetis valley. The strong Roman bases at Tarraco, New Carthage and Gades, together with the settlement at Italica, already provided the outline of the two Roman provinces, which did not come into being in any sense for another decade.[145] Moreover the way in which he, his father and his uncle had set about the tasks of supplying themselves with money and provisions, and of determining relations between themselves, as the Roman presence, and the indigenous peoples of Spain, was to shape Roman policy and the emerging Roman institutions over the next century and a half.

[142] Livy 28.24.3.
[143] Livy 28.37.10, 32.2.5 (on which see E. Badian, *CP* 49 (1954) 250–2).
[144] Livy 23.5.2; for another *praefectus*, in Bruttium in 209, see Livy 27.12.4.
[145] See below, Ch. 4.

CHAPTER 4

Continuity and adaptation: 206–194

Between 218 and 206 there was neither need nor occasion for the Romans, either in Spain or in the senate, to question the value of a Roman presence in the peninsula. The only moment at which the matter might have been raised, when after the deaths of the Scipio brothers in 211 their replacement was a live issue in Rome, was one when the value of Spain to the Carthaginians, and the disastrous consequences of abandoning the struggle there, must have been self-evident to every senator.[1] The same was not true in 206. As the younger P. Scipio reminded the senate, meeting in the Temple of Bellona just outside the sacred boundary of the *pomerium* to hear his request for a triumph in the latter part of 206, he had been sent out to Spain to face four enemy commanders and four victorious armies; he had left not one Carthaginian there on his departure.[2]

Although the reason which had first attracted Roman attention to Spain, and had detained, in the later stages, some four legions there,[3] no longer pertained, there seems to have been no move to end Roman involvement. Indeed already before Scipio reached Rome, two men, L. Cornelius Lentulus and L. Manlius Acidinus, had been chosen to replace him.[4] The decision to sustain the military action in Spain was of course a decision of the senate, which must have allocated the area as a *provincia*. If Livy has correctly described the feelings of Scipio's mutinous troops earlier in the year, some Romans in Spain, as well as some Iberians, felt that once the Carthaginians had been driven out, there was no need for the legions to remain.[5] On the other hand there were obvious reasons why Spain might continue to be of concern at least for the time being: the war in Italy was still in progress, and the dangers of a resurgence of Carthaginian strength in Spain were considerable. There was also a

---

[1] Thus Livy reports that 'post receptam Capuam non Italiae iam maior quam Hispaniae cura erat' (26.18.1).

[2] Livy 28.38.3.   [3] Brunt, *Italian manpower* 679–80.

[4] Livy 28.38.1 has Scipio hand over his province to them directly; Polybius 11.33.8, as emended by Casaubon (cf. Walbank, *Commentary* II, 312), has Scipio transfer it to Silanus and Marcius.

[5] Livy 28.24.7, 24.3–4.

fundamental difference between the position in 218 and that of 206. Before the outbreak of the Hannibalic war, the only interest that Rome had in the peninsula seems to have been to keep watch over the Carthaginians there, and their only known link with any community, that with Saguntum, is best seen as a part of this. By 206, the Romans had been in Spain for 12 years, and the connections between Rome and Spain had of course become much closer. Almost the first act of P. Scipio as consul in 205 was to introduce into the senate an embassy from Saguntum. Though the speech which Livy gives to them clearly derives from an annalistic source, the context is likely enough. The Saguntines stress their own loyalty, and give thanks for the prolonged struggle carried on by P. and Cn. Scipio, and by the younger P. Scipio whom they have just seen installed as consul. Moreover they stress that not only has the Carthaginian menace been removed, but they are themselves in a far stronger position in relation to their neighbours. They wished to make a thank-offering to Jupiter Optimus Maximus, and to ask that those benefits which had been won for them by the Roman generals might be perpetuated by the *auctoritas* of the senate.[6] The details of this story may well owe much to the Roman annalistic historian from whom Livy has drawn his account, but the situation in Saguntum was probably as described by the envoys in Livy's account and is likely to have been repeated in other places which had thrown in their lot with the Romans. The inhabitants of Emporion, Tarraco, New Carthage and, of course, Italica, would no doubt have told similar stories, and all would have been equally desirous of Roman troops remaining in their area.

In addition to this external pressure, internal political developments must have encouraged the senate in their decision. Scipio himself intended that the Romans should stay in Spain, as is evident from his treatment of the Iberian tribes and the settlement of Italica before his return to Rome.[7] His reasons were no doubt in part strategic. Although the Carthaginians had been driven out of Spain, Hannibal was still in Italy, and the control of his former supply-base still important. In addition, the suspicion felt towards the Gallic and Ligurian peoples on both sides of the Alps continued beyond the end of the war in Italy.[8] The significance of the strategic factor can be seen from the attempts by the senate to reduce or even end the Roman presence in Spain after the defeat of Hannibal, which will be examined later in this chapter. However, even at this point, Scipio himself had other ideas than those of military

---

[6] Livy 28.39.1–16. On the source (probably Antias) see A. Klotz, *Livius* 189–90.
[7] Above p. 53.   [8] Above p. 29.

strategy. His establishment of his wounded veterans at Italica, far away from the most strategically significant area of the eastern route to the Pyrenees, shows that he was aware of the benefits which might accrue to individuals and to the state from the control of such fertile areas as the Baetis valley, to say nothing of his interest in the silver-mining areas of New Carthage and the Sierra Morena.[9] Doubtless he was also concerned to maintain the links between Rome and the peoples of Spain, which, in Livy's story, had been stressed by the envoys from Saguntum. It was, after all, Scipio who had been offered some sort of 'kingship' by the Iberians, and who had accepted from them the title of *imperator*. Such ties were evidently seen as personal by the local chieftains, and the encouragement of such a client–patron relationship promised much for Scipio and his family in the future.[10] In 206, with the Carthaginians defeated in Spain, Scipio's influence in Rome will have been great, and the consulship of 205 was a natural outcome. If there were any doubts in the senate about the wisdom of maintaining the army in Spain, such as were to appear over the next few years, Scipio's political influence must have helped to check them.[11]

'Cum imperio' but 'sine magistratu': the commanders in Spain, 206–197

Even though the political will was present, the constitutional means for continuing the Spanish command may have presented problems. The first twelve years of the Roman presence there had seen considerable experiment on the part of the senate, which seems to have tried to adapt the machinery of *imperium* and *provincia* to match military developments in this distant region. In consequence, there was no obvious parallel to follow when Scipio left his province in 206. In fact, no source records how Acidinus and Lentulus were selected, nor is their status in Spain in 206 or 205 directly attested. In the passage in which Livy describes Scipio's hand-over to them in 206, the Oxford text reads 'propraetoribus provincia tradita'.[12] 'Propraetoribus' here is in fact a suggestion made by

---

[9] Baetis valley: Strabo 3.2.1–8 (pp. 141–6); A. Schulten, *Iberische Landeskunde* I (Strasbourg 1955) 195–7. Mines: Polybius 34.9.8–11; O. Davies, *Roman mines in Europe* (Oxford 1935) 111–39. Note that Orongis which L. Scipio attacked in 207, is described by Livy as wealthy because of its mines (Livy 28.3.3).

[10] E. Badian, *Foreign clientelae* (Oxford 1958) 116–19. For a Saguntine monument to Scipio, probably originally erected in the late republic, see *ILS* 66 and F. Beltrán Lloris, *Epigrafía latina de Saguntum* (Valencia 1980) nos. 36–7.

[11] On Scipio's standing, see Scullard, *Roman politics*[2] 75–6.　　　　　[12] Livy 28.38.1.

C. F. Walters, and adopted by the Oxford editors, Conway and Johnson, and is based on a correction in the *codex Colbertinus* of the vulgate 'pro provincia', or simply 'provincia'. The emendation is neat, but cannot be correct. When Livy does first mention the two men in the context of provincial allocations, at the beginning of his account of the year 204, the matter is not decided by the senate but referred to the people. This is clearly the *comitia tributa*, as all the tribes are said to have voted that Lentulus and Acidinus should hold command there *pro consulibus*, as they had the year before.[13] This implies that in 205, they had held proconsular, not propraetorian *imperium*. The earlier passage therefore should be restored either to read 'pro consulibus'[14] or else (with Madvig and others) the word 'pro' should be omitted altogether, leaving no record of their status at all.

Any reconstruction of the mode of appointment of Lentulus and Acidinus in 206 must therefore be based on probabilities. The constitutional machinery used to continue their command in 204 was, as already noted, a reference by the senate to the *comitia tributa*.[15] In 203 Livy merely adds a note to the usual senatorial allocations of provinces that the Spains (*Hispaniae*, pl.) with their armies and *imperium* were decreed to the same commanders.[16] In 201, as Lentulus and Acidinus had been there for some years, the senate instructed the consuls to refer the matter to the tribunes, so that the *plebs* might decide which person should hold the *imperium* in Spain; and again in 199, it was the *plebs*, on the motion of the tribunes, who ordered that two new commanders should hold the *imperium pro consulibus*.[17] The recurrence of this unusual procedure of reference by the senate to some form of popular assembly, and its similarity to the method used to select Scipio for Spain in 210, suggests that this was how Lentulus and Acidinus were chosen in 206.[18]

The process was, of course, anomalous. Livy seems to describe the appointment of men with consular *imperium* by means of a plebiscite. Not only are the *plebs* not the whole Roman people, but even if Livy (or his

13 Livy 28.13.7.

14 So A. Klotz, *Livius* 189; Jashemski, *Proconsular and propraetorian imperium* 30 n. 7. Sumner (*Arethusa* 3 (1970) 89–90) reads 'propraetoribus', and assumes a Livian error; Develin (*Klio* 62 (1980) 361 and n. 42) reads 'propraetoribus' without discussion.

15 Livy 29.13.7.   16 Livy 30.2.7.

17 Livy 30.41.4–5 (201); Livy 31.50.10–11 (199).

18 So Mommsen, *StR* II³, 652; Jashemski, *Proconsular and propraetorian imperium* 30–1; Sumner [n. 14] 90, *contra* Develin [n. 14] 361. The only other instance of such a process is the reference by the senate to the *populus* of the prorogation of C. Aurunculeius, praetor in Sardinia in 209, for 208 (Livy 27.22.6; cf. Mommsen, *StR* II³, 211 n. 1). Note also the role of the *comitia tributa* (or possibly the *concilium plebis*) in the extension of *imperium* within the city to a returning pro-magistrate wishing to celebrate a triumph (Richardson, *JRS* 65 (1975) 58–60).

source) has confused the *concilium plebis* with the *comitia tributa*, the latter is not the assembly at which *imperium*-holding magistrates were customarily chosen. For this reason it has been assumed recently that these men were selected by a popular assembly, but that their *imperium* was given to them by delegation by the urban praetor.[19] There is, however, no evidence for this in the sources, and in any case, it would involve further anomaly: either the urban praetor would be delegating *imperium pro consule*, which, as a praetor, he was in no position to do;[20] or, by a two-stage process (for which there is no evidence), men given the *imperium pro praetore* by delegation were subsequently upgraded to the status *pro consule*, by some means unknown. As Livy is the only source for these events, it is safer to admit uncertainty as to the procedural details. Whatever happened over the appointment of these men, the whole matter shows the strains placed on the normal constitutional process by the maintenance of two independent commands at a great distance from Rome over a long period.

The procedure for appointment is not the only area in which anomalies appear. Livy is unclear about whether these men were given one or two *provinciae* between them.[21] Probably this is partly the result of a reading back by Livy's own sources from the pattern of the two Spanish *provinciae*, Hispania Citerior and Hispania Ulterior, which began to be established in 197. In part, however, it also reflects an uncertainty that is implicit in the senate's own decisions. The unresolved question at this stage was whether the military control of Spain was really one task or two. The sending of two men with *imperium pro consule* would suggest the latter, though even here there are indications of fluctuations in policy over the next few years. On the other hand, the description of Lentulus and Acidinus being sent to one *provincia* suggests that the work was seen as a single undertaking, rather like the sending of both consuls in a particular year to one *provincia*.[22]

So far as it is possible to reconstruct senatorial policy towards the fighting in Spain in 206–205, therefore, it appears that they understood the need to continue a military presence, and that this was a sufficiently important matter to require two commanders with consular *imperium*.

[19] So Develin, [n. 14] 355–67.

[20] Mommsen, *StR* I³, 683.

[21] One province: Livy 28.38.1 (206); 29.13.7 (204); two provinces: 29.13.7 (204); 30.41.4 (201); probably 31.50.6–11 (199); 33.27.1,3 (196).

[22] In 219, both consuls had been sent to Illyria, and in 197, 196 and 194, both were assigned Italia, to fight the Ligurian and Gallic tribes in the north (as Broughton, *MRR* 1, *sub annis*). This consideration tells against the ingenious but over-neat division of the Spanish commanders at this time into two separate commands, proposed by Sumner, [n. 14] 85–102.

However, the machinery used to achieve this was of an unusual type. Not only did they work through the agency of the popular assemblies (either the *comitia tributa* or the *concilium plebis*), but they assigned both men to one *provincia*. This is a different procedure from that used at the same time in the other areas in which there was a continuous Roman presence, that is Sicily and Sardinia/Corsica. In both these areas there was a succession of commanders with praetorian *imperium* from 227, with a consular commander in Sicily when the importance of the war there demanded it.[23] In the 30 years from 227 to 198, these were all men who had been elected praetor or consul, and, when necessary, had had their *imperium* prorogued after their year of office. This was not true of Spain from 210 to 198. Further, in Sicily, where there was often more than one commander present during the Hannibalic war, each seems to have had a clearly defined *provincia*. Thus, in 214–213, there may have been as many as four commanders present, each with a carefully distinguished command.[24] Again this is a far more precisely articulated pattern than that in Spain after the departure of Scipio in 206.

It is difficult to know how far this unusual scheme affected and was affected by the campaigning in Spain. It did allow the choice of a relatively experienced man in the case of L. Manlius Acidinus, who had been *praetor urbanus* in 210, and had served as an ambassador to Greece and Macedonia in 208, and a commander, of unspecified status, guarding the Apennine passes, during the Metaurus campaign of 207.[25] L. Cornelius Lentulus may have been praetor in Sardinia in 211, though his case is complicated by the simultaneous existence of two men of the same name,[26] According to Livy, this Lentulus was elected to the curule aedileship of 205, and held office, despite his absence in Spain.[27] The only account we have of their activities concerns 205. In that year Indibilis, king of the Ilergetes, who had been defeated by Scipio the previous year, felt encouraged by the latter's departure to attack the Romans again, and roused the neighbouring tribe of the Ausetani as well. He brought

---

[23] Conveniently listed by Jashemski, *Proconsular and propraetorian imperium* 114–21. Consular commanders in Sicily were M. Claudius Marcellus (214–211), M. Valerius Laevinus (210–207) and P. Scipio (205).

[24] T. Otacilius Crassus, praetor and then propraetor in charge of the fleet; P. Cornelius Lentulus, praetor and then propraetor in the 'provincia vetus'; M. Claudius Marcellus, proconsul in Hiero's former Kingdom, taking over in 213 from Ap. Claudius Pulcher, propraetor there in 214, who seems to have joined Marcellus' staff in a subordinate capacity (Livy 24.10.5, 21.1, 27.4–6, 44.4; Polybius 8.3.1; on Ap. Pulcher, see de Sanctis, *Storia* III.2², 268 n. 38).

[25] Livy 26.23.1, 27.4.4, 27.35.3–4, 27.50.8.

[26] Livy 25.41.12–13; Munzer, *RE s.v.* Cornelius (187) and (188); Sumner [n. 14] 89; Develin [n. 14] 361–2.

[27] Livy 29.11.12, disbelieved by Sumner [n. 14] 89.

together his army in the territory of the Sedetani, just south of the Ebro. Lentulus and Acidinus joined forces and, in the ensuing battle, Indibilis was killed. A council summoned by his brother Mandonius compelled him to sue for terms, which were granted, on condition that he and the other ringleaders of the uprising should be handed over, and the tribes make a formal surrender. Peace was then established, money and other supplies were exacted from the defeated Spaniards, and hostages taken.[28]

The story well illustrates the need for flexibility in the deployment of troops in Spain at this period. Lentulus and Acidinus, whose forces had presumably been in separate winter-quarters, were able to combine to face the threat from Indibilis. The command structure of two proconsuls in one *provincia*, although it may have seemed anomalous viewed from Rome, mirrored the necessities of the situation, within which Roman allies were recent and unreliable, and close to essential strategic points, such as the coastal route from New Carthage to Tarraco. Subsequent developments, however, suggest that the senate was more concerned about the possibility of reducing their commitment to Spain than flexibility on the ground. Apart from the extension of their command in 204,[29] nothing more is heard of the activities of these two men before the senate again refers their commands to the *plebs* at the beginning of the consular year 201. On this occasion it was decreed that the consuls should ask the tribunes to enquire of the *plebs* which man should hold the *imperium* in Spain; and that he should amalgamate the two armies to form one legion from the Roman soldiers and 15 cohorts of Latin allies, the remainder of the veterans being brought back to Italy by the returning proconsuls.[30]

This senatorial decree indicates clearly an intention to run down the military presence in Spain, not only in terms of numbers of troops but also by reducing the commanders to one. This partial withdrawal, following the final defeat of Hannibal the previous year, would suggest that the arrangements that had been made in 206 were simply a stop-gap modification of the decisions taken when Scipio had been sent out in 210, rather than being specially designed to meet the needs of Spain and its particular circumstances after his departure.

Whatever the senate intended, no withdrawal was achieved. Certainly one man, C. Cornelius Cethegus, was selected, and when Lentulus

---

[28] Livy 29.1.19–3.5; cf. Appian, *Ib.* 38.156–7 and Diodorus 26.22, who have elements of the same story.

[29] Livy 29.13.7.   [30] Livy 30.41.4–5.

returned from Spain, he brought troops back with him.[31] Acidinus, however, remained until he was recalled in 199, at the same time as Cethegus, who had been elected curule aedile for that year.[32] It is not likely that he was left with no soldiers whatsoever after Cethegus' arrival, presumably in 201. Moreover, further veterans were clearly expected to return with Cethegus and Acidinus, for C. Sergius, the *praetor urbanus* of 200, had his *imperium* prorogued for the purpose of providing land for those soldiers who had served for many years in Spain, Sicily and Sardinia.[33] Even so, forces must have been maintained in Spain, since Cn. Cornelius Blasio, one of the proconsuls who succeeded Cethegus and Acidinus, celebrated an *ovatio* on his return in 196, and his colleague, L. Stertinius, though he did not attempt to gain a triumphal celebration, thought well enough of his own military achievements to construct two arches, one in the Forum Boarium and one in the Circus Maximus, from his personal share of the booty he brought back.[34] The senate's proposal about the reduction of forces was linked with and perhaps depended upon the reduction in the number of commanders. As there were throughout this period two men in Spain with *imperium pro consule*, there must also have been more than one legion and fifteen auxiliary cohorts,[35] though Livy's silence as to the nature and number of the forces there makes it impossible to be certain about them. Indeed the absence of a detailed account of this whole affair makes its interpretation difficult. It is tempting to see here another instance of the gap between the thinking about Spain which went on in Rome, and in particular in the senate, and what was actually happening on the spot. The problem is that in this instance it is impossible to know by whom and at what point the senate's original intention was frustrated. It may be that when the consuls, Cn. Cornelius Lentulus and P. Aelius Paetus, presented the senate's decree to the tribunes, or, when the tribunes in turn made their *rogatio* to the plebs, the decision was taken to withdraw only one of the two men then in Spain. In such a case, the change of policy may have been of too little importance, and have aroused too little controversy to have attracted the

---

[31] The choice of Cethegus is not recorded, but he is mentioned as winning a battle in the *ager Sedetanus* in 200 (Livy 31.49.7). Lentulus distributed 120 *asses* per man to the troops after his *ovatio* in 200 (Livy 31.20.7).

[32] Livy 31.49.6–11; 32.7.4.   [33] Livy 32.1.6.

[34] Livy 33.17.1–4. On Stertinius' arches, see F. Coarelli, 'La porta trionfale e la via dei trionfi', *Dialoghi di Archeologia* 2 (1968) 55–103, esp. 82–3, 88–93. A. Schulten (*CAH* VIII, 311–12) is surely wrong to believe that Stertinius had not fought in Spain. On the entry in the *Fasti Capitolini* recording Blasio's triumph, see the fresh reading presented by G. V. Sumner, *Phoenix* 19 (1965) 24–6.

[35] So A. Afzelius, *Die römische Kriegsmacht* (Acta Jutlandica 17, Copenhagen 1949) 34–5; contra Brunt, *Italian manpower* 661.

attention of the annalistic historians on whom Livy relied for Spanish affairs during this period.[36] There is, however, one consideration which suggests that the reversal occurred in Spain rather than in Rome. If it had been intended at the end of the sequence of events which resulted in Cethegus being sent to Spain in 201, that he should be one of two commanders *pro consule* rather than the sole pro-magistrate as the senate had suggested, then it would surely be expected that he would have gone with another pro-magistrate, and that both the commanders then in Spain would be replaced, rather than just one of them. It may be that it was not until after he had arrived to take up his *provincia*, that the decision was made to continue with two proconsuls and two armies. If so, this incident would emphasise the inevitable gap between the senate and the Spanish commanders already noted.

If the proconsuls in Spain were for geographical reasons beyond the control of the senate, the same was not true when such men returned to Rome. Not surprisingly, it was then that the anomalous nature of their constitutional position became particularly apparent. The first was P. Scipio himself, who on his arrival in Rome in 206 made his report to the senate in the hope of being allowed to celebrate a triumph.[37] However, though Polybius and Appian both record that Scipio did triumph,[38] Livy reports, surely correctly, that his request was refused, and indeed that Scipio hardly expected otherwise, since no-one up to that time had celebrated a triumph who had conducted his campaign without a magistracy. This expression (*sine magistratu*) is an odd one since it clearly does not mean that no-one had triumphed who had not won his victory while a magistrate, as several had previously celebrated while holding *imperium pro consule*. In any case a proconsul who had already been consul was no more a magistrate than Scipio, both properly speaking being *privati*.[39] Livy must mean that the objection to Scipio was that he had not held a higher magistracy; and indeed until the year 200, the triumph was virtually confined to those who had already held the consulship.[40] Scipio's request for a triumph thus placed in particularly sharp focus the anomaly of a commander holding consular *imperium*, at the head of an

---

[36] Cf. the remarks of Klotz, *Livius* 189.

[37] Livy 28.38.2–4.

[38] Polybius 11.33.7; Appian, *Ib.* 38.156; Scullard's suggestion (*Roman politics*[2] 75, n. 2) that Scipio celebrated 'in monte Albano' explains both accounts, but must be no more than guesswork. Broughton's hypothesis (*MRR* I, 299) that he celebrated an *ovatio* is difficult in view of the similar case of L. Cornelius Lentulus (see below p. 71) for whom even an *ovatio* was said to be unprecedented (Livy 31.20.5).

[39] As remarked by Mommsen, *StR* I[3], 642; II[2], 652; cf. Livy 38.42.10.

[40] See J. S. Richardson, *JRS* 65 (1975) 50–7.

army of consular proportions, who had not gained his status through the usual process of election to a magistracy.

The same question recurred with the return of L. Cornelius Lentulus in 200.[41] This request to the senate for a triumph, on the grounds that he had campaigned with valour and success for many years, was met with the reply that, although his achievements were worthy of a triumph, it would be unprecedented for anyone who had not acted as dictator, consul or praetor to triumph, and that he had held his *provincia* in Spain *pro consule*, not as consul or praetor. An alternative proposal, that he should be allowed the lesser celebration of an *ovatio*, was threatened by the veto of the tribune, Ti. Sempronius Longus, who argued that this also would be unprecedented. Longus, however, withdrew under the weight of senatorial opinion.

Of the two men who returned in 199, C. Cornelius Cethegus did not, as far as is known, apply for a triumph or *ovatio*, despite being credited by the annalists with a major victory. Perhaps the brevity of his time in Spain, from which he was recalled to act as curule aedile in 199, made such an attempt unlikely to succeed.[42] L. Manlius Acidinus, who did request a celebration, was prevented by the veto of the tribune P. Porcius Laeca, and not permitted even an *ovatio*. He seems to have been less fortunate than Lentulus had been in using senatorial pressure, despite his long service.[43] The final pair to hold these commands *pro consule* but *sine magistratu*, Cn. Cornelius Blasio and L. Stertinius, fared unequally on their return, though both evidently believed that they were worthy of some recognition. Blasio alone celebrated an *ovatio*.[44]

The arguments which beset the repeated requests for triumphs, and the compromise used by the senate in the award of the *ovatio*, or 'lesser triumph',[45] indicate clearly that the unusual position of the Spanish proconsuls was recognised in Rome. Though there was no better precedent, as the tribune Longus pointed out in 200, for giving the *ovatio* to a commander who had won his victory *sine magistratu* than for granting a full triumph, it provided a way of lessening the resentment created by the senate's use of an anomalous procedure for providing men to act *pro consule* in an area which required a continuous military presence.

In Spain itself there is, however, no sign that these constitutional problems affected the activities of the two proconsuls. As already noticed,

---

[41] Livy 31.20.1–7.   [42] Livy 31.49.7, 50.6.   [43] Livy 32.7.4.

[44] Livy 33.27.1–4. Blasio is called Lentulus by Livy at 31.50.11, but this appears to be an error (A. Degrassi, *Inscriptiones Italiae* XIII. 1 (Rome 1947) 552). On Stertinius, above n. 34.

[45] Dion. Hal., *Ant. Rom.* 8.67.10; cf. Richardson [n. 18] 52–7; E: Pais, *Fasti triumphales populi romani* (Rome 1920) XXIV.

the fighting seems to have gone on throughout the period, though little is known about who the enemy were. The only names mentioned are those of the Ilergetes, whom Lentulus and Acidinus defeated in 205, and the unspecified 'Hispani' routed by Cethegus in 200.[46] Both of these campaigns are located by Livy in the *ager Sedetanus*, the section of the eastern seaboard south of the Ebro. Although little is heard of administrative developments, it must be assumed that the pattern set by the Scipios continued. The reason for those arrangements had been the presence of the army, and the need to pay, feed and supply it. The army was still present, and it is likely that those who led it would wish to meet its requirements as far as possible within Spain. When in 205 the Ilergetes had been defeated, the terms exacted from the pacified Spaniards included double the *stipendium* for that year, six months' supply of corn, and Spanish cloaks and togas (*sic*) for the army.[47] The context within which *stipendium* is mentioned here shows that it refers to pay for the army which was collected by Lentulus and Acidinus just as it had been by Scipio the previous year.[48] The word does not mean here, as it did later for taxes levied in Spain, a fixed annual sum drawn from the province, since the amount is described as 'stipendium eius anni duplex' i.e. twice the *stipendium* for that year. Although there were the beginnings from which grew the more systematic taxation described by Roman writers from the first century BC onwards, at this stage *stipendium* seems to be still an *ad hoc* levy to pay the Roman soldiers.[49]

This does not mean, of course, that there was no attempt to profit from the presence of Roman troops. In the case just mentioned, the penalty suffered by those tribes who had gone into revolt was in part a payment in money and in kind. Moreover, in 203, not only was corn and clothing sent from Spain to Scipio in Africa, but the price of corn in Rome was reduced because of a large quantity sent from Spain, which was sold cheaply by the curule aediles to the people.[50] Although Livy does not state that this corn had been gathered by the proconsuls, its cheapness indicates that it was not purchased from private shippers, and indeed the same rate was asked in 201 for grain sent from Africa by P. Scipio, which was certainly collected on behalf of the Roman state.[51] Though there is no more evidence of an organised collection of corn than of money, no doubt

---

[46] Livy 29.1.19–3.5; 31.49.7.   [47] Livy 29.3.5; Appian, *Ib.* 38.157.
[48] Livy 28.25.9, 29.12, 34.11; above p. 54.
[49] See further J. S. Richardson, *JRS* 6 (1976) 147–9. For 'stipendium eius anni' meaning army pay for the year, see Livy 5.27.15; 5.32.5; 9.41.7; 10.46.12. (*contra* van Nostrand, *ESAR* III, 127; A. Schulten [n. 34] 308).
[50] Livy 30.3.2, 26.5.   [51] Livy 31.4.6.

both were taken on an *ad hoc* basis, as in the cases recorded in the sources, and such supplies as reached Rome will have provided a further argument for continuing the Roman presence in Spain.

Such continuity also entailed an extension and an alteration of the relationship with the native population established by the younger Scipio. It was inevitable that there should be change, for Scipio had built his alliances on a personal adherence to himself (or possibly to his family) and on a common interest in the expulsion of the Carthaginians from Spain. Already, before his departure from his *provincia* in 206, this pattern had been modified as a result of the final defeat of Hasdrubal son of Gisgo and the need to use Roman forces to control Spanish communities which had favoured the Carthaginians, as well as unreliable allies such as Indibilis and Mandonius.[52] It was indeed the return of Scipio to Rome, and the desire not to replace Carthaginian domination by Roman which, according to the annalistic sources, inspired the final revolt of the two leaders of the Ilergetes in 205.[53] Clearly there was no possibility of maintaining the close and continuous family connection between the Scipios and Spain, which seems, whether consciously or not, to have reflected that of the Barcids before them. Although three of the five men who followed P. Scipio between 206 and 197 were also members of the *gens Cornelia* (i.e. L. Lentulus, C. Cethegus and Cn. Blasio), and Cethegus and Blasio have been thought to have political links with Scipio,[54] the size and complexity of the Cornelian family make it hazardous to propound any view of 'dynastic succession' in Spain. The Roman method of selecting and appointing men to *provinciae*, even in the unusual form used in Spain at this time, made the development of such an intimate association between a particular overseas territory and a single family impossible over a prolonged period, at least at the formal level of magistrates and pro-magistrates. This, after all, was the intention of the principles of collegiality and short-term tenure of *imperium*.[55] Instead more direct methods of controlling allied and hostile groups in Spain would be necessary.

As with so much else in the 'administration' of the area at this date relations with foreign communities seem to lack the formal legal structures that were to become so notable a feature of the life of the Roman provinces before the end of the Republic. Already there were treaties of some kind with Gades and Saguntum, but in neither case was the full-scale

---

[52] Above pp. 58–61. On the 'personal' nature of the agreements with Spanish chieftains at this date, see Badian [n. 10] 117–19.   [53] Livy 29.1.19–26; Appian, *Ib.* 38.156.
[54] Scullard, *Roman politics*² 95 and 104–6.   [55] Mommsen, *StR* I³, 27.

foedus used. Cicero makes it clear that the original treaty with Gades, made when the city surrendered in 206, did not become a *foedus* until 78 BC and this is confirmed by the manner in which the senate in 199 dealt with a request from the Gaditanes to be relieved of the presence of a Roman *praefectus*, and, presumably, a Roman garrison. The treaty of 206 was no more (in Badian's phrase) than a 'military convention'.[56] Similarly in the case of Saguntum, the embassy of 205, though bearing witness to a close and continuing alliance of some sort, makes no claim that there was a formal treaty between the Saguntines and Rome.[57] The two Massiliote colonies of Emporion and Rhode may have had a more binding alliance with Rome, as Massilia itself had, but there is no evidence of the fact.[58] Although there are occasional mentions of towns and tribes being brought into 'alliance' (*societas*), such arrangements seem always to have been concluded by, and were thus presumably at the disposal of, the military commander on the spot.[59]

The decade which followed Scipio's departure from Spain in 206 was a period in which the developments of the previous twelve years came to fruition almost without any need for formulation of policy either by the senate or by the commanders. The crucial decision was whether or not to remain in Spain for the time being, and once that was taken (almost, it would seem, by default), it simply remained for those entrusted with the task to continue to maintain and perhaps to extend Roman control, and to ensure the upkeep of the forces under their command. This was achieved by a continuation of the *ad hoc* methods employed by the three Scipios; and, although it was impossible to deal with the leaders of the Spanish tribes through the highly personal system of allegiance they had developed, a loose, non-formal series of arrangements seems to have served adequately.

As had been the case during the 'Scipionic' period, it was at Rome that problems arose. Although the method of their selection and appointment was anomalous, this caused no difficulties to commanders in Spain, so long as they had adequate manpower at their disposal. The comparative freedom of action that they enjoyed, and the ability to extract from the

---

[56] Cic. *Balb.* 15.34, Livy 32.2.5; E. Badian, *CP* 49 (1954) 250–2; *id.* [n. 10] 118–19; W. Dahlheim, *Struktur und Entwicklung* 58; *contra* J. Briscoe, *Commentary xxxi–xxxiii* 170–1.

[57] Livy 28.39.1–22. The only evidence that Saguntum ever had a *foedus* is Cicero's linking of it with Massilia and Gades in *Balb.* 9.23, and its history in this respect may well be similar to that of Gades.

[58] So Badian [n. 10] 118.

[59] Thus Livy 27.7.2 (towns defecting after the capture of New Carthage in 210); Polybius 10.38.5 (Indibilis *et al.*): Livy 28.24.4 (Suessetani and Sedetani described as *socii*) cf. Knapp, *Aspects* 40–1.

Spaniards themselves more than sufficient grain, clothing and money to satisfy their soldiers, gave them scope to pursue their own policies. Only at Rome, at the moment of appointment and allocation of the *provincia*, or on their return with a request for recognition in the form of a triumph or *ovatio*, did the curiosities of their constitutional position become an issue. It was the decisions about these recurring issues which in effect constituted the formulation of any senatorial attitude towards Spain during these years; and it was the need to resolve the problems caused in Rome which seems to have promoted the major alteration in Roman policy which took place in 197.

Praetors and *provinciae* 197–195

In 198, at the elections for the following year, the *comitia centuriata* for the first time elected six men to the praetorship. The reason which Livy gives is that the *provinciae* were now growing, and the *imperium* was spreading further afield.[60] The reference is certainly to Spain, for two of the praetors chosen were given *provinciae* there.[61] The significance of this new method of selection of men to command the Roman forces in Spain was considerable. When C. Sempronius Tuditanus arrived in Hispania Citerior and M. Helvius in Ulterior, in 197, this was the first time Roman magistrates in their year of office had been present in the peninsula. On one previous occasion, Hispania had been a magistrate's *provincia*, for P. Scipio during his consulship in 218, but, as we have seen, he was prevented from reaching Spain until the following year.[62] For the next 20 years, the Roman commanders had held the *imperium*, almost always *pro consule*, and usually with no connection with a city magistracy. In 197 not only are two magistrates sent, but the number of magistracies is increased by adding two praetors to the previously existing four, an alteration which indicates an intention to continue sending such men to Spain on a regular basis. Compared with the anomalous and cumbersome arrangements which had been employed from the sending of the younger Scipio in 210 down to the selection of Blasio and Stertinius in 199, the appointment of praetors in 197 indicates a change of attitude to Spain by the senate. The earlier policy seems to have left room for an easy reduction or even withdrawal of Roman troops; the new arrangements point to support for a permanent Roman presence, which, as has been

---

[60] Livy 32.27.6: 'crescentibus iam provinciis et latius patescente imperio'.
[61] Livy 32.28.2.   [62] Above pp. 31–7.

seen, was already foreshadowed by the activities of the younger P. Scipio in 206.

The creation of additional praetorships to cover the need for overseas commands was not, of course, new. In 227 the number of praetors had been increased from two to four in order to provide men for Sicily and for Sardinia and Corsica.[63] Spain, however, evidently required somewhat different treatment. Livy, in his reports on the activities of the commanders there over the next 30 years, refers to them somewhat inconsistently as praetors, propraetors or proconsuls. The *Fasti Triumphales*, which lists the triumphs and ovations celebrated by many of them on their return to Rome, describes them as *pro consule*. It is probable that at least by the end of their tenure their *imperium* was *pro consule*, and that Livy's sources, knowing that such men were elected to the praetorship, simply assumed wrongly that after the end of their year of office they held *imperium pro praetore*.[64] That they held the *imperium pro consule* from the beginning of their holding of their *provincia*, is indicated by Plutarch's remark that Aemilius Paullus, leaving for Hispania Ulterior in 191, the year of his praetorship, had with him 12 lictors and the other insignia of the consulship.[65] This would be in accord with the previous senatorial view that commanders in Spain should exercise consular *imperium*, no doubt because of the serious nature of their military activities. When in 195 events in Spain seemed to be deteriorating, the senate decided to send one of the consuls to Hispania Citerior, on the grounds that a consular general with a consular army was required.[66] The implication is that, as the situation became worse, even a praetor *pro consule* would be insufficient, and that full consular status was necessary.

The intention of this constitutional change was clearly to bring the sending of commanders with consular *imperium* within the regular pattern of city magistrates. The difference between the new and the earlier pattern is emphasised by the note in the *Fasti Capitolini Triumphales* attached to the record of Cornelius Blasio's *ovatio*, celebrated on his return to Rome in 197. According to a new reading of the stone by G. V. Sumner, Blasio is described as having held his *imperium* 'extra ordinem'.[67] Blasio, with L. Stertinius, was one of the last two commanders sent *pro consule* without holding a magistracy, and this note in the *Fasti*

---

[63] Livy, *per.* 20; Pomponius D.1.2.2.32; Solinus 5.1.
[64] U. Kahrstedt, *Die Annalistik von Livius B. XXXI–XLV* (Berlin 1915), 2ff; Jashemski, *Proconsular and propraetorian imperium* 40–7; A. H. McDonald, *JRS* 43 (1953) 143–4.
[65] Plut. *Aem. Paull.* 4.1.
[66] Livy 33.43.2–3.
[67] G. V. Sumner, *Phoenix* 19 (1965) 24–6.

seems to reflect senatorial dissatisfaction with the previous anomalous method of appointment.

At the same time as they regularised the constitutional position of the Spanish commands, the senate appears from Livy's account to have ordered that the new praetors should fix the boundaries of their *provinciae*.[68] This apparently straightforward instruction has caused problems for modern scholars. By the end of the second century, the geographer Artemidorus of Ephesus described the boundary as running just south of New Carthage and by way of the source of the river Baetis, and this position is confirmed by other writers.[69] Certainly a boundary further inland than this could not have been fixed in 197, as the area north of the Sierra Morena was not under Roman control. For the same reason, there would be no need for a precise frontier at this date.[70] It has been argued that there was at some earlier stage a boundary at the Ebro, which was moved further south in 197 to reflect the extension of Roman control, but the evidence for this is extremely weak. In four places, the lexicographer Stephanus of Byzantium refers to towns and peoples in northern Spain as being 'inside' or 'outside the Ebro', and, as Stephanus is known to have drawn on Artemidorus, it has been thought that the geographer may have been describing an earlier division.[71] However, Stephanus does not mention Artemidorus as source, and in three of the four examples cites Polybius. In fact one passage of Polybius mentions all four of the names listed by Stephanus, and also their position relative to the Ebro. This describes Hannibal's sorties against various tribes and settlements in the area of the Vaccaei in 220.[72] This makes it most unlikely that Polybius was thinking of Roman administrative divisions. The precise location of Hannibal's exploits in the area was important for quite a different reason, which was certainly in Polybius' mind, the dispute over the Ebro treaty of 226. The nature of the fighting during the Carthaginian war, and the temporary arrangements made by the senate between 206 and 197 would in any case suggest that the establishment of a boundary was neither necessary nor desirable earlier. Moreover, the nature of the country over which the line between Citerior and Ulterior was eventually

---

[68] Livy 32.28.11: 'et terminare iussi, qua ulterior citeriorve provincia servaretur'.

[69] Artemidorus *ap.* Steph. Byz *s.v.* Ἰβηρία. Livy 40.41.10 places the boundary at New Carthage in 180, and Caesar, *BC* 1.38.1 describes it as being marked inland by the 'saltus Castulonensis' Cf. P. P. Spranger, *Historia* 7 (1958) 95–112. These passages make untenable the view of E. Cavaignac, *Histoire de l'antiquité* III (Paris 1914) 325, that the Ebro was the frontier after 197.

[70] So F. Braun, *Die Entwicklung der spanischen Provinzial-grenzen* (Berlin 1909) 82ff; E. Albertini, *Les Divisions administratives d'Espagne romaine* (Paris 1923) Ch. 2.

[71] Steph. Byz. *svv.* Ἐλμαντική, Καρπήσιοι, Ἀβρουκάλη and Ὀλκάδες. P. P. Spranger, *MM* I (1960) 128–41, esp. 130–4.   [72] Polybius 3.14.

to pass does not lend itself easily to the fixing of such a boundary, for the watershed between the Segura and the Guadalquivir, with its contributories, is masked by the parallel valleys of the Segura, Guadalquivir and Guadalimar, running north-east/south-west between high mountains. On the other hand there is no reason to doubt Livy's account, as Sumner does.[73] The record of events in Spain in 197 and the two years following is certainly confused, and indeed through to the end of the 190s it appears that, if there were any boundaries fixed, the proconsuls in Spain took little notice of them; but this does not mean that the senate did not decree that the boundary should be established in 197. As has already been noted, what was decreed in Rome did not *ipso facto* occur in Spain. In this case, the fixing of a boundary would have taken time and attention which neither praetor had to spare, for both were involved in fighting local tribes. Indeed, some of the confusion in Livy's account of these years seems to have arisen precisely from the attempt of the senate to interpret the actions of the proconsuls in Spain in terms of provincial boundaries, which bore little relation to the realities of the war.[74]

In the event both M. Helvius in Ulterior and C. Sempronius Tuditanus in Citerior were involved in fighting against the inhabitants of their *provinciae* to a greater extent than the senate had envisaged when they left Rome in 197. Each praetor took with him 8,000 allied infantry and 400 cavalry so that they might send back the troops serving there.[75] No doubt the provision of a relatively weak garrison force for the two Spains was partly due·to the difficulty which had been experienced in recruiting men for the army ever since the end of the Hannibalic war, especially in the case of the Macedonian campaigns.[76] The senate seem none the less to have been optimistic for the immediate future of the Spanish *provinciae*, which helps to explain why they thought the praetors of 197 would have time to determine their boundaries. Their judgement proved sadly mistaken.

Late in the year 197 a letter was received from Helvius, reporting that fighting had broken out between Roman forces and two kings, Culchas (who had been an ally in 206, though now apparently somewhat less powerful than he had been then) and Luxinus, ruler of two towns in the

---

[73] G. V. Sumner, [n. 14] 92–102. Sumner's position is challenged by R. Develin [n. 14] 364–7, who puts too much weight on a presumed distinction between praetors and proconsuls in Spain. As argued above, it is more probable that praetors too held *imperium pro consule* (above pp. 75–6).

[74] See below Appendix 1.

[75] Livy 32.28.11; 'praetoribus in Hispanias octona milia peditum socium ac nominis Latini data et quadringeni equites, ut dimitterent veterem ex Hispaniis militem.'

[76] Livy 31.8.5–6 (200 BC); 32.3.1–7 (199 BC); 32.9.1 (198 BC).

north-western sector of the Baetis valley. The defection had spread to the Phoenician towns of Malaca and Sexi on the southern coast.[77] Worse was to follow. At the very end of the year, a letter from Citerior recorded that Tuditanus had been defeated with the loss of many men, and the proconsul himself had been mortally wounded, and had since died.[78] The seriousness with which the situation was regarded in Rome is indicated by Livy's remark that the war in Spain now broke out in the fifth year after the end of the Punic war. His reason for stating this is not that he believed there had been no fighting in Spain over the past four years, for a few sentences later he records the *ovatio* given to C. Cornelius Blasio whom he describes (somehwat anachronistically) as having held Hispania Citerior before Tuditanus.[79] The implication is that, although fighting had been going on before, it was not a full-scale war, such as had now begun.

In recognition of the difficult plight faced by the Roman armies in both provinces, Q. Fabius Buteo and Q. Minucius Thermus, both praetors in 196, were sent with more substantial forces. Each (Buteo in Ulterior and Thermus in Citerior) was allotted a legion out of the four which the consuls had levied, and in addition 4,000 allied infantry and 300 cavalry.[80] It is clear, however, that they did not meet with rapid success, for by the time the provincial allocations came before the senate again at the beginning of the following year, the senators decided that, because the war in Spain had escalated to such an extent, it was necessary to send a consular general with a consular army; the consular provinces for 195 were decreed to be Hispania Citerior and Italy. The consul who received Spain was to take with him two legions, 15,000 allied infantry, 800 cavalry and 20 warships. This was the command which fell to M. Porcius Cato.[81] The senate appears not to have been convinced, however, that even these substantial forces were sufficient to meet the needs of the Spanish war, for they also sent a praetor, P. Manlius, to Citerior, to take over the legion commanded by Minucius Thermus, as well as sending to Ulterior Ap. Claudius Nero, who was to receive the legion which Fabius Buteo had commanded. Each man took a further 2,000 foot and 200 horse.[82] If the senate could be accused of having underestimated the dangers of the Spanish war before this, they were clearly determined not to do so now.

---

[77] Livy 33.21.6–9 In 206 Culchas is said to have controlled 28 towns, in 197 only 17 (Livy 28.13.3).
[78] Livy 33.26.5.   [79] Livy 33.27.1.
[80] Livy 33.26.3–4. On the succession of praetors in the two provinces, see below Appendix 1.
[81] Livy 33.43.1–5.   [82] Livy 33.43.7–8.

Cato in Spain 195–194

The period which Cato spent in Spain is of particular importance for an examination of the development of the Spanish *provinciae*. The main reason for this is the relative fullness of the sources, compared with the brief notices given to events in the peninsula both before and after 195 by Livy, our main source for Spanish affairs in the early second century. It is clear that Livy's account of Cato's campaign is largely derived from Cato's own, though whether from one or more of Cato's writings, or from some intermediary annalist using Cato is uncertain.[83] The light thus shed both on Cato's own view of what he was doing in his *provincia*, and on the commander's relations with the senate in Rome is invaluable.

There was some delay between Cato's entering his consulship and receiving his *provincia* from the senate on the Ides of March, and his departure for Spain. This was partly due to his activities as consul at the beginning of his year of office, which included the supervision of the religious ceremonies of the *ver sacrum* which was declared this year, and participation in the contentious debate over the repeal of the lex Oppia, a sumptuary law introduced during the Hannibalic war;[84] partly also it was caused by dislocation of the calendar, which resulted in the Ides of March 195, the date of the beginning of the consular year, occurring at the beginning of December or end of November 196, in terms of the Julian calendar.[85] This meant that three months of the official year would have passed before the seas would be safe for sailing.[86] In fact, despite Cato's later emphasis on the speed of his preparations, he does not seem to have reached his province before the middle of the summer.[87] Before

---

[83] See the excellent discussions by A. E. Astin, *Cato* 302–7 and Briscoe, *Commentary xxxiv–xxxviii* 63–5. The story of Helvius (34.10) derived from Valerius Antias (34.10.2), is inserted into a basically Catonian narrative, or narratives (34.8–9 and 11–21). Livy's description of Cato as 'haud sane detrectator laudum suarum' (34.15.9) is echoed by Plutarch, who, in a different context, says of him ἀεὶ μέν τις ἦν ὡς ἔοικε τῶν ἰδίων ἐγκωμίων ἀφειδής (*Cato maior* 14.2). This may indicate a common intermediary source. (My thanks are due to Dr T. J. Cornell for this reference.)

[84] Livy 33.44.1–2; 34.1.1–8.3.

[85] See discussion by P. Marchetti, *Ant. Class.* 42 (1973) 473–96 and *BCH* 100 (1976) 401–26; P. S. Derow, *Phoenix* 27 (1973) 345–56 and 30 (1976) 265–81; Briscoe, *Commentary xxxiv–xxxvii*, 17–26.

[86] J. Rougé, *REA* 54 (1952) 316–25; F. Braudel, *The Mediterranean and the Mediterranean world in the age of Philip II*[2] (London 1975) 248–53.

[87] So Astin, *Cato* 308–10. Briscoe, *Commentary xxxiv–xxxvii* 65–6 places his arrival in the late summer, arguing that Livy's reference to *castra hiberna* not long after Cato reached Emporion implies that the winter was then close. This is difficult, both because he arrived at Emporion in harvest-time, and thus not later than early August (34.9.12; cf. de Sanctis, *Storia* IV. 1, 368 and 388); and because Livy describes the setting up of the camp as at a time when fighting was possible (34.13.2). This is an odd phrase, but most inappropriate at the onset of winter. For Cato's own description of his rapid preparations, see Cato fr. 28 (ORF³).

he left Italy from Portus Lunae, north of Pisa, the situation in Spain, at least as far as it was viewed from Rome, had altered substantially, and with it the consul's prospects for his campaign.

Some time after the beginning of the consular year, when, according to Livy, people were expressing surprise that nothing had been done about the war in Spain, a communication arrived from Q. Minucius, stating that he had met and defeated two Spanish commanders, Budar and Baesado, at Turda; and that 12,000 of the enemy had been killed, Budar captured, and the rest routed and dispersed.[88] The result of this information was to reduce anxiety about the position in Spain and the previous expectation of a large-scale war. All attention was now turned to the activities of Antiochus, and the settlement of Greece in the wake of the defeat of Macedonia under Philip V. This must have been a bitter disappointment to Cato. He had acquired a province within which there had been the prospect of a major campaign, and of all the attendant prestige which a successful conclusion to such a campaign could bring. Moreover, the position in Spain was in the forefront of people's minds in Rome to a greater extent than at any point in the past decade. Suddenly Minucius Thermus' letter had changed the picture, and Cato and his province lost importance compared with the events of Greece and the eastern Mediterranean. It is tempting to believe that the chagrin Cato must have felt later manifested itself in the series of attacks which he launched against Minucius Thermus between 194 and 188, a major theme of which was Thermus' alleged exaggeration of military successes in Liguria.[89]

Seen against such a background, the unstinting self-praise which colours much of Cato's account of his activities in Spain is readily understandable.[90] Not only was it important to be successful; his success had also to be recognised in Rome. This must have been uppermost in his mind when, having sailed with a fleet of 20 ships from Portus Lunae to a rendezvous at Portus Pyrenaei, he moved south by sea towards Emporion, disposing of a native stronghold that was dominating the Massiliote port of Rhode (modern Rosas) as he went.[91] Emporion in fact

[88] Livy 33.44.4.4–5.

[89] Cato frs. 58–65 (ORF³). On these speeches see D. Kienast, *Cato der Zensor* (Heidelberg 1954) 50–2; Astin, *Cato* 63–4.

[90] Cf. Livy's assessment of Cato as 'haud sane detrectator laudum suarum' (34.15.9). For Cato's campaign, see Scullard, *Roman politics²* 110–11; U. Schlag, *Regnum in senatu* (Stuttgart 1968) 33–6, for a sceptical view of Cato's achievements; Astin, *Cato* 28–50 is more favourable to Cato.

[91] Livy 34.8.4–7. On the origin of these towns, see above pp. 17–18. Emporion is the Greek name for the port: the Latin plural, Emporiae, probably reflects the presence of two separate communities there, one Greek and one native.

comprised two settlements at this date, one Greek originating from Massilia, one native Iberian. Of these the former lies on the coast, the latter some 5 kilometres inland. The two communities, linked together by the mutual advantages of trade which the Greek presence made possible, were wary of one another. The Greeks in particular excluded the Spaniards from their town, only venturing out at night on the landward side in substantial numbers.[92] Livy makes no mention of the attitude of the native community to the Roman army, but the Greeks welcomed Cato, as they had Cn. Scipio in 218.[93] The consul occupied his time in determining the location and size of enemy forces, and conducting a number of training raids into the countryside around his base at Emporion. As this was the time of year when the Iberians were harvesting and threshing out their corn, Cato was able to use these raids to provide the necessary foodstuffs for his troops. So successful was he that he was able to dismiss the *redemptores*, the Roman merchants who had followed him from Rome, hoping to gain the contract for provisioning the army, with the tart phrase that the war would feed itself.[94]

While he was engaged in these training raids and with establishing himself in the region round Emporion, he was approached by ambassadors from the king of the Ilergetes, now once again Roman allies.[95] They reported that they were under severe pressure, that their fortified settlements were under attack and that they could not hold out without assistance; 3,000 men would be sufficient to dislodge the enemy. Cato was unwilling to divide his forces, believing that a substantial force of the enemy was in his own immediate vicinity. He therefore devised an elaborate ruse, announcing to the ambassadors that, despite his own difficulties, he would help them, and issuing orders to his forces to board ship, as though preparing to move south to bring aid. Having dismissed the embassy with appropriate gifts, he then ordered the troops to disembark and to go into winter-quarters 5 kilometres from Emporion. The intention was that the enemies of the Ilergetes would be discouraged by the rumour of impending Roman assistance without the need for actual movement of troops.[96]

This piece of deception was followed by the major military encounter of Cato's period in Citerior. The setting up of the *castra hiberna* was followed by further plundering of the local inhabitants. Finally a night

[92] Livy 34.9.1–9. Cf. M. Almagro, *Las fuentes escritas referentes a Ampurias* (Barcelona 1951) 47–60; id. *Ampurias: history of the city and guide to the excavations* (Barcelona 1956).
[93] Livy 34.9.10.　　　　　　　　　　　　[94] Livy 34.9.11–13.
[95] On the earlier frequent defections of the Ilergetes, see above pp. 53–4; pp. 67–8.
[96] Livy 34.11–12; Frontinus, *Strat.* 4.7.31.

march brought the Roman forces round behind the enemy camp, from which position, after an encouraging word from Cato, first to the officers and then to the troops, one legion launched into an attack against the Spanish forces drawn up in defence of their base. After a close-fought battle, the Spaniards were forced back towards the camp, at which point Cato sent in his second legion, who had taken no part in the conflict thus far, to storm the fortifications. The day after the battle saw a return to the plundering of the vicinity by the Roman troops, and the submission to Cato of the native inhabitants of Emporion, and of many other individuals from other communities who had fled there. The consul treated them kindly, and sent them home.[97] He then moved his base down the coast to Tarraco; there he heard that a rebellion had broken out among the Bergistani, a people who seem to have lived in the foothills of the Pyrenees, following a false rumour that he had left for the south of Spain. The rising was quickly suppressed but broke out again just before he did leave for Turdetania. This time those involved were sold into slavery, to discourage any repetition.[98]

Cato's campaign has received very different evaluations from modern scholars.[99] Those favourable to the consul have assumed that the region of Emporion was the heartland of the troubles which had beset the province in the past two years. There is in fact little reason to believe this. The site of Tuditanus' defeat is unknown,[100] but Minucius, if he was fighting against Turdetani in Citerior, won his victory in the south of his province, near the boundary with Ulterior.[101] This is confirmed by the fact that P. Manlius took over Minucius' troops and also those of Ap. Claudius, which were assigned to Ulterior, and immediately moved into Turdetania, in the further province.[102] This suggests that at the end of his tenure, at the time he reported his success to the senate, Minucius and his legion were at the southernmost end of the coastal strip which

---

[97] Livy 34.13.1–16.5. The analysis of the battle which appears in Livy, 34.16.1–2, occurs in only one manuscript, and may be a late addition (H. Tränkle, *Gnomon* 39 (1967) 374 n. 3).

[98] Livy 34.16.7–10. This may be a doublet with a later passage describing a revolt of the Bergistani (34.21.1–8; so Kienast [n. 89] 44–5, contra Klotz, *Livius* 36 n. 1). Astin has recently argued against this, and in particular the view that the second revolt of the Bergistani took place after Cato's expedition to Turdetania (Astin, *Cato* 304–5). This does not exclude the possibility that *both* revolts occurred before Cato left for the south, which is what 34.16.7–10 states. The later passage, tacked on to Cato's final sorties against tribes in Citerior, reads oddly after the emphatic statement that the second rebellion had been harshly suppressed 'ne saepius pacem sollicitarent' (34.16.10). The Bergistani are probably identical with the Bargusii, mentioned by Polybius 3.35.1 (cf. Briscoe, *Commentary xxxiv–xxxvii, ad loc.*).

[99] See above n. 90.

[100] Livy 33.25.8.

[101] Livy 33.44.4; see Appendix I.

[102] Livy 34.17.1.

comprised most of Citerior at this date. Cato, at Emporion, was by contrast at the northern end of this strip. Further, Livy, drawing on Cato's own account, describes his enemies in the battle near Emporion, as 'Emporitani Hispani'.[103] If these people had been in open conflict with the Romans when Cato arrived, it is extraordinary that they took no action against him when he first reached Emporion, and placed his troops in a series of small encampments outside the city. Their own settlement was after all only 5 kilometres distant.[104] In fact the first signs of hostility from the local tribes near Emporion came only after repeated plundering expeditions mounted by Cato, for the training and provisioning of his army. Although it may be excessively sceptical to suggest that these people were friendly to the Romans before Cato's arrival, there is no reason to believe that the area was in full revolt. Indeed the appeal from the Ilergetes suggests that any trouble that there was in this part of the province was considerably further inland. If Cato had not so much exaggerated as inflamed the hostility of the local tribes in the region of Emporion, his deceit in dealing with the appeal from the king of the Ilergetes takes on a different aspect. It seems that Cato wanted a spectacular victory, and that he wanted to choose where and against whom he won it.

Two other episodes from Cato's time in Citerior, one placed by Livy immediately before his expedition to Turdetania, one immediately after, show him involved with tribes north of the Ebro, and also the devious means he employed in order to achieve spectacular results. After putting down the revolt of the Bergistani, he demanded of the other tribes of the area that there should be no arms held north of the Ebro. This provoked considerable protest, many of the tribesmen considering that they would rather die than be forbidden to bear arms. Cato then summoned the tribal leaders, informed them in extremely patronising terms that rebellion was even less in their interests than the Romans', and requested their help in a manoeuvre to make resistance impossible. The leaders were given time to consider, but when a second congress produced no answer, the consul ordered all city walls to be destroyed on a single day. Unable to co-ordinate, all but one city obeyed, and that (called Segestica by Livy)

---

[103] Livy 34.16.4.

[104] Livy 34.9.2. For the small encampments, see Cato fr. 35 (ORF³): 'interea aliquot ⟨p⟩au⟨ca⟩ castra feci. Sed ubi anni tempus venit, castra hiberna...' For the siting of the Spanish settlement Livy 34.9.2. These people were the Indiketai, the Iberian inhabitants of Emporion (Strabo 3.4.8 (p. 160)), who are not known to have been hostile to the Romans at any time before or after 195. It is probably at this time that the town of Ullastret was destroyed (see above Ch. 2 n. 18).

he took by storm.[105] The other venture consisted of an assault on yet another tribal capital in the foothills of the Pyrenees, that of the Lacetani.[106] Cato, returning from fighting the Turdetani with a mere seven cohorts, and having captured a number of towns north of the Ebro, received the submission of the Sedetani, Ausetani and Suessetani. He then proceeded against the Lacetani, who had been harrying their neighbours during Cato's absence in the south. For this purpose, his small Roman forces were complemented with troops drawn from his Spanish allies. Relying on the known contempt of the Lacetani for the Suessetani, he mounted a frontal attack against their city with a group of the latter and, when they were repulsed by a wild sally from within the town, sent in forces he had held in reserve to capture the gate, which was still standing open. By the time the Lacetani had recovered themselves, their town was in his hands, and they were forced to surrender.

These two stories show once again Cato's delight in deceiving the enemy, and thereby gaining the maximum effect with the minimum effort. They also show that his reports of his activities claimed more than he actually achieved. The whole point of his actions before going to Turdetania was not merely to repress rebellion, but to make its resurgence impossible, and he claimed, if not to have disarmed all the tribes north of the Ebro, then at least to have destroyed all the fortifications of their settlements.[107] On his return not only did he have to receive the submission of some of the major tribes of the area, but the Lacetani were able to conduct their harassment from a walled town, out of which they had to be lured in order that Cato might bring them to surrender.

The events in Turdetania which took Cato south after the defeat of the Bergistani had begun earlier in the year with the campaign of P. Manlius, the praetor assigned with Cato to Hispania Citerior. Why he was involved at all is not clear. Turdetania is clearly placed by Strabo in the valley of the Baetis, and, although there are signs of Turdetani in the southern part of Citerior, the region which carries the name 'Turdetania' is always

---

[105] Livy 34.17.5–12; Plut. *Cat. Mai.* 10.3 (quoting Polybius, but describing the area involved as north of the Baetis; cf. de Sanctis, *Storia* IV. 1,453 n. 157). Other sources (Frontinus, *Strat.* 1.1.1; Polyaenus 8.17; Zon. 9.17.6; *de vir. ill.* 47.2) report Cato as writing a letter to the cities.

[106] Livy 34.20.1–9. E. Hübner, *Hermes* I (1866) 337–42, argued that the Lacetani did not exist, and were the result of a palaeographical confusion between the Iacetani and the Lacetani. G. Barbieri, *Athenaeum* N.S. 21 (1943) 112–21 has shown that the evidence is consonant with the existence of three separate tribes, in three locations north of the Ebro. On the Suessetani and Sedetani in the Ebro valley, see G. Fatás, *Arch. Español de Arqueologia* 44 (1971) 111–25.

[107] Livy 34.17.11–12.

located in Ulterior.[108] Minucius Thermus fought against the Turdetani the previous year, almost certainly in Citerior,[109] but there are other indications that Manlius pushed the war across the provincial boundary. When the praetor arrived in Spain, he added to the supplementary troops which he had brought with him both the army formerly under the command of Minucius Thermus, and also what Livy describes as the 'old' army of Appius Claudius Nero from Hispania Ulterior.[110] It has generally been assumed that Ap. Claudius co-operated with Manlius in the war against the Turdetani, but this is not what Livy says. The parallel, in Livy's account of Manlius' arrival, between the position of Minucius and Claudius, and the description of the two bodies of troops with the words 'exercitu vetere' and 'vetere item exercitu' respectively, imply that Nero was no longer in his province, and that Manlius in some sense took over from him. The absence of any mention of Nero in the report of the fighting in Turdetania confirms this. Moreover when, in 182, Manlius held a second praetorship, and was assigned to Hispania Ulterior, Livy describes this as the province which he had held in his previous praetorship.[111] The error is more explicable if Manlius had in fact commanded in Ulterior in 195.[112]

Livy's account certainly suggests that Manlius was conducting his campaign in Ulterior. This leaves the role of Ap. Claudius quite unclear. He is mentioned three times only in connection with the events in Spain in 195. First, he, like Manlius, was voted 2,000 infantry and 200 cavalry to add to the forces he would take over from his predecessor, Q. Fabius Buteo;[113] secondly, he provided an escort of 6,000 men to accompany M. Helvius out of the province, and it was with this force that Helvius won the victory which gained him an *ovatio* on his return to Rome;[114] finally, Claudius is mentioned in the passage discussed above, as having

---

[108] Strabo 3.2.1–15 (PP. 141–51). For the view that these operations took place in Citerior, see Schlag [n. 90] 33 n. 60; Briscoe, *Commentary xxxiv–xxxvii* 80. The evidence for another tribe of Turdetani in the area of Saguntum rests on Livy 21.6.1, where it may be a loose expression, covering the Spanish tribes in the southern half of the peninsula (cf. J. Vallejo, *Emerita* 11 (1943) 153–68; P. Fraccaro, *Opuscula* 1, 224 n. 15; Astin, *Cato* 41 n. 32; R. C. Knapp, 'Cato in Spain 195/194 B.C.', in C. Déroux (ed.), *Studies in Latin literature and Roman history* 11 (Brussels 1980) 21–54.

[109] See Appendix 1.

[110] Livy 34.17.1: 'interim P. Manlius praetor exercitu vetere a Q. Minucio, cui successerat, accepto, adiuncto et Ap. Claudi Neronis ex ulteriore Hispani vetere item exercitu, in Turdetaniam proficiscitur.'

[111] Livy 40.16.7. See Appendix 1.

[112] A further argument from the mention of the Baetis in the Plutarchian *Apophth. Cat. Mai.* 24 is less strong, being a geographical reference out of context (Astin, *Cato* 41 n. 32; Briscoe, *Commentary xxxiv–xxxvii* 80).

[113] Livy 33.43.7.   [114] Livy 34.10.1–6; see Appendix 1.

been the commander of forces which Manlius took under his command.[115]
If Manlius *was* in Ulterior, it is difficult to imagine that Claudius
remained there while someone else commanded his own troops within the
province assigned to him.[116] It is possible that he left the area early,
having handed his troops over to Manlius, perhaps to join Flamininus in
Greece.[117] He plays no further part in affairs in Spain.

Initially Manlius had little difficulty with the Turdetani, who were
notoriously unwarlike.[118] After their first defeats, however, they hired
10,000 mercenaries from the Celtiberians from further north.[119] At this
point Manlius called on Cato for assistance. Having settled affairs in the
region north of the Ebro, Cato proceeded south. After a few skirmishes
with the Turdetani, he resorted to a form of diplomacy not unlike that
he had already practised in Citerior. Noticing that the Celtiberians and
the Turdetani maintained separate encampments, he sent his military
tribunes to the former to make three offers: if they joined the Romans
he would give them twice what the Turdetani had paid; or if they
preferred, they could return to their homes unmolested, and their
association with the enemies of the Romans would not be held against
them; or, if neither proposal was acceptable, they were to name the day
and place for a set-piece battle. The Celtiberians could not agree among
themselves, so Cato took the opportunity to plunder the surrounding
area. He is also said to have sent a few cohorts of light-armed troops on
an expedition to Segontia, in the heart of Celtiberia, where he had been
told the stores of the mercenaries were being held. The result of this raid
is unknown, but on his return Cato, discovering that the situation had
not changed, paid his troops and those of the praetor, before returning
north, taking with him just seven cohorts, and leaving the remainder, an
army of some four legions, under Manlius' charge.[120]

---

[115] Livy 34.17.1.
[116] Briscoe, *Commentary xxxiv–xxxvii* 80, deduces from this that Manlius fought in Citerior.
[117] Livy mentions an Ap. Claudius as one of Flamininus' legates both in 195 (34.28.10) and in
194 (34.40.10). Unfortunately, there were two Ap. Claudii in this period, both of whom were in
Greece in 198 and one of whom is specified by Polybius as Nero (Polybius 18.8.6, 10.8; cf. E. Badian,
T. Quinctius Flamininus (Cincinnati 1970) 44–5). The other is usually supposed to be Ap. Claudius
Pulcher, *cos.* 185, and it is *this* Ap. Claudius who is assumed to be Flamininus' legate in 194.
(Broughton, *MRR* I, 332 n. 4; Schlag [n. 90] 112–13.
[118] Livy 34.17.3; cf. Strabo 3.2.15 (p. 151).
[119] Livy 34.17.4.
[120] Livy 34.19.1–10. See Astin, *Cato* 43–6. How any of these moves relate to the speech which
Gellius describes as having been spoken 'Numantiae apud equites' (fr. 17 (ORF³); Gellius, *NA*
16.1.1) is totally unclear. There must be a suspicion that Numantia, renowned for its later part in
Roman history, became attached to this speech because Cato had been in Citerior.

The fullness of the sources makes possible an assessment of the character of Cato's style of government, at least as Cato himself saw it. Throughout the account runs an evident desire to be seen to be careful over the expenditure incurred. His refusal to buy corn for the army when he could seize it by plundering local farmers has already been noted.[121] An anecdote in Plutarch, about the use of Spanish troops, and probably relating to Cato's time in Turdetania, is in a similar vein. Cato is said to have offered the Celtiberians 200 talents for their assistance, and when upbraided for so un-Roman a practice, replied that this was no disgrace, since, if he were defeated, the mercenaries would have no-one from whom they might claim their pay, while, if successful, he would have plenty of booty from which to provide the necessary funds.[122] In his speech on his consulship he also made much of the extent to which he was able to cut down on his own expenses.[123] His success in raising money by the practice of almost continuous plunder is shown by the very substantial sum deposited in the *aerarium* at the time of this triumph; and also by the generous donative he was able to distribute to his soldiers.[124] He is also said to have introduced measures which brought in a large amount of money from the iron and silver mines of the area.[125]

The second feature of the account of Cato's campaigns is his apparent disregard both for the boundaries established between the two Roman *provinciae* of Ulterior and Citerior, and for the alliances previously made by Roman commanders. The only allies he used are those who yielded to him (though it must be said that it is not clear they were previously in revolt),[126] and the only mention of previous allies is of the Ilergetes, whom Cato deliberately duped into believing that he was coming to their aid, when he had no intention of doing so.[127] The results were satisfactory for Cato, and brought the spectacular series of successes which led to his triumph. However, such tactics were unlikely to satisfy Rome's friends or overawe her enemies in the long term. Though Cato might claim that his *provincia* was pacified,[128] the history of the next 30 years was to show that the claim was an empty one.

In the forefront of Cato's mind throughout his time in Spain must have been the need for him to be seen as having dealt successfully with a crisis which, at the time of his entry to office, had seemed to be of major

---

[121] Livy 34.9.12–13.
[122] Plut. *Cat. Mai* 10.2.
[123] Cato frs. 51–9. (*ORF³*).
[124] Livy 34.46.2–3. For comparisons, see Astin, *Cato* 53–4.
[125] Livy 34.21.7; Gellius, *NA* 2.22.28.
[126] Livy 34.20.1–3.
[127] Livy 34.11–12.
[128] Livy 34.21.7.

proportions. From Cato's point of view this need will not have become less urgent when the letter from Minucius alleviated the anxiety of the senate. That Cato was able to conduct the idiosyncratic form of campaign he did, again reflects the selective concern of the senate for the events in Spain. Their response to what was seen as a threat to the Roman position in Spain was unusual and substantial: the provision of two magistrates, a consul and a praetor, for Citerior, and of two additional legions, to add to those, one in each province, which had been sent the previous year.[129] However, despite their apparent intention only two years before to fix the boundaries of the two *provinciae*, these were in fact ignored by both Manlius and Cato. Nor was it the case that the senate was uninterested in the question of boundaries. When M. Helvius eventually returned to Rome in 195, having been sent to Ulterior as praetor in 197, and subsequently delayed through illness, his request for a triumph was met with an offer only of a lesser celebration, the *ovatio*. The reason given for this by Livy was that he was fighting under the auspices of another magistrate in someone else's province. The *Fasti Urbisalvienses* show that he still held the *imperium pro consule* at the time of his entry to Rome, so that the objection was almost certainly to Helvius having fought outside his province with troops lent to him by Ap. Claudius Nero to escort him to Cato's camp *en route* for Rome, and therefore no doubt technically under Nero's command and auspices.[130] This incident certainly demonstrates senatorial concern about the limits of the areas of proconsular responsibility; but it also shows, especially when compared with the campaigns of Cato and Manlius, that in practice it was only when the commander was back in Rome, and the senate needed to consider his actions during his tenure of his *imperium*, that the question of exactly where he had been was even raised.

The exaggerations which have been detected in Cato's account of his Spanish campaign raise another question about the senate's involvement in the affairs of the two *provinciae*. In this period the senate was dependent for its information about what was happening in Spain on the reports from the governors. The senate is recorded as discussing Spain

[129] Livy 33.43.3, 26.3–4.
[130] Livy 34.10.1–5 Degrassi, *Inscr. It.* 13.1, 338. See discussion in Appendix 1 p. 182. Iliturgi, the site of Helvius' victory, is clearly placed by Livy outside of Hispania Ulterior and is probably a town of that name south of the Ebro (A. Schulten, *Hermes*, 63 (1928) 288–301, despite the doubts of J. Vallejo, *Emerita* 11 (1943) 175–7). The suggestion of J. M. Gazquez, *Pyrenae* 10 (1974) 173–9, that the *ovatio* was awarded for a victory won in Citerior in 197 after the death of C. Sempronius Tuditanus ignores the close connection in Livy's account between the *ovatio* and the successful fight in 195; also there is no mention at all of Helvius' intervention in the north in 197 (Livy 33.21.7–8, 25.8–9).

only when the provinces were allotted, when a triumph was requested, or, on one solitary occasion, when Helvius' letter was received in 197, when the matter was referred to the next praetor to whom the province would be assigned, with instructions to bring the question to the senate's attention again later.[131] Each time the war in Spain was discussed, the reports on which senatorial action was based seem to have originated from the Roman commander in the field, or, as with the letter which reported the death of C. Sempronius Tuditanus, no doubt from the senior officer on his staff.[132] While this reliance on the Spanish proconsuls was no doubt inevitable, it placed the senate in a vulnerable position, especially at a time when, as the case of Helvius shows, they were concerned to regulate to some extent the activities of these very people. The full implications of this weakness were to become evident in the disputes over triumphs in the next twenty years, and still more during the period of the Numantine and Viriathic wars.

There are indications that Cato himself, despite the excellent account he seems to have given of his activities in Spain, was faced with a dispute on his return to Rome. Both Nepos and Plutarch record a quarrel between Cato and Scipio Africanus, who, as consul for 194, is said to have wanted to replace him in Spain.[133] Plutarch indeed states that Scipio actually went to Spain, and that Cato's attack on the Lacetani did not take place until after Scipio had set out thither. According to Livy, the senate decided that as the wars both in Spain and in Macedonia were at an end, the consuls of 194 should take Italy as their *provincia*. Scipio did protest about this, but it was Macedonia, not Hispania Citerior to which he wanted to go.[134] The story in Nepos and Plutarch may be a confusion of this dispute with a charge levelled at Cato over the attack on the Lacetani; and the confusion will have been helped by the fact that a P. Scipio did indeed go to Spain in 184, for Africanus' cousin, P. Scipio Nasica, was assigned as praetor to Hispania Ulterior.[135] Cato seems to have got the better of the quarrel, but it is interesting, in view of the disputes in the years which followed, to note that the complaint was centred on the manner of Cato's departure from his province, and is reminiscent to that extent of the objections to Helvius' triumph.

It has often been assumed that this period, including as it does the regularisation of the constitutional position of the Spanish governors, and the presence of the consul Cato, saw the establishment of many of the

[131] Livy 33.21.7–9.
[132] Livy 33.25.8–9.
[133] Nepos, *Cato* 2.2; Plut. *Cat. Mai* 11.
[134] Livy 34.43.3–9.
[135] This problem is discussed by Astin, *Cato* 51–2.

administrative and financial arrangements of the two provinces.[136] The direct evidence is very slight. Cato is said by Livy to have set up large *vectigalia* from the iron and silver mines, which led to the province becoming daily more wealthy.[137] It is probable that this refers to Cato's activity north of the Ebro, both because Livy links his notice to Cato's 'pacification' of the province, and particularly the suppression of the Lacetani, which undoubtedly took place in the foothills of the Pyrenees; and because Cato himself, in a passage quoted by Gellius, wrote admiringly of the iron and silver mines north of the Ebro, and also of an inexhaustible mountain of salt, identified by Schulten with the deposits in the area of Cardona, north-west of Barcelona.[138] If this is correct, then Cato's organisation was of a limited nature, for, although the mineral resources of this region were far from negligible, they were not comparable with the large deposits of silver and lead north of the Baetis and the area of New Carthage, nor with the iron of the Cantabrian mountains, or of the Celtiberian region in the north-east of the *meseta*.[139] Cato's action is important, because it is the first direct evidence of Roman interest in the exploitation of Spanish mineral resources by the state, but there is no need to assume that he set up a complex system of taxation, involving the censors at Rome, and large-scale companies of *publicani*.[140] Cato, as has been seen, had little time to organise anything in the course of his continuous campaigning, and yet whatever steps he did take clearly showed profits immediately, for, as Livy records, the province grew daily more profitable as a result. This certainly does not suggest that contracts were placed in the hands of the censors in Rome to be let there, particularly as the new censors did not take up office until the following year, too late to show a daily increase in *vectigal* during Cato's governorship.[141] It is more likely that Cato, or his quaestor, collected the money due directly from those who were digging out the silver and iron ores.[142]

It has also been suggested that at this time, either in 197 or in Cato's

[136] Van Nostrand, *ESAR* III, 126–37; Sutherland, *The Romans in Spain* Ch. 3; E. Badian [n. 10] 120–1; M. H. Crawford, *NC* 9 (1969) 79–93; R. C. Knapp, *NC* 17 (1977) 1–18.

[137] Livy 34.21.7: 'pacata provincia vectigalia magna instituit ex ferrariis argentariisque, quibus tum institutis locupletior in dies provincia fuit.'

[138] Gellius, *NA* 2.22.28; Schulten, *FHA* III, 186.

[139] R. Way and M. Simmons, *A geography of Spain and Portugal* (London 1962) 155–8; A. Schulten, *Iberische Landeskunde* II (Strasbourg 1957) 487–91, 510–15.

[140] J. S. Richardson, *JRS* 66 (1976) 139–47, *contra* P. A. Brunt, in ed. Seager, *The crisis of the Roman republic* (Cambridge 1962) 105, and E. Badian, *Publicans and sinners* (Oxford 1972) 32ff.

[141] Livy 34.44.4. Cato seems, from Livy's account (34.46.2) to have returned early in the consular year.

[142] On this see further pp. 120–3 below.

governorship, the payment of *stipendium* was regularised. The evidence given for this belief is the appearance among the booty declared by commanders returning from Spain in 195 and 194 of coined money, described by Livy as 'argentum oscense'.[143] It has been suggested that this refers to the so-called 'Iberian denarii', coins with an Iberian legend on the Roman weight standard.

The collection of money on the scale which would be implied by the minting of a silver coinage specifically for the purpose would indicate a far more complex set of financial obligations by the Spanish tribes to the Romans than has been seen in the literary evidence up to this date. There are, however, difficulties with so early a dating. The coins themselves, from indications of usage, can only give a very approximate indication of their date, and the only reason for placing their introduction at the very beginning of the second century is the mention of 'argentum oscense' by Livy.[144] Yet, if they were introduced to pay Roman taxes in 197, the notices in Livy are very odd, for there they appear among the booty of proconsuls who governed Spanish provinces in 197, 196 and 195. This would imply that coins, minted for the first time in 197 on Roman instructions, were immediately captured in substantial quantities from rebellious tribes. It is in any case difficult to imagine Iberian denarii being used at this date to pay the *stipendium* demanded by Roman governors. As has been seen, *stipendium* at the end of the third century was seen, in the Spanish context, as payment for Roman soldiers in the area, and it is likely that this was still the case, at least until the end of the 180s.[145] In this case, the expectation would be that the *stipendium* would be paid in bronze, rather than in silver, since the soldiers appear to have been paid in bronze until the 140s.[146] The *argentum oscense* of Livy is probably some other local coinage, such as the Iberian coins struck in imitation of the drachmas from Emporion, and their appearance in the 190s is no evidence for the existence of a complex system of taxation at this date.[147]

[143] Crawford [n. 136] 79–93 (it should be noted that Crawford now gives a later date to the introduction of the Iberian *denarii*; see below pp. 121–2). M. Helvius (Livy 34.10.4) brought back 119, 439 in 195; Q. Minucius Thermus 278,000 in the same year (Livy 34.10.7); and Cato himself 540 in 194 (Livy 34.46.2). The only other mention of 'argentum oscense' is in the booty of Q. Fulvius Flaccus, who returned in 180 with 173,200 (Livy 40.43.6).

[144] Arguments based on the similarity of the weight of the Iberian denarii to the weight of the early denarii minted at Rome in the latter years of the second Punic War, are of little help, as it is clear that Roman coins took several decades to reach Spain (Crawford [n. 136] 79–80). It is difficult therefore to know what coins were used by Spanish coiners as comparison-pieces at any particular date.

[145] See index *s.v. stipendium*; also *JRS* 66 (1976) 147–9.

[146] M. H. Crawford, *RRC* II, 621–31.

[147] On the date and purpose of the Iberian denarii, see below pp. 121–3.

That exploitation by the state of the riches of Spain was still very much an *ad hoc* business, is indicated by another incident in Cato's period there. Although by the end of the 170s the Romans had instituted a 5 per cent tax on grain, it seems clear from Cato's dismissal of the *redemptores* who were proposing to act as supply agents for the provisioning of his forces that no mechanism for collecting a half-tithe of grain existed in 195.[148] For Cato, the alternative methods of feeding his soldiers were buying grain or seizing it as plunder, and this despite the fact that the incident occurred when the grain was on the threshing floor, precisely the moment at which, under the Sicilian system, the grain-tithe was assessed and collected.[149]

It is probable that Cato made no alteration to the administrative arrangements within his province, apart from the institution of income from the silver and iron mines in the north of his province.[150] For the most part, the *ad hoc* arrangements of his predecessors sufficed, and were applied by Cato with a characteristic blend of violence and opportunism. He did not after all come to Spain to reorganise the administration; he came to fight a war and to win victories. These form the content of the accounts of his governorship, and must have filled completely the year he spent there. In this his attitude was complementary to that of the senate, whose interest, at least so far as can be told from the record Livy gives us, was in equipping and dispatching large enough forces and commanders with adequate powers to lead them, and in receiving reports of their military activity, whether by letter or in person, when a proconsul requested a triumph on his return. When questions arise about the governor's conduct of himself and his army, they relate to the extent of his success or failure in terms of numbers of casualties and amounts of booty, and to whether constitutional proprieties (such as the limitations of the magistrates' area of responsibility, whether geographical or chronological) have been observed. The financial and administrative arrangements, the treatment of friends and enemies within the *provincia*, even the precise nature and location of the campaigns undertaken, all these seem to have been of little concern.

It is impossible to know to what extent Cato's view of the task of a Spanish proconsul was typical of the period, and how far the product of his own style and character. Two points, however, indicate that many of the attitudes that can be seen from the accounts of his tenure of Hispania

---

148 Livy 34.9.12–13. Cf. Richardson [n. 49] 150.
149 Cic. *II Verr.* 3.14.36–7.
150 This is the conclusion also of R. Bernhardt, *Historia* 24 (1975) 421.

Citerior were at least in line with those of most of his contemporaries. First, as has been noted, his single-minded concentration on his *provincia* as a place where he was sent to fight coincides with what we know of senatorial policy, and indeed with the views of the majority of Romans about the military activity of the state.[151] Secondly the history of continuous warfare in Spain for the first 20 years after the decision to send praetors annually, the sporadic and almost inconsequential nature of the fighting that went on, and the attitude of the senate to that fighting all seem to fit a similar picture. The change in senatorial policy that took place in 197 certainly represents a new commitment to a continued military presence in Spain, but the emergence of anything resembling a coherent administrative pattern, of provincial government as we know it from the first century BC onwards, was still in the future.

[151] The best exposition of this is Harris, *War and imperialism* Ch. 1.

CHAPTER 5

The shaping of the *provinciae*: 193–155

The praetorian commanders 193–155

Cato claimed that, by the end of his tenure of the *provincia* of Hispania Citerior, the area was at peace. The senate, in recognition of this, voted him a three-day *supplicatio* in thanksgiving to the gods and, on his return, a triumph.[1] They also decided that the army which Cato had commanded in Spain, consisting of two legions with the usual complement of auxiliary infantry and cavalry, should be withdrawn. Although the wisdom of this action has been questioned, it was an inevitable concomitant of the senate's acceptance of Cato's account of his own successes, and the award of a triumph.[2] However, as the following years demonstrated, the senate was undoubtedly wrong to believe Cato.

Both the praetors sent out to Spain in 194[3] had connections with the peninsula. P. Cornelius Scipio Nasica, who was sent to Ulterior, was the son of Cn. Scipio who had been killed with his brother Publius in the disasters of 211. Sex. Digitius was present with Publius' son, the younger P. Scipio, at New Carthage in 209, where, as a *socius navalis*, he won the distinction of a mural crown,[4] and in all probability gained the citizenship. In 194, in the second consulship of P. Scipio, Nasica's cousin and Digitius' former commander, these two men were faced with the aftermath of Cato's victories. Digitius succeeded Cato, and, with forces less than half those at his predecessor's disposal, had to deal with a rash of small-scale rebellions. In one of these, he was heavily defeated and only saved by the assistance of Nasica, who, coming in from Ulterior, overawed the southern part of the province by a series of victories. The

---

[1] Livy 34.21.7–8, 42.1, 46.2–3.

[2] Livy 34.43.3, 43.8. Astin, *Cato* 47–8, calls this an 'astonishing decision' and a glaring error. On the relationship between the claim to have pacified a province, the removal of armies and the award of a triumph, see Richardson, *JRS* 65 (1975) 60–2.

[3] Livy 34.42.4, 43.7. On the connection between Digitius and the Scipios, see Münzer, *Röm. Adelsparteien*, 92–5.   [4] Livy 26.48.6–14.

departure of the consular army of Cato revealed clearly the instability which he had left. Digitius' defeat took place in the area between the Ebro and the Pyrenees, precisely the location of Cato's campaigns in the previous year.[5] In Ulterior, Scipio had no further problems with the Turdetani, but engaged the Lusitani, who had been causing devastation in the western part of the Baetis valley, and early in the following year defeated them near Ilipa before his successor arrived.[6]

This continuation of warfare in areas allegedly pacified, and the ignoring of the provincial boundaries, seen in the activities of Scipio Nasica in 194, demonstrate again the effects of the distance between Spain and Rome on the information which reached the senate about the true state of affairs in the two provinces, and on their control, or lack of control, over commanders actually present in Spain. The same can be seen still more clearly in the following years. Of the praetors for 193 M. Fulvius Nobilior was allotted to Hispania Ulterior, C. Flaminius to Citerior.[7] Like his predecessor, Digitius, Flaminius had been in Spain before, as quaestor to the younger Scipio in 209.[8] It may have been through his previous links with people there that he heard privately of the state of affairs in the province, and demanded that one of the urban legions should be assigned to him, on the grounds that an immense war had broken out in the province, that little was left of the army commanded by Digitius, and that these remnants were in a state of terror. The senate, however, refused to co-operate, on the grounds that they had had no news from Digitius himself, and that they could not act on the basis of idle rumours received from random individuals. Indeed they went so far as to state that unless the praetors themselves wrote from the provinces or legates brought reports to the senate, no account should be regarded as valid. Their response to Flaminius' request for soldiers was that, if it should prove that there was serious trouble in Spain, he could enrol 'tumultarii milites' outside Italy. It is not clear where these soldiers were expected to come from. The senate is said to have intended that Flaminius should draw them from Spain, but the number of Roman citizens in Spain at this date cannot have been large. However, Livy reports Valerius Antias as saying that Flaminius thwarted the senate's intention by levying troops in Sicily, and later landing in Africa, having been carried there by

[5] Livy 35.1.1–3. Scipio's successes are described as being won 'trans Iberum'. As there is no record of the two praetors joining forces, the natural interpretation of Livy's account suggests that Digitius was fighting north of the Ebro.

[6] Livy 35.1.5–12. For the site of Ilipa, see above p. 50.

[7] Livy 34.55.6.   [8] Livy 26.47.8, 49.10.

a storm, and conscripting various stray veterans left over from Africanus' final campaign nine years before.[9]

Whatever is believed about the conclusion of this story, the remoteness of Spain and the self-imposed limitation which the senate placed upon their sources of information make clear the difficulties that the senate would experience in keeping close watch on the activities of the proconsuls they had sent there, even if they wished to do so. The record of the activities of Flaminius and Nobilior confirms the impression. The war apparently turned out to be less of a threat than Flaminius had feared, and he was able to proceed against the Oretani, capturing the town of Inlucia.[10] The Oretani lived on the northern side of the Sierra Morena, within the province of Ulterior.[11] At the same time Nobilior was fighting a confederation of tribes from the northern part of the *meseta*, the Vaccaei, the Vettones and the Celtiberians at Toletum, the modern Toledo.[12] Unless all the names in Livy's account have been hopelessly distorted, Nobilior, the praetor sent to the further province, is fighting tribes at a point about 200 kilometres north of his colleague Flaminius, who is allegedly in charge of the nearer province. In 192, Nobilior is fighting the Oretani, Flaminius' enemy of the previous year, and again reaches Toledo; while Flaminius seizes the town of Licabrum, which is probably identical with Igabrum, a settlement south-east of Corduba in the Baetis valley.[13]

The reason for this disregard for the geographical division between the two areas of responsibility in Spain is linked to the movement inland of the fighting which the two proconsuls were undertaking. No clear pattern emerges from the two sets of campaigns, other than that there was always fighting going on, and that if the tribes within the area which was clearly the proconsul's *provincia* were not involved, then he transferred his attention to those beyond it. The motivation for such behaviour might

[9] Livy 35.2. On the urban legions conscripted in 193, see Livy 34.56.4. There are other instances of *tumultarii* being conscripted in the provinces, especially in this period of Livy 31.2.5–6 (201); 35.23.8 (193). On Romans in Spain, see E. Gabba, *Athenaeum* N.S. 32 (1954) 290–9.

[10] Livy 35.7.6–7.

[11] A. Schulten, *RE* XVIII, 1018–19. Inlucia has been identified with Ilugo, north-east of Castulo (Schulten, *RE* XIII, 2119 *s.v.* Lyco).   [12] Livy 35.7.8.

[13] Livy 35.22.5–8. On Licabrum/Igabrum, E. Hübner, *CIL* II, 215–16, A. Schulten, *FHA* III, 197. On these campaigns, see Schlag, *Regnum in senatu* (Stuttgart 1968) 36–9; she, however, places Licabrum in the territory of the Vaccaei, citing Weissenborn/Müller *ad. loc.* They in turn cite F. A. Ukert, *Geographie der Griechen und Römer*, II.1 (Weimar 1821) 432, who cites Ambrosio de Morales, *Coronica general de España* II (Alcala 1574) 56 and *Antiguedades de España* (Alcala 1575) 95. Morales placed the town near Segovia, on the grounds that a place named Britablo had occurred with Segovia and Cauca in a letter of Montanus, who was bishop of Toledo in the first half of the sixth century. This attribution was already doubted in the 1791 edition of the *Coronica general* III, 404.

sometimes be incursions into the territory already regarded by the Romans as under their control, or belonging to a tribe in alliance with them, but this was by no means always the case. Given the erratic and uncoordinated nature of the various attacks, it does not seem that there was any grand design for an eventual conquest of the entire peninsula. The appearance is rather that of an unsystematic hunt for peoples to defeat and booty to carry home.[14]

For more than a decade following the tenure of the two provinces by Flaminius and Nobilior, the fighting continued in Spain in the same sporadic but unceasing fashion. Flaminius himself remained in charge of Citerior for two more years, no doubt because of the exigencies of the war against Antiochus in the east.[15] Though nothing more is heard of his campaigning after 192, his new colleague in Ulterior, L. Aemilius Paullus, fought against the Bastetani, in the eastern part of his *provincia*, and the Lusitani in the west. In both cases he was unsuccessful, though the report of his total defeat and death, which Orosius gives, is clearly exaggerated.[16] He was able to redeem the situation because the praetor sent to succeed him in 189, L. Baebius Dives, had died at Massilia, having been ambushed by Ligurians while on his way to Spain. Paullus managed to defeat the Lusitanians before his eventual replacement, P. Iunius Brutus, arrived.[17] In fact neither Brutus, who had been praetor in 190 and was sent on to Spain after the news of Baebius' death, nor L. Plautius Hypsaeus, who as praetor in 189 went to Citerior and presumably replaced Flaminius there, is recorded as having undertaken any military engagements, though the senate took care, by the sending of *supplementa* for the armies, to keep up the strength of Roman forces stationed there.[18] This silence may be due to no more than a quirk in Livy's annalistic sources, though his remark that news of Paullus' final victory caused a quietening of matters in Spain perhaps indicates a lull in the fighting.[19] If so, it was the first since Cn. Scipio landed in 218, and the last until the mid-170s.

Their successors, L. Manlius Acidinus and C. Atinius, praetors of 188, brought further troops to Citerior and Ulterior. To the single legion in each *provincia*, the senate added a further 3,000 foot and 200 horse drawn from the allies.[20] In late 187, at the end of their second year, both men

---

[14] So Schlag [n. 13] 37–8 and 40; Dahlheim, *Gewalt und Herrschaft* 77–110.
[15] Livy 36.2.9; 37.2.11. This had been the reason for extending the tenure of Nobilior and Flaminius to a second year (Livy 35.20.8–13).
[16] Livy 37.46.7–8; Orosius 4.20.23.
[17] Livy 37.57.1–6; Orosius 4.20.24.
[18] Livy 37.50.8, 11–12.
[19] Livy 37.57.6.
[20] Livy 38.35.10, 36.3.

sent back letters telling of revolts among the Celtiberians and the Lusitanians, accompanied by the customary charges of plundering the territory of Roman allies. The senate deferred discussion of this until after the election of magistrates for the following year, and the allotment of provinces. In fact further news came through shortly after this had been done. C. Calpurnius Piso was about to leave the port of Luna on his way to Ulterior when he learned that the Lusitanians had been defeated at Hasta, in the south-western section of the Baetis valley, but that Atinius himself had died of wounds, following the attack on the town itself. At the same time a report from Citerior told of a defeat of the Celtiberians at Calgurris in the Ebro valley.[21]

Perhaps because of this rather mixed news from Spain Piso and his colleague in Citerior, L. Quinctius Crispinus, decided at the outset of the following year to combine their forces.[22] Together they commanded the largest army seen in Spain since Cato's departure, adding to the remains of the legions, which they took over from their predecessors, a further 3,000 Roman and 20,000 allied infantry, and 200 Roman and 1,300 allied cavalry.[23] It has been suggested that these huge numbers represent the *supplementa* for four legions, and that each of the two praetors had received an additional legion in 187.[24] This is quite possible, although Livy gives no details for the levying and distribution of armies in that year. The difference, however, between 187 and 186 was that, in the latter year, the two proconsuls combined their forces. If the numbers had been increased in 187, this would give them an army of four legions. With this united strength, they fought in Baeturia, that is in the eastern part of the Baetis valley, and later moved across the Sierra Morena into Carpetania, reaching Dipo (whose location is unknown) and Toledo. Here they first suffered a defeat, but subsequently themselves defeated their enemy in a major battle.[25] Livy does not name the peoples against whom they fought, but he notes that their triumphs, on their return in 184, were both over the Lusitanians and the Celtiberians.[26]

Though Livy commends the decision of these two men to act with common mind and plan, he does not seem to think it odd that they should do so.[27] It is in fact remarkable. They were independent commanders

---

[21] Livy 39.7.6–7, 21.1–10.

[22] Livy 39.30.1. The previous year they had had time only to move into winter-quarters (Livy 39.21.10). [23] Livy 39.20.3–4.

[24] A. Afzelius, *Die römische Kriegsmacht* (Copenhagen 1944) 40–1; Brunt, *Italian manpower* 661. The numeration of their legions in 185 and the arguments about their return show that Piso and Crispinus had four legions between them (Livy 39.30.12; 38.8–12).

[25] Livy 39.30–1.

[26] Livy 39.42.2–4. [27] Livy 39.30.1.

who had been assigned to separate *provinciae* by the senate, and apparently they only decided to join forces in the winter and early spring of 185, when they were far from the eyes and thoughts of the Roman senate. Once again, though perhaps on this occasion in a more constructive manner, the provincial arrangements, as understood by the senate, were simply ignored by commanders in Spain.

The experiment was not, however, repeated by the next two praetors. A. Terentius Varro and P. Sempronius Longus, respectively in Citerior and Ulterior, showed no signs of a desire to co-operate with one another. Ulterior is said to have been quiet for the two years of Longus' tenure (184–183) partly because of the successes of Piso and Crispinus the year before, partly because in the second year Longus himself was incapacitated by illness of which he died before he could return home.[28] As Livy remarks, the Lusitani were most fortunately peaceful while no-one was harassing them.[29] In Citerior Terentius won several victories, in 184 against the Suessetani, north of the Ebro, and in 183 against the Ausetani, in the coastal area south of the Pyrenees, and against the Celtiberians, capturing some of their towns.[30] It was Terentius who wrote to inform the senate of Longus' death, and on receipt of his letter early in 182, the new praetors, Q. Fulvius Flaccus for Citerior and P. Manlius for Ulterior, were instructed to proceed to their provinces with all speed.[31] Manlius, who had been Cato's second-in-command in 195, needed to spend his first campaigning season reassembling the army which had apparently scattered across the province. Flaccus, however, was able to move onto the offensive immediately, and attacked a town called either Urbicna or Urbicua by Livy. This action roused the Celtiberians to revolt, but after a stiff fight, Flaccus drove them off and captured the town.[32] In the following year the two praetors were sent *supplementa* of 3,000 Roman and 6,000 allied infantry, together with 200 Roman and 300 allied horse.[33] Fulvius added to these such allied troops as he could raise and marched south into Carpetania. Here he defeated a large force of Celtiberians at a town called Aebura and moved northwards through Carpetania to Contrebia, probably sited at Botorrita on the southern edge of the Ebro

[28] Livy 39.42.1, 56.2; 40.2.6.

[29] Livy 39.56.2: 'nullo lacessante peropportune quieverunt Lusitani'.

[30] Livy 39.42.1, 56.1.

[31] Livy 40.2.5. For the assignment of the provinces, Livy 40.1.2; for the *supplementa* sent to the legions in Spain, Livy 40.1.7.

[32] Livy 40.16.7–10. For the reading of the town's name, see Weissenborn and Müller *ad loc*. It may be identical with Urbiaca, placed by the *Itin. Ant.* p. 447.5 (Wess.) 98 miles south of Zaragoza.

[33] Livy 40.18.16.

valley, south of Zaragoza. Manlius won several skirmishes with the Lusitanians.[34]

Of the two praetors assigned to Spain in 180 Ti. Sempronius Gracchus was late reaching Citerior because of a dispute in the senate about Flaccus' proposal to withdraw his forces from the province, and because the senate had instructed him as a result to levy additional troops to make up for those Flaccus was to bring home.[35] Despite Gracchus' forethought in sending a message to Flaccus by way of L. Postumius Albinus, who had been assigned to Ulterior, to meet him at Tarraco, Flaccus had already undertaken an expedition into the depths of Celtiberia, and being unable to induce any of the Celtiberians to surrender, had contented himself with plundering the area, which, Livy reports, irritated rather than terrified the enemy. Flaccus set off for Tarraco, and, after dealing with an ambush laid for him by the Celtiberians *en route*, arrived there two days late. By the time the forces had been sorted out according to the formula laid down by the senate, there can have been little time left for further campaigning. Gracchus is said to have led his troops into Celtiberia, but with what result is not stated.[36]

In the next year, 179, and in the early months of 178 before their successors arrived, Gracchus and Albinus undertook a great deal of fighting and, more unusually, a considerable amount of administration. Precise chronology of these events is uncertain for Livy seems to have had more sources at his disposal than was usual for Spanish affairs, and describes their activities in 179 in a series of largely disconnected anecdotes. For 178, his account is lost in the lacuna at the beginning of book 41, and survives only in epitome. Certainly at the beginning of the campaigning season in 179 the two men reached agreement that Albinus would move north through Lusitania into the territory of the Vaccaei, and thence eastwards into Celtiberia; Gracchus would penetrate deep into Celtiberia. Gracchus' attacks against several Celtiberian towns are then described, but the names which Livy gives to them are of no assistance in identifying the area in which he was fighting.[37] For the following year,

---

[34] Livy 40.30.1–34.1. Cf. the stories in Appian, *Ib.* 42.171.4 and Diod. Sic 29.28, who have similar accounts, though with some material not found in Livy, and varying names for the towns. On the site of Contrebia, see G. Fatás, *Contrebia Belaisca II: Tabula Contrebiensis* (Zaragoza 1980) 46–57; A. Beltrán and A. Tovar, *Contrebia Belaisca I: el bronce de Botorrita* (Zaragoza 1982) 9–33.

[35] Livy 40.35.3–36.11.   [36] Livy 40.39–40.

[37] Livy 40.47.1–50.5. The towns are Certima, Munda, Alce and Ergavica. The first two cannot be the well known towns Munda and Cartima, in Ulterior, as they are said specifically to be Celtiberian. Appian says Gracchus fought at Caravis and Complega (*Ib.* 43.175–9), of which Caravis may be identical with Caravi, on the road between Numantia and Zaragoza (*Itin. Ant.* 443.1 (Wess.))

the Livian epitome of book 41 says no more than that he accepted the surrender of the Celtiberians. He was presumably active in the north-eastern part of the *meseta*, since he founded the town of Gracchurris in the upper Ebro valley in 178.[38] Stories relating to his campaigns are frequent, and they clearly covered much territory.[39] Of Albinus' activities we know even less. Livy seems confused about the date of his arrival in Ulterior, for, having stated that he was in Spain before Gracchus, in the following year he denies that he could have won victories against the Vaccaei, because he arrived too late in the province. The epitome of book 41 says he defeated the Vaccaei and Lusitani, and his triumph in 178 was 'ex Lusitania Hispaniaque', as opposed to that of Gracchus 'de Celtibereis Hispaneisque'.[40]

In view of the record of the praetors in Spain, more surprising than the extent of Gracchus' military activity are the stories in Livy of his negotiations with the Celtiberians, and the evidence of the introduction of civilian organisation on a larger scale than seen hitherto. The incidents related by Livy of his discussions with enemy ambassadors, and his personal contacts with the leaders of Spanish tribes are reminiscent of the relationships established by Scipio Africanus, and of nothing since.[41] It is clear that Livy had access to another tradition which wished to deny the effectiveness of these relationships by asserting that in fact the Celtiberians went into revolt as soon as Gracchus' back was turned, and that they were only subdued after a second defeat, and the destruction of their camp.[42] This version is the less probable. Gracchus was renowned for the large number of 'cities', or, more probably, forts that he captured, and many of these must have surrendered to him rather than having been besieged.[43] In view of the time available to him for campaigning, and the extent of his programme of reorganisation and settlement, it is unlikely that there was time for a full-scale revolt and repression as this second tradition suggests. Further, the evident respect and affection in which

(So Hübner, *RE s.v.*) Schulten (*FHA* III, 217–24) places all Gracchus' exploits in the Jalón valley, but the evidence is weak.

[38] Livy *ep.* 41, Festus 86 (Lindsay).

[39] Strabo 3.4.13 (p. 163), quoting Polybius and Poseidonius; Frontius 2.53, 2.5.14, 3.5.2; ps.-Frontius 4.7.33; Florus 1.33.9.

[40] Livy 40.39.3 (180), 50.6–7 (179); *ep.* 41 (178). For the triumphs, see Livy 41.7.1–3 and *Inscr. It.* 13.1.80–1. On Livy's error, H. Nissen, *Kritische Untersuchungen über die Quellen der vierten und fünften Dekade der Livius* (Berlin 1863) 237–8.

[41] Livy 40.47.3–10, 49.4–7; cf. above pp. 58–61. Compare also Cato's relations with the son of a chief of the Ilergetes, which seem, in context, to be an attempt to maintain cordiality while denying commitment (Livy 34.12.7).　　　　　　　　　　[42] Livy 40.50.2–5.

[43] Polybius, 25.1.1, (= Strabo 3.4.13) says he 'put down' 300 cities (τριακοσίας αὐτῶν καταλῦσαι πολείς), whereas Florus (1.33.9) says 150.

Gracchus and his measures were held subsequently suggest that his arrangements were accepted relatively freely by the Celtiberians.[44] The details of his arrangements will be discussed further below, but it is important to note, for the progress of the fighting in Spain, that it was he who, according to Appian, gave to the Spanish tribes precise treaties which made them 'friends' of the Romans. As will be seen, it is probable that this was not confined to the Celtiberians in Citerior alone.[45]

Of the praetors who went to Spain over the next decade, little is known but their names. The provincial *sortitio* for 178 is lost in the gap at the beginning of Livy book 41, but from the mention of *supplementa* sent, from the *Fasti Triumphales*, and from a later mention during the trials of Spanish governors in 171, it is clear that between 178 and 176 M. Titinius Curvus was in Citerior and T. Fonteius in Ulterior.[46] Although the record of Curvus' triumph proves he was involved with fighting, the size of both armies seems to have been reduced from two to one legion.[47] In 175 the *sortitio* is again lost from Livy's text, but at least the praetor in Citerior is known to have been Ap. Claudius, who returned in 174 to celebrate an *ovatio* over the Celtiberians. The *Fasti Triumphales* supply the cognomen Cento, a name which in literary sources is written 'Centho'.[48] It is probable that there was a successor to Fonteius in Ulterior this year, but his name has not survived, nor any record of his activity.

Beginning with Centho, the praetors for the next few years down to 172 are in Spain each for one year only. Little is known of the area after 175. In 174 P. Furius Philus went to Citerior, Cn. Servilius Caepio to Citerior, taking *supplementa* with them.[49] In 173, of the two praetors dispatched, only M. Matienus (Ulterior) arrived, his colleague, N. Fabius Buteo, having died at Massilia on his way to Citerior. As soon as the senate heard this they decreed that the two returning governors, Caepio and Philus, should draw lots to decide which of them should remain, and, as it turned out, Philus' tenure was extended for a year.[50] In the following

---

[44] Polybius 35.2.15; Appian, *Ib.* 43.179–44.183; Plut. *Ti. Gracch.* 5.2.

[45] Appian, *Ib.* 43.179: πᾶσιν ἔθετο τοῖς τῇδε συνθήκας ἀκριβεῖς, καθ' ἃ 'Ρωμαίων ἔσονται φίλοι. See below pp. 112–19.

[46] Livy 41.9.3, 15.11; 43.2.6; *Inscr. It.* 13.1.555 (Titinius' name appears in the Capitoline Fasti, the triumph both there and in the Urbisalvienses). As Titinius was accused by representatives from both provinces in 171, he may have been in control of both at some point during the period 178–176 (Livy 43.2.7).

[47] Brunt, *Italian manpower* 661–3, *contra* A. Afzelius [n. 24].

[48] Livy 41.26.1–5, 28.1–3. *Inscr. It.* 13.1.556.

[49] Livy 41.21.3.

[50] Livy 42.1.3, 4.1–3. For doubts about Matienus' praenomen (M. or C.) see A. Klotz, *Hermes* 50 (1915) 517 n. l.

year, 172, the first effects of the impending war with Perseus were being felt, and the two praetors chosen to go to Spain, M. Iunius Pennus to Citerior and Sp. Lucretius to Ulterior, were at first refused *supplementa*. When it became clear that hostilities would not break out that year, their continual demands persuaded the senate to provide them with the standard number required to keep their legions up to strength.[51]

By the time of the *sortitio* in 171, the war in the east had broken out in earnest and, in order to leave one praetorian command free to be assigned wherever the senate saw fit, they reduced the number of praetors sent to Spain to one.[52] This combination of the two *provinciae* was made still more economical by extending the *imperium* of the man who was sent, L. Canuleius Dives, for a second year.[53] In one of the two years, there was fresh trouble among the Celtiberians, led by a messianic figure, named Olonicus or Olyndicus, who brandished a silver spear, allegedly sent from heaven. The revolt petered out following his untimely death.[54] M. Claudius Marcellus, who in 169 again commanded in both provinces, and brought *supplementa* with him, is recorded as having captured a single town, Marcolica, whose whereabouts are unknown.[55] In 168, he was replaced by P. Fonteius Balbus, of whom nothing else is known.[56]

By 167, with the Macedonian war over, the senate decided to revert to the former pattern. Cn. Fulvius was sent to Citerior and C. Licinius Nerva to Ulterior.[57] In fact these are the last men known to have held the Spanish provinces before the beginnings of the major problems there in the mid-150s. Although a list of praetors for 166 survives in Livy, together with a notice of the senate's resolution that the two Spains should be among the provinces allotted, there is no indication of who went to which.[58]

Senatorial policy

(a) Military

This survey of the activities of the men who went as *praetor pro consule* to Spain between 194 and 167 illustrates clearly that, especially down to 178, their main role was that of military commanders. The same, of course

---

[51] Livy 40.10.13, 18.6–7; cf. Brunt, *Italian manpower* 662.   [52] Livy 42.28.5–6.
[53] Broughton, *MRR* I, 421; D. Wilsdorf, *Fasti Hispaniarum provinciarum* (Leipzig 1878) 92.
[54] Livy *ep.* 43; Florus 1.33.13.   [55] Livy 43.12.10–11, 15.3; 45.4.1.
[56] Livy 44.17.5, 10.   [57] Livy 45.16.1–3.
[58] Livy 45.44.1–2, Wilsdorf [n. 53] 94, conjectures that the lists of praetors and of provinces are parallel, and thus assigns A. Licinius Nerva to Citerior, and P. Rutilius Calvus to Ulterior (so Broughton, *MRR* I, 437). However, compare Livy 43.11.7–8 and 15.3 (for 169), where the lists are not parallel.

had been true of their predecessors, during and immediately after the Hannibalic war. Within the period examined in this chapter, the fighting seems to have been almost continuous down to the return of Gracchus and Albinus to Rome in early 178. Indeed of the 23 praetors and ex-praetors and 1 consul sent to the two provinces between 197 and the end of 179, 4 only are not specifically mentioned as involved in warfare. Ap. Claudius Pulcher, in Ulterior in 195, seems to all intents and purposes to have been deprived of his command on the arrival of Cato and P. Manlius. L. Plautius Hypsaeus and P. Iunius Brutus in 189 may indeed not have undertaken hostile campaigns, perhaps in part because Brutus was late arriving in Ulterior. The other, P. Sempronius Longus, in Ulterior from 184 to 183, was incapacitated by a prolonged illness. All the others, until the governorships of Gracchus and Albinus, spent their tenure of the provinces in fighting, and, so far as our record goes, only in fighting.

After 179, there appears to be a change, at least in the intensity and continuity of the warfare. The size of the Roman forces stationed in the two provinces, which since 187 had probably been four legions, seems to have been reduced to a single legion in each.[59] At the same time, there was a drop in the number of returning pro-magistrates who were permitted to celebrate a triumph or an *ovatio* in recognition of their military achievements. Of the twenty-two men who returned from Spain[60] between the return of the first ex-praetors *pro consule* in 195 and that of Gracchus and Albinus, seven celebrated a triumph and four an *ovatio*, that is one in two. Of the twelve men known or presumed to have returned from Spain between 177 and 166, one was awarded a triumph and one an *ovatio*, that is one in six. The contrast becomes still sharper if the period between 166 and 155 is taken into account. Although neither a Livian account nor any other source survives to describe events in Spain during this period, the *Fasti Capitolini Triumphales*, of which fragments are extant covering the entire 11 years, record not one triumph or *ovatio* from the two Spanish provinces.[61]

In view of the immense prestige accorded to those who were successful in war, and particularly anyone who was able as a result to lead a triumphal procession through the streets of Rome, it is not surprising that a similar picture emerges from a consideration of the progress made by

[59] Brunt, *Italian manpower* 661–3.
[60] For this computation P. Manlius (*pr.* 195 and 182) is counted twice; C. Sempronius Tuditanus (*pr.* 197), C. Atinius (*pr.* 188) and P. Sempronius Longus (*pr.* 184) all died in Spain.
[61] *Inscr. It.* 13.1.80–3, 556–7. On the triumphs in the second century, see J. S. Richardson [n. 2] 50–63. R. Develin, *Klio* 60 (1978) 429–38, adds little.

the Spanish commanders to higher office in the *cursus honorum*. Of the twenty praetorians who returned from Spain in the period down to 178,[62] ten subsequently reached the consulship, and of the ten who celebrated an *ovatio* or triumph,[63] seven subsequently became consul. As the ratio of praetors to consuls throughout this period was three to one, it is clear that the tenure of one of the Spanish provinces considerably enhanced the chances of advancing to the consulship. Again, this is no longer true after 178. Only three of the twelve who went to Spain between 178 and 167 managed to become consul, and, perhaps surprisingly, neither M. Titinius Curvus, who triumphed in 175, nor Ap. Claudius Centho, who celebrated an *ovatio* in 174, did so.

All this indicates both a reduction of the amount of military activity in Spain after 178, and a consequent lessening in the advantages to be gained by a praetorship spent in one of the two provinces there. This latter point is reinforced by clear indications that praetors were less anxious to make the long and dangerous journey to the west from the mid-170s. The decision of the senate when, in 173, they received news of the death of N. Fabius Buteo on his way to Citerior, that the two men about to return to Rome from Spain should cast lots to fill the vacancy,[64] is one instance. In the past when such emergencies had arisen, the senate had sent out from Italy a pro-magistrate already in office.[65] It is not surprising that the senate should wish to use a man already in Spain, but it is difficult to understand why they should go through the elaborate performance of the lot to decide which of the two provincial governors of 174 should replace Buteo. Unless Furius Philus had been in some way unsatisfactory, he was the obvious candidate; whereas if he had been unsatisfactory (as the accusations brought against him in 171 by the inhabitants of Citerior might lead one to suspect), then Caepio could take his place. In neither circumstance is the use of the lot explained. The simplest way to account for it is that Spain was so unpopular that it was assumed that neither commander wished to spend a second year there, and that the senate, unwilling to force one or the other, left the decision to chance.

A second incident, which illustrates still more forcibly the unpopularity of the Spanish provinces, occurred in 176. After the *sortitio* had taken place, two praetors requested that they should be excused from going to their provinces. M. Popilius Laenas argued that he should not be sent to

---

[62] Excluding Cato, who was already consul, and counting P. Manlius as one.
[63] Again, excluding Cato.　　　　　　　　　　　　　　　　[64] Livy 42.4.1–2.
[65] Thus C. Claudius Nero in 211/210, and P. Iunius Brutus in 189.

Sardinia, as the consul of the previous year, Ti. Gracchus, and his praetorian *adiutor* were proving very successful, and should not be interrupted. The strength of this argument was recognised. The other praetor, however, P. Licinius Crassus, swore on oath that he was prevented from going by religious duties. No sooner had Crassus taken his oath than another praetor, M. Cornelius Scipio Maluginensis, also remembered that similar religious scruples hindered him from proceeding to his province. He swore an oath on identical terms to that of Crassus, and was excused duty.[66] Both these men had been assigned to provinces in Spain, Crassus to Citerior and Scipio to Ulterior. There is evidence that in each of these two cases, doubt was cast on the sincerity of their religious professions. Scipio was expelled from the senate by the censors of the next *lustrum* in 174, at which point Livy describes him as the man who two years before had been praetor in Spain. The description is clearly false, but may originate from an explanatory note attached to the list of those expelled by the censors.[67] Crassus was not so harshly treated, but when as consul in 171 he wanted to go to the province of Macedonia and the war against Perseus, his colleague, C. Cassius Longinus, demanded that the province be assigned to himself without use of the lot, on the grounds that Crassus could not take a province without breaking the oath he had made while a praetor. The senate replied that it was not for them to deny a province to a man elected consul by the Roman people, and ordered the *sortitio* to take place.[68] It seems that in one, and perhaps in both these cases, a praetor was prepared to take an oath of somewhat dubious propriety in order to avoid going to a Spanish province.

There was, then, an alteration in the situation in Spain in 178, which resulted in a change in senatorial policy, in the reduction of forces there, a change in military activity and political prospects of the men sent there, and in consequence, a change in the desirability or otherwise of a Spanish command. There can be little doubt that the cause of this was the success of Gracchus and Albinus, and the somewhat more settled conditions which followed the 'precise treaties' which Gracchus arranged. When in 154, on the verge of the Numantine war, Spanish tribes sent embassies to Rome, it was to the treaties of Gracchus and to the conditions specified by Gracchus that they referred.[69] It is noteworthy that, given the

[66] Livy 41.15.6–10.

[67] Livy 41.27.2. Compare the action of the censors of 70, who, in expelling C. Antonius from the senate, wrote underneath a list of his crimes (Ascon. 84 C.). On the appearance of material from censorial records in Livy, see K. Gast, *Die zensorischen Bauberichte bei Livius und die röm. Bauinschriften* (Göttingen 1965).

[68] Livy 42.32.1–5.   [69] Polybius 35.2.15; Appian, *Ib.* 44.180–3.

significance of these agreements, they appear to have originated with Gracchus himself, rather than with the senate in Rome, and indeed there is no record of the senate even having ratified the treaties. Appian, the only source who gives any details of what happened, states that negotiations were concluded by an exchange of oaths between the Spaniards and Gracchus himself; and in 154 a distinction is drawn between the agreements of Gracchus, and later concessions given by the senate.[70] Once again the style of Gracchus' relations with the Spanish tribes is reminiscent of Scipio Africanus, whom the Spaniards swore to follow and to obey.[71]

Lack of interest by the senate in the detailed arrangements for the internal management of the area should not cause surprise. Up to this point there had been no indication of central military planning, nor indeed, so far as we know, were there any discussions about or instructions on the way in which the proconsular governors should proceed during the apparently haphazard series of annual campaigns between 197 and 178. This absence is the more remarkable because Livy does relate in some detail a series of debates involving the Spanish commanders. On three occasions during the 180s debates took place in the senate about the applications of proconsuls returning from Spain for the celebration of a triumph. In 185, L. Manlius Acidinus was refused a triumph and allowed only an *ovatio* on the grounds that he could not triumph unless he had brought back his army and handed over his province, completely subjugated and pacified, to his successor.[72] The following year C. Calpurnius Piso and L. Quinctius Crispinus had the forethought to send *legati* to the senate before they left their provinces, asking that honour be given to the gods for the victories they had won, and that they should be permitted to bring their armies home. This second request gave rise to a great dispute between supporters of Piso and Crispinus and the praetors already assigned as their successors. Each side was supported by one consul and a group of tribunes, and each threatened disruption of the processes of government if their demand was refused. Eventually a compromise was reached allowing Piso and Crispinus to return with some of their troops, and thus to celebrate their triumphs.[73] The third case was in 180, when Q. Fulvius Flaccus sent back a deputation with a request almost identical to that of 184, that the gods should be honoured and Fulvius be permitted to bring home his army. Once again, his successor, Ti. Gracchus, objected strongly, on the grounds that he could not be

---

[70] Appian, *Ib.* 43.179; 44.183.
[72] Livy 39.29.4–7.

[71] Polybius 10.38.5.
[73] Livy 39.38.4–12.

expected to control an unsettled and warlike province with an army of raw recruits. Once again, as had happened four years earlier, a compromise was reached, and Flaccus was allowed to return with part of his army to celebrate his triumph.[74]

These debates make clear the senate's attitude towards the triumph, and, in so far as the triumph was the highest accolade available to a military commander, its view of what was the most acceptable form of military action. It is clear that what was needed to win such a reward was to defeat enemies in battle. It is true that in 180 M. Baebius Tamphilus and P. Cornelius Cethegus celebrated a triumph for having, without bloodshed, moved the Apuani from their homes in Liguria to Samnium, but Livy remarks on this extraordinary event that they were the first ever to triumph without waging war; and it is probably in this context that a rule was introduced that at least 5,000 enemy should be slain before a triumph could be awarded.[75] The completeness of the victory was certified by the withdrawal of the army. It is important to note, as, according to Livy, Ti. Gracchus pointed out in 180, that this approval of a proconsul's success is not related to the value of that success in extending the territorial possessions of the Romans. Indeed, the repeated insistence on the removal of forces from the area in order to celebrate a triumph was likely to work against any stability in the area thereafter. The collapse of the peace which Cato claimed to have brought about once his large and experienced army was withdrawn from Citerior, demonstrated a pattern which recurred several times over the next fifteen years. The senate did not learn the lesson, perhaps because they were not aware there was a lesson to be learnt. The negative results of their regulations point in the same direction as their positive requirements. What was expected from a holder of *imperium* was military success, not the extension or stabilisation of the territory within which that success was achieved. In short, the senate's attitude towards the applicants for triumphs in Spain shows that it was aggression not imperialist expansion that they were concerned to encourage.

(b) Constitutional

The senate was also active during this period in what had always been seen as their proper sphere, the adjustment of the arrangements for the sending of men to govern the provinces. When two extra praetors were elected in 197, the intention was presumably to make possible an annual

---

74 Livy 40.35.3–36.12.
75 Livy 40.37.8–38.9. For the rule, Val. Max. 2.8.1; see J. S. Richardson [n. 2] 60–2.

command for each of the two men in Citerior and Ulterior. Appian indeed explicitly states, with characteristic chronological imprecision, that from shortly before the 144th Olympiad (i.e. 204/3 BC), the Romans sent annual praetors (*strategoi*) to those tribes they had conquered.[76] This is confirmed by the practice of sending two praetors to the Spanish provinces from 197 to 193 inclusive, even when (as in 195) a consul was also sent to Citerior.[77] In 192 this pattern was abandoned, under pressure from the need for commanders in the war with Antiochus, and the praetors of 193, C. Flaminius in Citerior and M. Fulvius Nobilior in Ulterior, had their *imperia* prorogued for another year. From then until the late 170s, with one exception in 189, none of the men in command of the Spanish provinces was there for less than two years, and in one case, that of C. Flaminius, who was in Citerior from 193 to early 189, the period was extended to four.[78] There are obvious advantages in a scheme which allowed more time than a single year for tenure of a province which was far from Italy, and where a praetor might well have difficulty in establishing himself and getting to know the terrain by the end of his first year.

The emergence of this pattern of commands may also explain the intention behind the mysterious lex Baebia *de praetoribus*. This law is mentioned directly only in a passage of Livy, describing the election of the praetors for 179. In that year, he explains, there were only four praetors, under the provisions of the lex Baebia, which prescribed that four praetors should be elected in alternate years.[79] The law cannot have been passed long before, and the most likely magistrate to have proposed it is M. Baebius Tamphilus, the consul of 181. The fact that this law seems only to have affected the praetors elected in 179 and 177, combined with the survival of a fragment of a speech of Cato, opposing the repeal of a part of a lex Baebia, has led scholars to believe that the regulation to which Livy refers was part of the lex *de ambitu*, proposed by Baebius and his colleague P. Cornelius Cethegus.[80] The difficulty about this suggestion is that the law did not become operative until the election of the praetors for 179, and for this reason the connection with Baebius

[76] Appian, *Ib.* 38.152.

[77] Livy 32.28.2 (197); 33.26.1–2 (196); 33.43.5 (195); 34.43.6–7 (194); 34.55.6 (193).

[78] Livy 34.55.6 (193); 35.20.11 (192); 36.2.9 (191); 37.2.11 (190). His successor was L. Plautius Hypsaeus, praetor in 189 (Livy 37.50.8).

[79] Livy 40.44.2.

[80] Livy 41.8.1 gives six praetors in 177, but two of the names are almost certainly interpolations (Münzer, *Röm. Adelsparteien* 198 n. 1; Broughton, *MRR* I, 399 nn. 1 and 2). On Cato's speech (frs. 136–8 (*ORF³*)), see P. Fraccaro, *Opuscula* (Pavia 1956) i, 227–32. On the *lex Cornelia Baebia de ambitu*, Livy 40.19.11; cf. Scullard, *Roman politics²* 172.

Tamphilus has been doubted.[81] One possible explanation, that the law was passed after the praetors for 180 had been elected, is unlikely, as Livy places the enactment of the lex *de ambitu* at the beginning of the year, before the consuls left for Liguria. In fact only Baebius returned before the end of the year, and then only to hold the elections.[82] If the law was passed in 181, the delay in its implementation was probably due to its connection with the government of the Spanish provinces. Mommsen suggested that the measure originated from the need for praetors in Spain to spend two years there before returning, and that under these circumstances, six praetors each year would be two too many in alternate years.[83] The section of the law about the number of praetors might well have been intended as a reasonable adjustment, given the fact that Spanish governors had been holding their provinces for biennial terms since 193.[84] In this respect, it would be like the decision to send praetors to Spain in 197, or indeed like the lex Villia *annalis* of 180, which, in requiring that no one should proceed to the consulship without first holding the praetorship, was putting into law what had been the case in practice since 197.[85] If this was the intention of the lex Baebia, the delay in its first use is readily explained. The governors in the two provinces in 181, Q. Fulvius Flaccus and P. Manlius, were already in their second year in Spain, and to have only four praetors in 180 would have entailed leaving them there for a third year. The postponement of the first four-praetor year to 179 brought the new cycle into phase with that which was operating when the law was introduced.

That the lex Baebia was connected with the Spanish praetors is confirmed by the events following its presumed partial repeal in 177 or 176. In 176 two praetors were assigned to the Spanish provinces to replace M. Titinius Curvus in Citerior and T. Fonteius Capito in Ulterior, who had been there since their praetorships in 178, though in fact neither went.[86] Thereafter, at least for so long as the Livian narrative survives, one-year tenures became the rule, even though from 171 to 169 the two provinces are combined under one magistrate.[87] Once again the number

---

[81] L. Lange, *Röm. Alterthümer* II³ (Berlin 1879) 259, followed by Klebs, *RE* II, 2728.

[82] Scullard, *Roman politics*² 173 n. l; cf. Livy 40.19.11, 35.1.

[83] Mommsen, *StR* II³, 194 n. 4.   [84] Above pp. 95–101.

[85] This answers the objection of A. Afzelius *Class. et Med.* 7 (1945) 197–8, that the lex Baebia would be unnecessary *vis-à-vis* Spain. For the lex Villia and its background, Livy 40.44.1, A. E. Austin, *Latomus* 16 (1957) 588–613 and 17 (1958) 49–64; G. Rögler, *Klio* 40 (1962) 76–213.

[86] Livy 41.15.9–10.

[87] The one exception is L. Canuleius Dives, who, in the midst of the war with Perseus, seems to have governed both provinces from late 171, until he was replaced by M. Claudius Marcellus, in 169 (above p. 104).

of praetors required each year and the length of tenure by men sent to Spain seem to be interdependent. It would seem that, about 177, it was decided that a more satisfactory solution to the numerical incongruity between praetors and provinces if governors were in Citerior and Ulterior for two years, was to reduce the period in Spain rather than reduce the number of praetors. The reasons for this conclusion are unknown, but it may be that, despite Cato's opposition to the repeal, many members of the senatorial class preferred to have a larger number of magistracies to compete for rather than a smaller, especially once the lex Villia had made explicit the need to hold the praetorship before becoming a candidate for the consulship.

Shaping the *provinciae*: the contribution of Ti. Gracchus

Attention in Rome, so far as it was directed at all to the affairs of Spain, seems to have concentrated on the status of the governors, the provision of troops and the granting of recognition for success by a triumph or *ovatio*. This by no means exhausts the developments within the two provinces during this period. The most notable change seems to have come about, as has already been shown, as a result of the fighting undertaken by Ti. Sempronius Gracchus and his colleague L. Postumius Albinus between 180 and 178, and the agreements between them and various of the Spanish tribes once the fighting was over. Appian is the only source to describe these agreements in any detail, though Livy, as mentioned above, records negotiations between Gracchus and the Celtiberians, and may well have included an account of the treaties in the lost chapters at the beginning of book 41.[88] References to Gracchus by Polybius, Plutarch and Appian, in the context of the war against Numantia, make it clear that later his work was seen as laying the basis for relations between the Romans and those tribes involved in the Numantine war.[89]

Appian's brief description is not of much help when attempting to determine the extent of Gracchus' arrangements. Having mentioned victories at Complega (an unknown site, apparently in the Ebro valley), including the capture of the town and its surroundings, Appian says that Gracchus provided a settlement for the destitute, and distributed land to them; and then provided precise treaties for all those in the area,

---

[88] Appian, *Ib.* 43.179; Livy 40.47.3–10, 49.4–7. See also the fragment of Polybius, identified by S. Szádeczky-Kardoss (*Oikumene* 1 (1976) 99–107).

[89] Polybius 35.2.15; Plut. *Ti. Gracchus* 5.2; Appian, *Ib.* 44.182–3.

according to the terms of which they would be friends of the Romans. He then gave and received oaths which, according to Appian, were frequently looked back to with longing during the wars of the later period. The content of these treaties emerges in the following chapter, which deals with the negotiations between the senate and the Celtiberian town of Segeda which led to the outbreak of war in 153. There Segeda is described as a large and powerful city, which was included in the Gracchan agreements. The immediate cause of the dispute was the construction by the Segedans of a wall around their city, following the resettlement of various smaller communities within it. It is clear from the discussion which followed that Gracchus laid down that they should not found new cities, though nothing, according to the Segedans, was said about not walling existing ones: and also that they should pay defined amounts of tax, and serve with the Roman army.[90]

Although Appian's account concentrates on Gracchus and the Celtiberians, there are other indications that his measures covered a far wider area. Two settlements of native populations by Gracchus are known in Spain. One, at Gracchurris, in the upper Ebro valley, is north of Celtiberia, in the region of the Vascones. Although their town had Latin rights by the time of Augustus, it was probably no more than a peregrine community at the time of its foundation.[91] A recently discovered inscription, found near Mengibar on the banks of the Guadalquivir (the ancient Baetis), indicates a second Gracchan settlement. This stone, which dates probably from the Julio–Claudian period, records a dedication 'Ti. Sempronio Graccho / deductori / populus Iliturgitanus'.[92] The description of the dedicators as 'populus Iliturgitanus' suggests that here too, as at Gracchurris, the settlement was of natives, with no legal status within the Roman constitution.[93] If Gracchus was active here, he was establishing communities not only outside Celtiberia, but outside his own province, since the Baetis valley was undoubtedly part of the province of Hispania Ulterior.

Other evidence also suggests that the terms which were given to the

---

[90] Appian, *Ib.* 44.180–3.

[91] Livy, *per.* 41; Festus 86 (Lindsay). Galsterer, *Untersuchungen* 13; Knapp, *Aspects* 108–9.

[92] A. Blanco and G. La Chica, *Arch. Español de Arqueologia* 33 (1960) 193–5; A. Degrassi, *Scritti Vari di Antichità* III (Venezia–Trieste 1967) 129–34. On the date of the inscription, and its genuineness, see Knapp, *Aspects* 110 n. 18, and the exhaustive, if inconclusive, investigation by R. Weigels, *Madrider Mitteilungen* 23 (1982), 152–221, and the brief note by M. José Pena Gimeno, *Estudios de la Antigüedad* I (1984) 54–5.

[93] Though doubt has been cast on the authenticity of the inscription (see last note) a Gracchan foundation for Iliturgi may also be indicated by Festus' remark that Gracchurris was originally called 'Ilurcis', a name not otherwise known, and which may result from a confusion with Iliturgi. (So A. Tovar, *ANRW* II.3 (1975) 430–1.)

Celtiberians were imposed more widely. In 171, seven years after Gracchus and Postumius Albinus returned to Rome, an embassy came to the senate from 'certain of the peoples' of Spain, complaining of the greed and arrogance of Roman magistrates, and asking that they should not allow Roman allies to be plundered more viciously than their enemies. As it was clear that a charge of extortion, of *pecuniae captae*, was involved, the senate ordered L. Canuleius, the praetor to whom the two provinces had just been assigned, to set up boards of five senatorial *recuperatores*, and to provide the embassies with patrons whom they themselves wished to represent them. The first case under this procedure seems to have involved legations from both provinces against M. Titinius, who was eventually acquitted after two adjournments. A disagreement arose between the two sets of ambassadors, and as a result the *patroni* split into two pairs, with M. Cato and P. Scipio representing Citerior, and L. Aemilius Paullus and C. Sulpicius Galus representing Ulterior. The former brought a case against P. Furius Philus, the latter against M. Matienius. In these cases, after a first adjournment, both accused went into voluntary exile, Furius at Praeneste and Matienius at Tibur, and it is by no means clear what satisfaction if any the Spaniards gained from the proceedings. Certainly it was suspected that the *patroni* had been prevented by powerful forces within the senate from making the accused suffer the punishment they deserved, and this feeling was exacerbated by the hasty departure of Canuleius for his province.[94]

These events have attracted a considerable amount of scholarly attention, for this is the first occasion on which complaints from provincials were dealt with by a judicial, or at least quasi-judicial procedure of this kind.[95] The use of *recuperatores* and the reference to *pecuniae captae* suggest that, in some sense, these 'trials' were precursors of those later conducted by the *quaestio de repetundis* under the law fully developed by C. Gracchus and his successors. This is confirmed by the decree of the senate which followed the departure of Canuleius, that no Roman magistrate should be permitted to impose his own valuation on the corn which the Spanish farmers were required to supply, thereby increasing the amount of money which he would receive from the local communities should he permit them to pay cash rather than handing over

[94] Livy 43.2.1–11.
[95] Th. Mommsen, *Röm. Strafrecht* 707–9; J. L. Strachan-Davidson, *Problems of the Roman criminal law* II (Oxford 1912) 1–4; W. W. Buckland, *JRS* 27 (1937) 40–1; E. S. Gruen, *Roman politics and the criminal courts* (Harvard 1968) 10; W. Eder, *Das vorsullanische Repetundenverfahren* (Munich 1969) 34–41; C. Venturini, *Studi sul 'crimen repetundorum' nell'età repubblicana* (Pisa 1979) 221–2; A. W. Lintott, *ZSS* 98 (1981) 168–71.

the grain. The same decree forbade a Roman magistrate to force the Spanish communities to sell off the half-tithe of one-twentieth of the crop which was apparently due to the Romans, and to impose his own officers (*praefecti*) on the communities in order to extract money from them by force. It is clear that, by 171, the senate was having to deal with abuses of a taxation system which were to cause continuing problems for local populations in the Roman provinces throughout the history of the Roman empire.[96]

Such abuses of course presuppose the existence of a system to abuse, and it is noteworthy that the three men whose activities led to the promulgation of this decree were all governors of the Spanish provinces in the period immediately following the return of Gracchus and Albinus from the peninsula. It cannot be stated with any certainty that the half-tithe on corn was instituted by Gracchus, although, as noted above, it appears that it did not exist at the time of Cato's tenure of Citerior in 195,[97] and there is no obvious occasion for the introduction of such a system between then and 180. If it was Gracchus' rationalisation of the previous *ad hoc* collection of grain which provided the opportunity for the extortion of which the Spanish ambassadors complained in 171, then it is clear that his arrangements applied in both Citerior and Ulterior.

There is no reason to doubt that Gracchus organised more effectively the financial contributions from the native communities in Spain, for this is attested by Appian, who mentions the 'taxes determined by Gracchus'.[98] Whether or not these included the half-tithe on corn, it is probable that they did lay down the rules for the payment of the fixed tax known as *stipendium*. In the first century BC Cicero mentions the Spaniards together with the Carthaginians as paying a 'vectigal certum, quod stipendarium dicitur', a fixed payment, as opposed to the other forms of *vectigalia*, whether assigned by the censors at Rome for collection by *publicani*, or allotted within the province, as were the Sicilian tithes.[99] Florus, writing in the second century AD, asserted that Spain was made a 'stipendiary province' by Scipio Africanus, but, as often with Florus, the remark appears to be a rhetorical flourish rather than a piece of

---

[96] Livy 43.2.12; Ps.-Ascon, 203 (Stangl) (a reference to Cato's speech against P. Furius 'propter iniquissimam frumenti aestimationem'). For later abuses Cic. *II Verr.* 77.178; Tac. *Agricola* 19; Ammianus 28.1.18; R. T. Pritchard, *Historia* 20 (1971) 224–8. Nicola Mackie believes that the *vicensuma* was a quota which the Spaniards had to sell to the Romans (*JRS* 71 (1981) 187); but *vicensuma* elsewhere always means a 5% *tax* (cf. *OLD s.v.* vicensumus; and Cic. *II Verr.* 2.26.63 for 'decumas vendere' = 'sell off corn collected as tithes').

[97] Above p. 93.

[98] Appian, *Ib.* 44.182: φόρους...τοὺς ὁρισθέντας ἐπὶ Γράκχου.

[99] Cic. *II Verr.* 3.6.12.

history.[100] Not only is there no sign of the collection of a 'vectigal certum' before 180, but the *stipendium* which was levied during and after the Hannibalic war was clearly a variable *ad hoc* amount to cover the pay of the troops stationed in Spain.[101] The final instance of the word used in this sense of army pay collected locally, and apparently on the initiative of the governor, occurs in Livy's report of the application in 180 by Q. Fulvius Flaccus for permission to celebrate a triumph. He stated that not only had he been entirely successful in his province but that there had that year been no need for the *stipendium* which was usually sent out, nor for corn to be brought in for the army.[102] The implication is that still in 180 *stipendium* was not a fixed tax imposed on the Spaniards, but that it was pay for the army which normally would be expected to be brought from Rome to Spain. No doubt in 180 the Celtiberians, over whom Flaccus celebrated his triumph, supplied the necessary funds. Appian's reference to the 'taxes determined by Gracchus', which formed part of the 'precise treaties' which were intended to regulate relations between Rome and at least some of the Spanish communities, is the first appearance in the Spanish context of any form of payment corresponding to the *stipendium* which Cicero describes, a 'vectigal certum'. It is not difficult to see why this might have been introduced at this point. If the previous form of *stipendium* had been used to pay the army, Gracchus' victories, which might be expected to lead to a reduction in the size of the forces in Spain (and, it seems, actually did so), provided an appropriate moment for the reconsideration of the somewhat erratic methods by which such funds had been extracted. The introduction of a more systematic pattern of payments, on a fixed fiscal basis, would make good sense in 179, and would also have complemented the reorganisation of the corn-levy which may well have been part of Gracchus' arrangements.

If these changes in the taxation practice of the Roman commanders in Spain are correctly attributed to Gracchus, this confirms the opinion, already noted in the sources, that the treaties which he concluded formed a watershed in the development of the Roman presence in Spain. Up to this point, the main concern of the commanders in Spain had been with fighting, and such information as has survived on the collection of grain and of cash is connected explicitly with their use of the former to feed

---

[100] Florus 1.33.7: 'quasi novam integramque provinciam ultor patris et patrui Scipio ille mox Africanus invasit, isque statim capta Carthagine et aliis urbibus, non contentus Poenos expulisse, stipendariam nobis provinciam fecit.'

[101] See above pp. 57–8, 72–3; cf. J. S. Richardson, *JRS* 66 (1976) 147–9.

[102] Livy 40.35.4.

and the latter to pay their troops. No doubt this was not the only use to which such supplies were put. In the last years of the third century, grain was sent from Spain to Africa and to Rome. As for money coming out of the peninsula, Livy provides a series of figures for the sums brought back to Rome by returning commanders, from Scipio in 206 down to M. Claudius Marcellus in 168.[103] The amounts cited are very considerable indeed, but they represent not income from taxation but accumulated booty.[104] This is hardly surprising given the nature of the activities in which these pro-magistrates had been involved. It is not easy to determine how much surplus money was left from the exactions on Rome's allies, and from the *vectigalia* levied on iron and silver mines such as those instituted by Cato.[105] Only one figure survives which seems to relate to such income. In 185 L. Manlius Acidinus, returning from Citerior, requested from the senate permission to celebrate a triumph. As part of his argument, he reported that he himself had brought back 52 golden crowns and 132 pounds of gold, and 16,300 pounds of silver; moreover his quaestor, Q. Fabius, had brought back 80 pounds of gold and 10,000 of silver, which Acidinus was about to deposit in the *aerarium*.[106] If the cash which Acidinus brought himself was booty, as all such sums, reported in the context of applications for triumphs, seem to be, then the amounts which were in the hands of his quaestor were probably the excess of his other receipts over the expenditure he had made during his tenure of the *provincia*. The figure is, of course, a final total, and gives no indication of how much came into the quaestor's hands from different sources. It is likely that the amount is unusually high. Fulvius Flaccus, five years later, seems to have been pleased to report that money had not had to be sent out from Rome to pay his soldiers, which would suggest that he had done well to break even,[107] although comparison with Acidinus is difficult, as we do not know whether the latter had received financial support from the *aerarium* for the wages of his army. None the less, the fact that he mentioned the silver and gold which his quaestor had brought back suggests that a profit of this size was out of the ordinary.

Gracchus' innovation seems to have been the regularisation of the demands for contributions from those tribes and communities which were 'friends' of the Romans. His policy of settlement also mentioned by

---

[103] Conveniently tabulated by van Nostrand, *ESAR* III, 129 (where, however, note that Cato returned with 540 'Oscan' denarii, not 5040).

[104] P. A. Brunt in *The crisis of the Roman republic* (ed. R. Seager) (Cambridge 1962) 105; E. Badian, *Publicans and sinners* (Oxford 1972) 32; Richardson [n. 101] 140–1.

[105] Livy 34.21.7.

[106] Livy 39.29.6–7.   [107] Livy 40.43.6.

Appian[108] was probably also an extension of methods employed by some at least of his predecessors. A bronze tablet, found near Alcala de los Gazules, about 40 kilometres east of Cadiz, records an edict of L. Aemilius Paullus, dated 19 January, probably in the year 189.[109] This edict ordered that those slaves of the inhabitants of Hasta who lived in the 'tower of Lascuta' should be free, and should hold and possess the land which at that moment they possessed, for so long as the people and senate of Rome agreed. Although it is impossible to be certain about the status of the 'servei' to whom freedom and land are granted by this document, it is probable that Paullus was creating a separate settlement for a dependent part of the population of Hasta, who were perhaps previously serfs of some kind.[110] The action of Aemilius Paullus seems to be similar to that of Gracchus a decade later. The same practice of settlement of native populations recurred in the aftermath of the wars in Spain in the 150s and 130s.[111]

The final clause of Paullus' edict, making the settlement dependent on the passive assent of the people and senate, implies that the arrangement was made on his own initiative.[112] This seems to have been the case also with Gracchus' agreements, which were ratified by an exchange of oaths between himself and the Spaniards;[113] there is no sign here of prior approval by the senate, though in both cases it would be open to the authorities in Rome to revoke such arrangements at will. Similarly the little known about Gracchus' settlements suggests that, like that of Paullus at Hasta, they were set up on the initiative of the commander. The name Gracchurris clearly indicates that this was Gracchus' foundation, while the apparent lack of any distinctive status given either to Gracchurris or Iliturgi at the time is at least a negative argument for the non-involvement of the senate and people of Rome in the process.[114]

---

[108] Appian, *Ib.* 43.179.

[109] *CIL* II, 5041; I², 614 (= *ILLRP* 514). The inscription describes Paullus as 'inpeirator', not praetor, and is presumably therefore dated later than 28 February 190, the last day of his holding of the praetorship. Paullus remained in his province until well into 189, because of the delay in sending his successor (above p. 98). A. Deman, *Latomus* 35 (1976) 805–7, believes the inscription may be dated as late as 19 January 188. 'Inpeirator' probably here means 'holder of imperium' (cf. above p. 41) and D. Kienast, *ZSS* 78 (1961) 408; *contra* Mommsen, *Hermes* 3 (1869) 261–7). [110] So Knapp, *Aspects* 108 n. 11.

[111] Galba's specious offer in 150 (Appian *Ib.* 59.249ff); the unsuccessful offer of Vetilius, probably in 146 (*ibid.* 61.255–6); the settlement of Lusitanians after Viriathus' death (*ibid.* 75.325; Livy, *per.* 55). [112] So Degrassi, *ILLRP* no. 514 n. 3.

[113] Appian, *Ib.* 43.179. Cf. also the same phrase in *tab. Alcantarenis*, lines 11–12 (below Appendix v).

[114] Galsterer, *Untersuchungen* 13; Knapp, *Aspects* 108–11.

Though it is difficult to be certain, in view of the lack of evidence, it is in any case improbable that the senate would have given its sanction to a town whose name so explicitly enhanced the prestige of its founder.

The evidence that survives from the only other two Roman settlements which belong to this period confirms the suggestion that there was a distinction between those founded by the local commander and those in which the senate had a hand. Corduba is said by Strabo to have been the first Roman colony in this region (i.e. the Baetis valley) and to have been the foundation of Marcellus.[115] It is not certain whether this took place in 169/8, when Marcellus governed both provinces, or in 152 when, as consul in the province of Citerior, he wintered there.[116] In either case it is certain that Corduba did not become a *colonia civium Romanorum* then, but probably in the time of Caesar or Augustus.[117] As in the case of Italica, it seems that Corduba at its foundation was probably a settlement without any defined status, and comprised both Romans and natives.[118] The other settlement, at Carteia, near Algeciras, resulted from a direct appeal to the senate. In 171 an embassy arrived in Rome, representing over 4,000 men, the offspring of Roman soldiers and Spanish women who had no right of *conubium*, who asked for a town in which to live. The senate decreed that they should give their names to L. Canuleius, the praetor to whom the Spanish provinces had been alloted, and also the names of those whom they had manumitted and that a colony was to be founded at Carteia, into which the native inhabitants of Carteia could be enrolled. This was to be a Latin colony, and to be called 'libertinorum', 'of the freedmen'.[119] Although these men clearly had a moral claim on the Roman state for assistance, they were technically foreigners (*peregrini*), with the same status as Paullus' freed serfs at Hasta in 189 or Gracchus' poor in 178, since by the *ius gentium* the offspring of a male Roman and a female peregrine, where there was no *conubium*, were themselves *peregrini*.[120] In this case, however, because of the appeal to the senate,

---

[115] Strabo 3.2.1 (p. 141).

[116] Livy 43.15.3, 45.4.1 (169/8); Polybius 35.2.2 (152).

[117] M. Griffin, *JRS* 62 (1972) 17–19; Galsterer, *Untersuchungen* 9–10; Knapp, *Aspects* 120–4. Caesar, *BC* 2.19.3 and *B. Alex.* 58.4 call the Roman population there a *conventus* in the early 40s BC, which implies that it was not then a citizen colony (Wilson, *Emigration* 16–17).

[118] So Strabo, *loc. cit.* ᾠκησάν τε ἐξ ἀρχῆς Ῥωμαίων τε καὶ τῶν ἐπιχωρίων ἄνδρες ἐπίλεκτοι.

[119] Livy 43.3.1–4. I read 'manumisissent' with the *codex Vindobonensis*, rather than Grynaeus' conjecture 'manumisisset', which would imply that Canuleius had performed a manumission of a second group of petitioners before the *professio* of the names. For an explanation of the passage, on the basis of Grynaeus' conjecture, see M. Humbert, *MEFRA* 88 (1976) 221–42.

[120] Gaius 1.78; Ulpian, *tit.* 5.8.

both the settlement and its inhabitants acquired a status within the Roman system.[121]

Gracchus' measures, then, despite their importance in the history of the development of the two Spanish provinces, seem to originate from his own initiative, and without any active part being played by the senate. Yet there are other signs, even despite the poverty of our sources, that in the period after the Gracchan treaties the exploitation of the area became more systematic and more efficient. Polybius describing the silver-mining area around Cartagena, probably as he had seen it himself on his journeys in Spain in the middle of the second century, writes of an area of some 100 square miles, with 40,000 men involved in the work of the mines, and producing 2,500 drachmae per day for the Roman people.[122] If Polybius' figures are accurate, and if the mines were worked every day, this account implies that each year over 10,800 pounds of silver were drawn by the Roman state from the Cartagena mines.[123] This is a considerable sum. Only 16,300 pounds of silver had been brought back in 185 by Q. Fabius, the quaestor of L. Manlius Acidinus, as surplus revenue from the whole of Hispania Citerior over two years, and, as argued above, that return was probably large.[124] We do not know, of course, what other sources were available to Acidinus, nor what expenditure had to be met by his quaestor during his tenure of the *provincia*, but the figures probably indicate a growth in the exploitation of silver in this region. Diodorus' description of a horde of Italians descending upon the silver mines of Spain following the Roman 'conquest', and using large numbers of slaves for the purpose, suggests a similar picture.[125]

Polybius' account also implies that the collection of the state's share of the workings from the mines was done on a daily basis. This at least is a reasonable assumption from the fact that his own computation of revenue to the Roman people is *per diem*. Such systems are known in other places and at other periods where a conquering power exploits precious mineral resources at a great distance from home.[126] This would require,

---

[121] A. N. Sherwin-White, *The Roman citizenship*[2] (Oxford 1973) 101; Galsterer, *Untersuchungen* 7–9; Knapp, *Aspects* 116–20. The doubts expressed by Ch. Saumagne, *Rev. Hist.* 40 (1962) 135–52 seem unnecessary. Probably the freedmen were explicitly included in the scheme because otherwise their status, as men freed by *peregrini*, would itself be anomalous.

[122] Polybius 34.9.8 (= Strabo 3.2.10 (pp. 147–8)). See J. S. Richardson [n. 101] 139–52; Walbank, *Commentary* III, 605–7. On Polybius' journeys, and their date, Polybius 3.59.7, 10.11.4; Walbank, *Commentary* I, 4–5; II, 212.

[123] This calculation also assumes that Polybius is equating the drachma with the denarius, on which Walbank, *Commentary* I, 176; Crawford, *RRC* II, 662–4. On the relationship of the silver denarius to the Roman pound, *ibid.* 594–5.   [124] Livy 39.29.6–7.   [125] Diodorus 5.36.

[126] For instance the Spaniards in Mexico and Peru in the sixteenth century (Richardson [n. 101] 144–7, 151–2).

of course, the establishment of a group of officials, under the direction of the quaestor, to supervise the weighing and collection of the silver. Though there is no need to assume, as some have done, the involvement of the great *societates publicanorum*, based in Rome, in this process,[127] there is no doubt that the management of such revenues implies a systematic fiscal exploitation of the Cartagena silver deposits.

Although Polybius' evidence relates only to the silver mines, and indeed to only one group of mines in the south of Citerior, there is one other indication that fiscal arrangements were more organised in the middle of the second century than they had been before Gracchus' time. By the end of the century, it is clear that several communities in Citerior were issuing silver coins, with inscriptions in the Iberian alphabet, on the same weight-standard as the Roman denarius.[128] It is highly likely that these coins were produced for the purpose of paying sums to the Romans, as some form of tax or tribute.[129] It is difficult to establish a date for the introduction of this coinage, and various suggestions have been made, most recently *c*. 202, 197 or *c*. 175.[130] The earliest Iberian denarii occur in hoards which may be dated, from the presence of Roman coins, to the last decade of the second century, though they show signs of considerable wear.[131] It is notable, however, that Iberian bronze coins, which were produced both in Citerior and Ulterior, are found in earlier contexts, as, for instance, in hoards and chance finds from the Roman camps at Numantia, dated to 153 and 134–133 BC, and the number and condition of these coins makes it certain that they had been introduced some considerable time before 153.[132] The sparse and sporadic nature of the

127 So P. A. Brunt, *Second International Conference of Economic History* (Aix-en-Provence 1962) I, 138–41 (= *The crisis of the Roman republic* ed. Seager (Cambridge 1962) 104–7); F. Badian [n. 104] 31–44. G. Calboli, *M. Porci Catonis oratio pro Rhodensibus* (Bologna 1978) 156–65, and M. R. Cimma, *Ricerche sulle società di publicani* (Milan 1981) find difficulty in envisaging any alternative to *societates publicanorum*.

128 G. F. Hill, *Notes on the ancient coinage of Hispania Citerior* (New York 1931); A. M. de Guadan y Lascaris, *Numismatica iberica e ibero-romana* (Madrid 1969); *id.*, *La moneda iberica* (Madrid 1980).

129 M. H. Crawford, *NC* 9 (1969) 79–93. R. C. Knapp, *NC* 17 (1977) 1–18, argues that there may be other purposes for the Iberian denarii; but it is probable that the minting of silver by the Iberian communities was for the purposes of *community* expenditure, of which the most obvious is Roman taxation. Compare the arguments of Crawford, *JRS* 60 (970) 40–8, for the reasons for the issue of Roman coinage.

130 Knapp [n. 129] 1–12; Crawford [n. 129] 79–83; G. K. Jenkins, *Am. Num. Soc. Museum Notes* 8 (1958) 57–8. R. Martin Valls, *Boletin de seminario de estudios de arte y arqueologia* (Valladolid) 32 (1966) 208–9) argued for a date following the sack of Numantia, but his argument depends on a date of 187 for the introduction of the denarius.

131 M. H. Crawford, *Coinage and money under the Roman republic* (London 1985) 90–1.

132 For a catalogue, and an attempted re-dating of the camps from numismatic evidence, see H. J. Hildebrandt, *MM* 20 (1979) 238–71. On the Iberian bronze coins, see esp. pp. 257ff. J. C. M. Richard and L. Villaronga, *Mél. de la Casa de Velasquez* 9 (1973) 105–31, survey bronze

evidence from the finds of coins precludes any firm conclusions, but the indications are that bronze coins were produced in both Citerior and Ulterior late in the third or early in the second century, while the silver coinage seems to begin in the middle of the second century, and then only in Citerior. Such a pattern would have an obvious explanation. As has been argued above, the *stipendium* collected by Roman commanders in Spain from 218 down to 180 was payment for the Roman troops serving there.[133] Down to the middle of the second century, Roman soldiers were paid in bronze, but thereafter in silver, and it is probable that the suspension of the production of bronze *asses* in 145 was connected with this change.[134] If the monetary payments by the Spanish communities had been fixed by Gracchus in 178, it would not be surprising if they began to pay in silver either then, or (perhaps more probably) after the change to silver payments to the Roman soldiers.[135] This is not to deny that other silver coins were circulating in Spain in the early second century. Roman denarii, *monnaies-à-la-croix*, drachmae from Emporion and Iberian imitations of such drachmae all occur in Spanish hoards before the end of the third century, as well as coins of Massilia and Carthage.[136] Moreover Livy's reports of booty brought back from Spain in the late third and early second century include coined silver (*argentum signatum*), often designated as Roman (*bigati*) or *argentum oscense*, a term whose meaning has been disputed since the eighteenth century, but which probably refers to some form of Iberian coinage.[137]

The fiscal arrangements, therefore, of which evidence has survived, and which were current in those areas of Spain controlled by the Romans in the middle of the second century, would seem to be as follows: (1) a sum was paid to the Roman state, probably in the person of the quaestor, by those who exploited the metal mines, which, at least in the case of the silver mines at Cartagena, seems to have been calculated on a daily basis,

issued in Spain before Augustus, and conclude that the earliest date to the late third century. The basis for this conclusion, however is the unproven correspondence between variations in the weight of the *as* in Roman and Iberian series. As Richard and Villaronga themselves admit the existence of both a heavy and a light series in Spain in the second century, which does not occur at this date in the Roman issues, this argument is not compelling. (cf. Knapp, *Aspects* 79–84; Crawford [n. 131] 90–3).

133 Above p. 116.   134 Crawford, *RRC* II, 621–5.
135 See now Crawford [n. 131] Ch. 6.

136 M. H. Crawford, *Roman coin hoards* (London 1969) nos. 33, 75, 91, 94, 104, 107, and 109. Richard and Villaronga [n. 132] 90–105; on the Punic coins, E. S. G. Robinson, in *Essays in Roman coinage presented to Harold Mattingly* (Oxford 1956) 34–53.

137 Livy 28.38.5; 33.27.2; 34.10.4–7; 34.46.2; 36.21.11; 40.43.6. cf. E. Florez, *Medallas de las colonias, municipios y pueblos antiguos de España* II (Madrid 1758) 519–23; J. M. Eckhel, *Doctrina Nummorum* I (Vienna 1792) 4ff; J. Amoros, *Numario Hispanico* 6 (1957) 51–71; Crawford [n. 129] 83; Knapp [n. 129] 4–6.

and thus presumably related to production (there is in fact no evidence for mines other than those in Citerior, but it is reasonable to assume that a similar system was employed in Ulterior also); (2) after the governor-ships of Gracchus and Albinus the collection of corn was regularised in at least some areas of both provinces into a half-tithe system of one-twentieth of the crop; (3) in Citerior at least, the *stipendium*, which had previously provided a contribution towards the pay of Roman soldiers stationed in the *provincia*, became a fixed sum. Although the account Appian gives of Gracchus' arrangements has been taken to apply only to the Celtiberians, against whom he had been fighting, it is likely that their effect was more widespread. Not only does Appian say that these 'precise' treaties were made with all, as a basis for their friendship with the Romans, but the silver coins, which were probably used in payment of the tribute demanded by these treaties, were minted in the coastal regions, the Ebro valley and the foothills of the Pyrenees as well as in Celtiberia.[138] The collection of tribute in Ulterior remains even more obscure, though the bronze coinage of the region may also have originated in pay for Roman soldiers. It seems certain that the inhabitants must at some point have begun to pay in silver, but there is no way of dating this change. Presumably, they did so using either Roman coins or those minted in Citerior.[139]

Roman policy in Spain: the senate and the praetors

The 40 years which separated the departure of Cato from Spain in 194 from the disputes in 154 which led to the Numantine war saw not only an immense amount of warfare, but also the development of various civil institutions which were to become part of the Roman understanding of the provinces. The war was virtually continuous down to 178, and there can be no doubt that the military role of the proconsuls was by far the most important part of their activity during these years, and indeed down to the end of the period. It is not surprising therefore that their 'civilian' arrangements also grew out of this military function. Taxation of the local communities seems to have begun as a levy of grain and coin for the feeding and payment of troops. Fiscal exploitation of the mines had not

[138] See the summary in Richard and Villaronga [n. 132] 94–7; again, their proposed chronology depends on the uncertain basis of comparative metrology of Iberian and Roman issues. For the metrological basis of the arguments, see de Guadan [n. 128] 17–28, and especially 21–24.

[139] For the sort of economic pattern which this may have involved, see M. H. Crawford, *Econ. Hist. Rev.* 30 (1977) 42–52, on the relations between Rome and the East.

begun before Cato's tenure of Citerior in 195–194, and, particularly in the case of the silver mines, no doubt grew with the increase in the number of private individuals, who came from Italy to make their fortunes in Spain.[140] The establishing of settlements also seems to have been a direct result of military responsibilities, whether these were, like Italica and Carteia, a consequence of the presence of Roman and Italian soldiers in the area, or, as with Gracchurris and Aemilius Paullus' action near Hasta, native resettlements, following a successful campaign. There were no doubt other demands on a proconsul, as the representative of the major power and, as the commander of the most formidable military force in the area, uniquely capable of enforcing his decisions. The most obvious, though there is little direct evidence, is the request for arbitration and judicial action, of which Aemilius Paullus' decree in 189 is an example.

In the making of these arrangements, little is heard of the activity of the senate, either in formulating policy or in making decisions about particular cases, or even in approving decisions made by the proconsuls. Three examples are recorded. The appeal which led to the foundation of Carteia, and the complaints against the three proconsuls over seizure of money and abuse of the corn levy, both in 171, have already been mentioned. The third involves an alteration to the tribute payments and troop levies laid down by Gracchus in 179. In the course of negotiations with the senate in 154, the Celtiberian tribes of the Belli and the Titthi argued that their obligations had been subsequently removed by the Romans, and it is clear from Appian's comment that this had been granted by the senate.[141] It is notable that in each of these cases the action of the senate followed on an application to them by provincials themselves. (This is explicitly stated in the two instances in 171, and may be presumed in the matter of the Belli and Titthi.) When the senate was approached in this manner, they showed no reluctance to act, but there is no indication that they took any initiative otherwise in the internal affairs of the two *provinciae*. Indeed the attitude taken by both Roman commanders and the Spaniards themselves to the conclusion of treaties and other 'international' relations, and the status of the settlements made by Scipio Africanus, Aemilius Paullus and Ti. Gracchus all indicate that the power of decision was in the hands of the commanders in Spain, and that the senate took no action even *ex post facto*.

Such independence of action is not surprising considering the power invested in a proconsul by his holding of *imperium*, the need for rapid

[140] Diodorus 5.36.   [141] Appian, *Ib.* 44.183.

decision within an area of continuous if sporadic warfare, and the virtual isolation of Spain from Italy caused by distance and poor communications. The senate was bound to confine its scrutiny of a proconsul's activity to the bestowing of approval and disapproval on his return to Rome. Here too the focus of attention appears to be on military activity, and debate centres on the giving or refusing of a triumph, for which the criteria are not the extent to which an area has been consolidated, or brought nearer to what in later times might have been called a 'forma provinciae'.[142] At least in Spain in this crucial period of the development of the Roman presence there, the senate only act to reprimand and correct a proconsul when direct complaints from the provincials draw their attention to his misdeeds, or when he falls short of their own conception of the proper activity of a military commander by failing to win battles. The emergence of the practices and institutions which were to shape these areas assigned to Roman commanders for the exercise of their *imperium*, the two *provinciae* of Hispania Citerior and Ulterior, into provinces of the Roman empire, resulted from the actions of those commanders, not from the policy of the senate. If it is appropriate to speak of an 'imperial policy' towards Spain at all in this period, such policy was in the hands of the praetors *pro consule* who commanded the forces within the two *provinciae*.

[142] Above, pp. 5–7.

CHAPTER 6

The consular *provinciae*: the wars in Spain 155–133

The next series of events in Spain which have left any substantial mark on the literary sources is the concatenation of wars waged against the Lusitanians and the Celtiberians from the mid-150s to the late 130s. For these events our only continuous account is that given by Appian in his *Ibērikē*, for that of Livy, whose comments on Roman activity in Spain provide most of the evidence for the late third and early second centuries, survives for this period only in the two epitomes, one known from manuscripts and one from fragments discovered among the papyri from Oxyrhyncus. Although there is considerable doubt about Appian's own sources and the historical value of his work, his narrative is coherent, and free from the excesses which from time to time mar the annalistic account given by Livy, most obviously when recording the campaigns of the Scipio brothers during the first half of the Hannibalic war.[1] Appian arranges his material province by province rather than year by year, but a reasonably secure chronology can be extracted from it.[2]

The first Spanish governors whom Appian mentions are the two praetors, Manilius and Calpurnius Piso, who were in Ulterior, probably in 155 and 154 respectively. These men were faced with a revolt by the so-called 'autonomous' Lusitanians, which was eventually put down by the ruthless and discreditable policies of Ser. Sulpicius Galba, praetor in 151, who held Ulterior in 151 and 150. The first bout of fighting in Hispania Citerior began in 153 when, after a disagreement between the senate and the town of Segeda, the consul Q. Fulvius Nobilior unsuccessfully attacked the Segedans and their allies. This conflict was concluded by the consul of the following year, M. Claudius Marcellus, early in 151, though one further consul, L. Licinius Lucullus (*cos.* 151) was involved in fighting against the neighbouring tribe of the Vaccaei, and in 150 combined with Galba in Ulterior against the Lusitanians.[3]

[1] On Appian as a source for this period, see below Appendix IV.
[2] On Appian's division, see Simon, *Roms Kriege* 13 n. 6 and 79 n. 6.
[3] Events in Citerior, 153–150: Appian, *Ib.* 44.180–55.233; in Ulterior: 56.234–75.322; in Citerior 143–133: 76.323–99.428. On the chronology, see below, Appendix II.

The end of Lucullus' campaign seems to mark a breaking off of hostilities. Appian at least takes this moment as the end of the first section of his account of the events in Citerior, and proceeds to deal with Ulterior, down to the death of the Lusitanian leader Viriathus in 139. His new starting-point is the campaign of Q. Metellus Macedonicus in 143–142. The recurrence of hostilities in the north is ascribed to the encouragement given to the Celtiberians by Viriathus. This remarkable man had emerged from the treacherous slaughter of the Lusitanians in 150, and is first recorded as leading them when he defeated the praetorian governor of Ulterior, Vetilius, in 145. After similar treatment had been meted out to two further praetors, Q. Fabius Maximus Aemilianus (*cos.* 145), succeeded in re-establishing the Roman position with a defeat of the Lusitanians. By 141 the situation had again deteriorated, and Fabius' adoptive brother, Q. Fabius Maximus Servilianus (*cos.* 142), was assigned to the *provincia*, to be succeeded in turn by his own brother, Q. Servilius Caepio (*cos.* 140), after his reverses had led him to conclude a peace. Caepio eventually persuaded the senate to reject this treaty, and though he too failed to defeat Viriathus, he did manage to arrange his assassination by three treacherous Lusitanians. With their leader dead the remaining rebels seem to have been quite willing to accept a grant of land from Caepio or his successor, D. Iunius Brutus (*cos.* 138), who then headed north-westwards to find new tribes to conquer.

Meanwhile in Citerior, the Celtiberians, spurred on by the example and the assistance of Viriathus, centred their resistance on the town of Numantia in the upper reaches of the Durius valley, which thwarted the attempts of a series of Roman consuls from Q. Macedonicus onwards to subdue it, until it was eventually sacked by Scipio Aemilianus in 133. Pompeius, Macedonicus' successor and consul in 141, failed to take the town despite repeated efforts and, hard-pressed by the severe conditions of a winter on the *meseta*, arranged a treaty, which was subsequently rejected by the senate. M. Popilius Laenas (*cos.* 139), who followed him, achieved little, while his successor, C. Hostilius Mancinus, was completely routed and compelled to surrender, with all his army, to the Numantines. His colleague as consul in 137, M. Aemilius Lepidus Porcina, was recalled in disgrace after an unauthorised attack on the neighbouring Vaccaei. Two more consuls, L. Furius Philus (136) and Q. Calpurnius Piso (135), held the *provincia* without success before Scipio, elected (despite a law forbidding iteration) to a second consulship in 134, brought the war to a conclusion in the following year.[4]

---

[4] For a detailed analysis of the historical narrative of this period, see Simon, *Roms Kriege*.

Even this brief outline of the events in Spain between 155 and 133 reveals one clear change in senatorial policy from what has been seen in the earlier part of the century. In the period from the first sending of praetors to the two provinces in 197 down to 166, where the extant portion of Livy's history ends, the men who commanded the Roman forces in the peninsula were, with only one exception, praetorian; and there is no reason to suppose that there was any alteration in this pattern before the late 150s.[5] By contrast the period which followed may fairly be characterised as consular. This is not to say that all the Spanish governors were consuls or ex-consuls. In Ulterior, only 4 of the 12[6] whose names have survived are consular; the other 8 are all praetors, and another 3 praetorians should probably be added to cover the years 149–147, for which no governors' names have survived. In Citerior, where the consuls were more continuously involved in the warfare, 11 of the 13 names found in the sources are those of consuls; to the two known praetors, perhaps 6 more should be added for the years 155–154 and 149–146.[7] In both provinces there is a marked increase in the use of consuls as governors.

This change of status among the commanders in Spain is a clear indication of a change of policy on the part of the senate, since it involved an alteration in the practice of the allocation of *provinciae* to magistrates, which had always been the point at which the senate had been most closely involved with the development of the Roman presence there. The sending of Q. Fulvius Nobilior to Citerior in 153 was an alteration to a pattern which had been established more than 50 years before, and had been employed with only minor and temporary variations ever since.[8] Moreover the sending of consuls instead of praetors to Spain did not only affect what was happening in the far west, but also caused changes at Rome, which illustrate the sheer administrative inconvenience involved in dispatching the chief magistrate so great a distance to his *provincia*.

Before 153, the consuls entered office at Rome on the Ides of March.[9] A remark in Cassiodorus records that in 153 this date was altered to the Kalends of January, and this is confirmed by a noted in the fragmentary

---

[5] The exception was Cato in Citerior in 195–194.

[6] Perhaps thirteen, if Quintus/Quinctius of 143–2 is two people; see Simon, *Roms Kriege* 81–3, and below, Appendix II pp. 189–91.

[7] See the *fasti* in Appendix II.

[8] Cato was in Citerior as consul in 195; from 171 to 168, both *provinciae* were under a single praetorian commander (Livy 42.28.5–6; 43.15.3).

[9] Livy 31.5.2; Th. Mommsen, *Die römische Chronologie bis auf Caesar*[2] (Berlin 1852) 102 and n. 186; *id.*, *StR* I[3], 599. The calendar year evidently began already on *Kal. Jan.* as Fulvius Nobilior (*cos.* 189) began each year of his *Annales* then (Varro, *LL* 6.33ff; A. K. Michels, *The calendar of the Roman republic* (Princeton 1967) 97ff).

fasti from Praeneste, and from a passage in the Livian epitome.[10] There is a connection, explicitly made by both Cassiodorus and the Livian epitomator, between this change in the dates of entry to office (and thus also of the election of the consuls) and the troubles in Spain,[11] and some scholars have argued that it was made so that the consuls could reach their *provinciae* early in the campaigning season, and thus be able to combine a full year in the field with the duties they had to perform at Rome before leaving.[12] A more detailed examination of the events of the following years suggests that the early entry-date was not merely desirable if the consuls were to fight in Spain, but was absolutely essential.

Fulvius' arrival in Citerior can be dated with unusual precision. First it is clear that Mummius, the praetor of 153 to whom Ulterior was assigned, arrived in the southern province earlier in the year. Appian describes how Mummius was defeated by the Lusitanians under their new leader Kaisaros in the early stages of his tenure of the *provincia*, and how they then carried their trophies, stripped from the Roman dead, round Celtiberia in mockery. Diodorus records that the defeat of 'Memmios' shortly after his arrival was the major factor in the decision of the Celtiberian Arevaci to fight against Rome. Appian says that the Segedans only approached the Arevaci for aid when they learnt that Fulvius was advancing against them, which must have been at the latest shortly after his arrival in Spain.[13] Secondly Appian says that once the appeal to the Arevaci had been accepted, the allies chose the Segedan Karos as their commander, and that on the third day after his election, he led them to victory against Nobilior, losing his own life in the aftermath of the battle; and that this occurred at the time when the Romans were keeping the festival of Hephaistos.[14] The date referred to is that of the Vulcanalia, which was celebrated on *viii Kal. Sept.*,[15] so that Nobilior's arrival should be placed about the beginning of August, despite the early date of his entry into the consulship.

[10] Cassiodorus (in *Mon. Germ. Hist.* IX.2 (Berlin 1894) 130) under the Varronian year 601. The *Fasti Praenestini* (*CIL* I², p. 231) reads 'ann]us no[[vus incipit] quia eo die mag. ineunt, quod coepit [[p. R.] c.a. DCI'. Livy, *per.* 47, places this under the year *a.u.c.* 598, which is equivalent to 601 on the Varronian reckoning (cf. G. Perl, *Kritische Untersuchungen zu Diodors römische Jahrzählung* (Berlin 1957) 20; E. J. Bickerman, *The chronology of the ancient world* (London 1968) 77).

[11] Cassiodorus [n. 10]: 'hi primi consules Kal. Ianuariis magistratum inierunt propter subitum Keltiberiae bellum.' Livy, *per.* 47: 'mutandi comitia causa fuit, quod Hispani rebellarunt.'

[12] Mommsen [n. 9] 102ff; Simon, *Roms Kriege* 17 and 19 n. 19, who suggests the situation in Lusitania may also have been a factor.

[13] Appian, *Ib.* 45.184, 56.237; Diodorus 31.42.

[14] Appian, *Ib.* 45. 185–7.

[15] Cf. *ILLRP* I, p. 35; *CIL* I², p. 215; M. Guarducci, *Bulletino della Commissione archeologica communale di Roma* 64 (1936) 32–4; H. H. Scullard, *Festivals and ceremonies of the Roman republic* (London 1981) 178–9.

The relative precision with which the date of Fulvius' arrival can be fixed is unusual, but it seems that others also had similar difficulty in reaching Spain before the season was well advanced. His successor, M. Claudius Marcellus (*cos.* 152), having recaptured the town of Ikilis which had been lost at the end of Nobilior's term of office, entered into negotiations which led to the Arevaci, Belli and Titthi sending ambassadors to the senate in Rome. It is clear from Polybius' account of the hearing in the senate that these embassies were not received until the year 151, as he states that the two consuls of 151, Aulus Postumius and L. Licinius Lucullus, were both present.[16] In this case it is probable that Marcellus did not reach Citerior until fairly late in 152.

Lucullus himself, who went to Citerior in 151, also probably did not arrive before the middle of the year. He faced problems over the levy, and even if he was not, as the Livian epitomator believes, imprisoned by the tribunes as a result, this will have caused delay.[17] Certainly the ambassadors of the Arevaci, Belli and Titthi had returned to Spain, learnt from Marcellus that the senate had decided to continue the war, received another attack by Marcellus on Numantia, and made a formal surrender, all before Lucullus arrived.[18] The next consul to be sent to Citerior, Q. Metellus Macedonicus in 143, did not reach the area until fairly late in the season, since his first action was to attack the Vaccaei while they were harvesting.[19] It may be that he had spent the earlier part of his consular year putting down a slave revolt at Minturnae.[20] For quite different reasons Q. Fabius Maximus Aemilianus (*cos.* 145) arrived in Ulterior only at the end of the campaigning season. The praetor, C. Plautius, to whom the *provincia* had originally been assigned, retired into winter-quarters at midsummer, following a defeat by Viriathus, and

---

[16] Polybius 35.2.1–3.7; Appian *Ib.* 48.198–49.208; Simon, *Roms Kriege* 30–41. A lex Pupia, dated by Mommsen to *c.* 154, forbade the senate to meet on comitial days, which would have reduced the number of possible days for senate meetings in January to ten, and made likely the reception of embassies in February (Mommsen, *StR* III, 922–3; R. Y. Tyrrell and L. C. Purser, *Correspondence of Cicero* II (London 1886) 115; G. Rotondi, *Leges publicae populi Romani* (Milan 1912) 399). It may be that the lex Gabinia, which in the Ciceronian period ordered that the senate receive embassies in February, was already in existence in the second century (Hassall, Crawford and Reynolds, *JRS* 64 (1974) 218 n. 27; *contra* Giovannini and Grzybek, *Mus. Helv.* 35 (1978) 46–7).

[17] Livy, *per.* 48. This account seems based on that of Polybius (35.3.7.7–4.14), but neither he nor Appian (*Ib.* 19.209) mentions imprisonment. Orosius 4.21.1, probably using Livy here, also omits it. Perhaps the epitomator has confused this occurrence with the similar one in 138 (cf. Livy, *per.* 55), of which Cicero, *de leg.* 3.20, specifically says that such an imprisoning of consuls by tribunes had never occurred before.

[18] Appian, *Ib.* 50.211–14.

[19] Appian, *Ib.* 76.322, reading Οὐακκαίων, with the manuscript, rather than Ἀρουακῶν with Schweighaeuser and Viereck. See Schulten, *Numantia* I, 143; Simon, *Roms Kriege* 106 n. 9.

[20] Orosius 5.9.4. Badian, *Historia* 6 (1957) 321, places this in 133, but the Orosius passage gives no indication of date.

it was only after the news had been received in Rome that a decision was taken to send the consul.[21] Fabius himself had time only to undertake some training of the soldiers before himself going into winter-quarters.

In the first ten years after the introduction of the early date for entry to office by the consuls, it would thus appear that none of the consular governors in either province arrived before the middle of the campaigning season, and some only at the end. So far as Citerior is concerned the next ten years saw more variation. For three of the consular governors, Q. Pompeius (*cos.* 141), M. Popilius Laenas (*cos.* 139) and Q. Calpurnius Piso (*cos* 135) it is impossible to determine even approximately when in their consular year they reached their *provincia*.[22] Two others, M. Aemilius Lepidus Porcina (*cos.* 137) and L. Furius Philus (*cos.* 136), certainly arrived late, but in each case this was because they were replacing others to whom the *provincia* had already been allotted for that year, respectively C. Hostilius Mancinus and Lepidus Porcina himself.[23] Of the two remaining consular governors, Mancinus at least completed his disastrous efforts in time to be recalled while still consul, but this must have been towards the end of the year, since his successor, Lepidus, undertook his first attack against Pallantia during the discussion of Mancinus' surrender in the senate, and in his capacity not as consul but *pro consule*.[24] Scipio Aemilianus in 134 at least managed to discipline and train his troops, conduct a preliminary attack on the Vaccaei and establish himself outside Numantia before the end of the year.[25] Both cases suggest a fairly early start to the fighting in those two years, though how early is impossible to say.

In Ulterior, the picture is somewhat different. The next two consular governors, Q. Fabius Maximus Servilianus (*cos.* 142) and Q. Servilius Caepio (*cos.* 140) both began their time in the *provincia* at or just before the beginning of a campaigning season, but in each case, this was the year following their consulship, a pattern more common in the next century.[26] D. Iunius Brutus (*cos.* 138) did reach Ulterior during his consulship, but probably not until late in the year. He had difficulties with the levy, rather

---

[21] Appian, *Ib.* 64.271–65.277. On the chronology, see below, Appendix II.

[22] On these men, see Simon, *Roms Kriege* 108–16, 127–38, 169.

[23] Lepidus: Appian, *Ib.* 83.358–359; Livy, *per.* 56; Orosius 5.5.13. Furius: Val. Max. 3.7.5; Dio Cassius fr. 82; cf. Simon, *Roms Kriege* 168–9.

[24] Appian, *Ib.* 80.349–350 (stressing Lepidus' eagerness and avoidance of delay); Livy, *per.* 56.

[25] Appian, *Ib.* 84.365–90.400; Livy, *per.* 57; Plut. *apophth. Scip.* 16ff; Val. Max. 2.7.1; Front. 4.1.1, 5; 4.3.9; Polyaenus 8.16.2–4; Aelian, *var. hist.* 11.9; Veget. 3.10; Eutropius 4.17.2; Orosius 5.7.4–6; cf. Simon, *Roms Kriege* 171–80.

[26] Fabius: Livy, *per. Oxy.* 171; Appian, *Ib.* 67.283. Caepio: Appian, *Ib.* 70.296. On the chronology, see below Appendix II.

like those of Lucullus in 151, and the only action of his which can be placed in 138 is the foundation of Valentia (modern Valencia).[27]

It would seem that if the change of entry-date for the consulship introduced in 153 was to enable consuls to reach the peninsula early in the year, it was a signal failure. However, it follows that if the entry-date had remained the Ides of March, few if any of the consuls would have reached their *provinciae* within their consulship at all. In this case the change was an essential prerequisite for the implementation of a policy of sending consuls in their year of office to the two provinces.[28] This suggests that what happened in 153 was indeed a conscious change of policy on the part of the senate to provide consular governors. Such an alteration, as with that of 197, requires some explanation.

The Spanish wars in the context of the middle of the second century

The most obvious and plausible explanation for an increase in the status of the commanders in Spain and thus also the size of the armies from the praetorian norm of one legion to the consular army of two legions,[29] is that there was a serious war going on which required the attentions of a consul. Such had been the reason for the *provincia* of Hispania Citerior being assigned to Cato in 195,[30] and the language used by Livy of Cato is almost exactly the same as that which the epitomator employs to explain the sending of Q. Fabius Maximus Aemilianus to Ulterior in 145.[31] Aemilianus was the first consular ever to be sent to the farther province, and he had to face a resurgence of Lusitanian marauding, led by Viriathus, so that the Livian explanation makes some sense here. It is much less clear that this is the reason for the beginning of the 'consular' policy, with the sending of Fulvius Nobilior against Segeda in 153.

Those sources which give a reason for the outbreak of war in 153 link the sending of the consul with the problems caused by the town of

[27] Livy, *per.* 55. This seems to be in a different year from the crossing of the river Oblivio, which is dated to 137 by the Oxyrhyncus epitome (Livy. *per. Oxy.* 200–17).

[28] Note that when Cato had been sent in 195, dislocation of the calendar made it possible for him to enter office on *Id. Mart.* and still reach Spain about midsummer (above pp. 80–1). This dislocation had been partly corrected by the middle of the century (Bickerman [n. 10] 46; P. S. Derow, *Phoenix* 27 (1973) 355–6).

[29] On the troops in Spain in this period, Brunt, *Italian manpower* 427–9.

[30] Livy 33.43.2: 'quoniam in Hispania tantum glisceret bellum ut iam consulari et duce et exercitu opus esset'.

[31] Livy, *per.* 52: 'tantum terroris is hostis [*i.e.* Viriathus] intulit, ut iam consulari opus esset et duce et exercitu.'

Segeda.[32] Appian, whose account is the fullest, describes it as a large town of the Belli, one of the tribes which had signed the agreement with Gracchus in 179. The Belli absorbed the smaller towns near Segeda, and forced the neighbouring tribe of the Titthi to join also, putting a wall about the whole settlement that was 40 stades long. The senate learnt of this and ordered them to stop, as their action was contrary to the terms of the agreement with Gracchus; they also insisted that the Segedans should pay the taxation and provide troops, as had been laid down in 179. The Segedans replied that they had been forbidden to found new cities, not to fortify old ones, which was all they were doing; and further that, subsequent to the agreement with Gracchus, they had been allowed to stop paying the tribute and supplying soldiers. Appian adds that this was indeed true, but that the senate always made such concessions with the proviso that they should last only for so long as it pleased the senate and people. As a result Nobilior was sent against them, with an army of almost thirty thousand men, that is a consular army of two legions, with *auxilia*.

The name Segeda is common enough among towns in Spain, but in this instance is probably to be identified with a partially walled site, 10 kilometres south-east of Calatayud, in the mountains which fringe the north-eastern edge of the *meseta*, and which at some point issued Iberian denarii bearing the legend 'Segaisa'.[33] Appian's account contains some difficulties in his presentation of the relations of the Belli, Titthi and Arevaci with Rome, which becomes more obvious later in the war, but the course of the negotiations which he describes is probably accurate. Certainly concessions made by commanders in Spain could contain provisos of the type which he mentions, as may be seen from the famous decree of L. Aemilius Paullus from Hasta and the *deditio* of 104 BC, recently discovered near Alcántara.[34] However the story is reconstructed, the most puzzling feature remains the sending of the consul to deal with the difficulty.

Even in the version given by Appian, the decision of the senate seems rather abrupt. According to Diodorus the matter appears even more odd. He represents the Segedans as trying hard to be conciliatory, assuring the ambassadors that were sent to them that, while they reserved the right to continue building, they were faithful allies of the Romans, and would obey all other instructions with alacrity, and emphasising this resolve with

[32] Appian, *Ib.* 44.180–3; Florus 1.34.3; Diodorus 31.39 calls it Begeda.
[33] On the location of Segeda, see A. Schulten, *Hommagen a Martins Sarmento* (Guimaraes 1933) 373–5.
[34] On the divergent traditions about these tribes, see below Appendix IV. On the Hasta decree, above p. 118; and on the Alcántara *deditio*, below Appendix V.

a vote taken by their popular assembly. However, when the ambassadors reported back to the senate, the agreement (presumably that of 179) was set aside, and war declared.[35] It seems clear that action of this sort had been the senate's intention from the start, particularly as it would have been necessary to introduce the early date for the entry of the consuls into office at some point in the previous year, and the intention of this change was to allow a consul to go to Spain. This implies both that a war in Spain was foreseen, and that the expectation was that a consul would be sent. This is surprising not only because a war decision preceded the negotiations but because the practice of the senate up to this point would suggest that the more usual reaction to difficulties of this kind was to send a praetor. When the Celtiberians had been brought under Roman control previously, in the wars which had ended with the treaties now in question, the Roman commander, Ti. Sempronius Gracchus, had been of praetorian status, and that seems to have been far more widespread a rising than the difficulty over Segeda. At the same time as Fulvius was in charge in Citerior, the commander in Ulterior, who was engaged in putting down a group of Lusitanian insurgents which had already inflicted crushing defeats on two praetorian armies in as many years, was the praetor, L. Mummius.[36] It is probable that the reason for the senate's decision to send a consul to Citerior in 153, already taken in principle in 154, must lie outside the situation in Spain itself, and the practices developed over the past half-century for selecting Spanish commanders.

If the cause of this shift in senatorial policy does not obviously emerge from an examination of the events in the *provincia*, it should perhaps be sought in the consulship itself. It is easy to forget that the office which was the peak of a political career was above all else a military command, and that the *imperium* which the consul held was primarily the power of an army commander.[37] It is of course true that a consul had other important duties and opportunities, but the essence of the magistracy is summed up by Cicero's observation that at the consular elections it was generals, not expounders of words that were elected.[38] This close association of the senior army command with the highest political position

[35] Diodorus 31.39.

[36] On Gracchus, above pp. 101–3. On Mummius, Appian, *Ib.* 56.236–57.242; Simon, *Roms Kriege* 20–5.

[37] Thus Mommsen, *StR* I³, 116; '*Imperium*, dasselbe Wort welches technisch die Gewalt des Oberbeamten überhaupt bezeichnet, wird weit haüfiger in nicht minder technischer Weise in eminenten Sinn verwendet für das militärische Commando.' Cf. the remark of J. P. V. D. Balsdon, on the position in the first century BC: 'the primary function of the ex-praetor was to govern...; the primary function of the consul and ex-consul, outside Rome, was to fight' (*JRS* 29 (1939) 64); see also Harris, *War and imperialism* 15–16.   [38] Cic., *pro Murena* 18–38.

in the state helps to explain the immense prestige that attached to successful military activity, and to its recognition in the celebration of a triumph. As has been noted already, the tenure of the two Spanish *provinciae* by praetors in the first decades of the second century coincided with and was responsible for the great increase in the proportion of triumphs awarded to men who had not reached the consulship which took place in those years. The situation had been altered by the relative stability which seems to have followed the Celtiberian wars of the early 170s, and when fighting is again recorded with the campaign of Manilius in Ulterior in 155, there had not been a celebration from Spain since the *ovatio* of Ap. Claudius Centho in 174.[39] The effects of this change on the overall number and pattern of triumphs and *ovationes* can be seen by a comparison of the period between 200 and 170 with that between 169 and 82, the year in which Sulla returned to Rome and began his legislative review of the powers of provincial commanders. In the earlier period, 36 celebrations were held, half of them by non-consulars, in 31 years; in the next 88 years, there were only 52 such celebrations (taking those recorded on the *Fasti Triumphales*, and those conjectured by Degrassi),[40] of which only 10 were by men who had not already held the consulship.[41] It would seem that at the time of Fulvius Nobilior's assignment to Citerior the fundamentally consular nature of the most important military commands, and of the triumph as a reward for success in the field, was even more part of the Roman understanding of their own institutions than had been the case earlier in the same century.

If it was both the right and duty of a consul to command Roman troops, it was necessary for the senate to assign military areas as consular provinces. In practice, this usually meant that one such *provincia* had to be found, as usually one consul in this period seems to hold *Italia* as his area of responsibility, and to work with the senate on the affairs of Rome and Italy.[42] At least one consul each year seems to have expected a war to fight, and in the middle of the second century there was some difficulty in fulfilling this need. The clearest instance of this problem occurred in 156. Polybius states that a major consideration in the senate's thoughts, when deciding to send the consul C. Marcius Figulus to fight the Dalmatians, was that they did not want the men of Italy to become effeminate because of the long peace, since this was now the twelfth year

---

[39] J. S. Richardson, *JRS* 65 (1975) 50–63.

[40] Degrassi, *Inscr. It.* 13.1.556ff.

[41] Richardson [n. 39] 56–7. The prestige gained from the now less frequent triumph may account for the increased use of triumphal cognomina in the second half of the second century (cf. I. Kajanto *The Latin cognomina* (Helsinki 1965) 52). [42] Mommsen, *StR* III, 1212–13.

since the war against Perseus.[43] The 'long peace', which the senate at
least saw as a reason for war, must have caused problems for the senatorial
nobility as well as weakening the moral fibre of the Italian population,
and, from this point of view the situation was deteriorating. The
Dalmatian war was finished by the consul of the following year, P. Scipio
Nasica Corculum, who celebrated a triumph in his consulship as a
result,[44] and in Liguria, which had provided a consular *provincia* for
much of the first half of the century and, in the immediate past, a triumph
in 158 and 155, there was also an absence of military activity. After the
victory of Q. Opimius over the Transalpine Ligurian peoples, the Oxybii
and the Deciatae, in 154, no other consul is known to have fought in the
area until the sending of M. Fulvius Flaccus in 125.[45] The shortage of
places in which Romans might fight must at least have made the senate
aware of the possibility of sending consular armies and consular commanders to fresh pastures, and it is probably no accident that the decision
to alter the consular entry-date was made in the same year that Opimius
brought the war against the Ligurians to a temporary halt.

The link between the sending of consuls to Spain and the lack of other
suitable *provinciae* is confirmed by the otherwise inexplicable pause in the
fighting after 150. Lucullus, the consul of 151, finding that his predecessor,
Marcellus, had effectively ended the fighting against the Celtiberians,
attacked the neighbouring Vaccaei, and also aided the praetorian commander in Ulterior, Ser. Sulpicius Galba, against the Lusitanians.[46] In
neither area was there an evident conclusion, and although the blood-bath
which marked the end of Galba's period in his *provincia* seems to have
stunned the Lusitanians, there would have been ample excuse for
dispatching a consul to either. Instead the fighting seems simply to have
been broken off. In 149 however, unlike 153, there was another war in
prospect. Not only were both the consuls of the year sent to fight against
the old enemy, Carthage, at last provoked into retaliation against Rome's
client Massinissa, but one consul in each of the next two years was also
given the *provincia* of Africa. While Scipio Aemilianus was ending this
war with the razing of Carthage, L. Mummius (*cos.* 146) had been
assigned the *provincia* of Achaea and was in the process of destroying

[43] Polybius 32.13.6–7; cf. Harris, *War and imperialism* 233–4.

[44] *Inscr. It.* 13.1.82 and 557.

[45] Triumphs in 158 and 155: *Inscr. It.* 13.1.82 and 557. Opimius: Polybius 33.10. Flaccus: Livy,
per. 60, Plut., *C. Gracchus* 15.1. Sp. Postumius Albinus (*cos.* 148) was probably active in the area,
as his name appears on a milestone between Genoa and Cremona (*ILLRP* 452).

[46] Citerior: Appian, *Ib.* 55.232. Ulterior: Appian, *Ib.* 59.247–60.254. Cf. Simon, *Roms Kriege*
55–9.

Corinth and the Achaean League.[47] It was only then that the disastrous situation which had resulted from Galba's and Lucullus' activities in south-western Spain merited the attention of a consul, and late in 145 Q. Fabius Maximus Aemilianus was sent to Ulterior.[48] Now that wars elsewhere had subsided, Hispania Ulterior became the consular *provincia* of the moment, and there was competition to be sent there. Valerius Maximus relates that both the consuls of 144, Ser. Sulpicius Galba and L. Aurelius Cotta were anxious to obtain the Spanish command, but were prevented by the intervention of Scipio Aemilianus, who succeeded in securing a further year's command for his brother, Fabius.[49] For the next ten years, from 143 to 134, one consul in every year went to one or other of the Spanish provinces, and in 137, as a result of Mancinus' disaster, both the consuls of the year were assigned to Citerior.[50]

In this period in the second half of the century, as was the case from the late third century onwards, the senate's policy towards the events in Spain was expressed through their allocation of *provinciae* year by year, and the change in that policy in 153 was a change in the status of the men to whom those *provinciae* were assigned. Given this similarity, it is not surprising that there is little more attention to what is actually happening in Spain in the later period than in the earlier, at least so far as the initiating of wars is concerned. Once again, senatorial action seems to be directed towards the needs and behaviour of the magistrates and pro-magistrates who were, or who wished to be, sent to the peninsula. However, the involvement of the senate in Spanish affairs was undoubtedly greater during the period 153 to 133, and certainly extended beyond the basic matter of allotting the *provinciae*. It is to the establishment of the *quaestio de repetundis* and to the series of protracted debates about the claims of returning commanders to have finished wars and concluded peace treaties that we must look for clarification of the senate's attitude to these westernmost parts of the Roman empire at this time.

The *quaestio de repetundis* and the Spanish provinces

In 149 BC the tribune L. Calpurnius Piso proposed a law *de rebus repetundis*, which was not only the first to establish a permanent *quaestio* procedure, with a jury manned by senators, but which also provided a

---

[47] References in Broughton, *MRR* I, 458–67.
[48] Appian, *Ib.* 65.273–4; Livy, *per. Oxy.* 151.   [49] Val. Max. 6.4.2.
[50] References in Broughton, *MRR* I, 471–90. See below Appendix II.

means by which magistrates and pro-magistrates, who had used their power wrongly to acquire property belonging to others, might be compelled to make restitution. It was from this beginning that there emerged the long series of laws, which were to be of such political importance throughout the last century of the republic, and which provided a remedy of sorts for non-Romans in the provinces who had suffered the depredations of Roman governors.[51] The introduction of this law has been linked by many scholars with the attempt in the same year to impose some punishment on Ser. Sulpicius Galba for having sold a large number of Lusitanians into slavery in 150, at the end of his tenure of Hispania Ulterior.[52] These events, taken together, would suggest an interest in the well-being of the provincials, and a willingness by at least some members of the senate to take an initiative to protect them. If this is correct, it represents a significant change of attitude compared with the lack of concern shown hitherto, except in those cases where specific application had been made directly to the senate.

Although the story of the proceedings taken against Galba and of his escape scot-free is told in several sources, there is disagreement about precisely what happened. Although some use language appropriate to the law-courts (especially about Galba's use of his children and ward in order to arouse pity), others refer to these events in a legislative context.[53] There is no doubt that there was an attempt by the tribune L. Scribonius Libo to introduce a *rogatio* that the Lusitanians who had surrendered to Galba, and who had been taken to Gaul, should be set free, and that this proposal was supported by M. Porcius Cato and opposed by Q. Fulvius Nobilior, and subsequently defeated.[54] It is probable that Galba was never brought before a court at all and that the later sources have imported judicial vocabulary into the debate about the *rogatio*, which, had it become law, would have been tantamount to a condemnation. But, irrespective of the

---

[51] Cic., *Brut.* 27.106; *ad Att.* 12.5(b); Livy, *per. Oxy.* 98–100 (cf. Livy, *per.* 49). On the history of the *leges repetundarum*, see J. P. V. D. Balsdon, *PBSR* 14 (1938) 98–114; A. W. Lintott, *ZSS* 98 (1981) 162–212.

[52] The bibliography on this topic is large. See, for instance, W. S. Ferguson *JRS* 11 (1921) 93–4; F. Munzer, *RE* IVA, 762–3; E. Badian, *CR* 72 (1958) 216; D. C. Earl, *Athenaeum* N.S. 38 (1960) 292; Simon, *Roms Kriege* 66; L. R. Taylor, *JRS* 52 (1962) 24; A. J. Toynbee, *Hannibal's legacy* (Oxford 1965) II, 496–7; A. E. Astin, *Scipio Aemilianus* 58–60, 318–19; E. S. Gruen, *Roman politics and the criminal courts 149–78 BC* (Cambridge, Mass. 1968) 12–13; W. Eder, *Das vorsullanische Repetunden- verfahren* (Munich 1969) 51–7; Lintott [n. 51] 166–7.

[53] For the judicial setting: Livy 39.40.12; Appian, *Ib.* 60.255; Gellius, *NA* 1.12.17; Ps.-Ascon. 203 (St.), on Cic. *Div. in Caec.* 20.66. For the legislative setting: Cic. *Brut.* 23.89; *de or.* 1.53.227–8; Livy, *per.* 49; Quint. 2.15.8. Val. Max. 8.1.2 and Livy, *per.* 49 use 'trial' language of Libo's *rogatio*. Cf. Astin, *Cato* 111–13; Lintott [n. 51] 166–7.   [54] Livy, *per.* 49.

form taken by these accusations, it is important to note that the content does not relate to *res repetundae*. Libo's proposal was that the Lusitanians should be restored to liberty, while the charge under the *lex de repetundis*, to judge by later examples, will have related to 'pequniae...quod ablatum captum coactum conciliatum aversumve siet'.[55] It is difficult to see how such a charge could be made to apply to massacre and enslavement, such as that alleged against Galba. Of course money and property had changed hands as a result of the outrage, but it is hard to see who would bring an action against the offending proconsul under a *lex de repetundis*. The Lusitanians had lost their freedom, and the loss of property which they had doubtless suffered at the same time seems to be an unimportant matter by comparison. Only the purchasers of the slaves, who were subsequently declared free, would seem to have been improperly deprived of money. In fact there is no reason to believe that any such claim was contemplated; and even if it were, to institute a *quaestio de repetundis* in order to deter governors from such monstrous actions as those which Galba seems to have perpetrated would be absurdly circuitous.

The difficulty in fitting the complaints against Galba into a context of *res repetundae* is not the only reason for questioning the modern assumption that the events of his period in Ulterior were the immediate cause of the lex Calpurnia. The story of his escape from justice was notorious and popular among the writers of the next two and a half centuries, and yet none of them link it with Calpurnius Piso's measure. Although it is always dangerous to argue from the silence of the ancient sources, and it may be pointed out quite properly that the first *lex de repetundis* was a less colourful and attractive topic than Galba's scandalous conduct, we might at least have expected that Cicero, who frequently alludes to *causes célèbres* of the second century, and also uses the history of the *quaestio de repetundis* to bolster his forensic arguments, would not neglect an association between an important judicial development and so ripe an outrage.

From one point of view, the separation of the lex Calpurnia from the case of Galba is not of great importance. It is clear that the 150s were a time of increasing concern at Rome over the behaviour of magistrates and pro-magistrates in the provinces, of which Libo's attempt to censure Galba is simply one further instance. L. Lentulus (*cos.* 156) was, according to Valerius Maximus, prosecuted on a *repetundae* charge under

---

[55] Livy, *per.* 49: 'ut Lusitani, qui in fidem populi R. dediti ab Servio Galba in Galliam venissent, in libertatem restituerentur'. Cf. *lex rep.* (*FIRA* I², 7) lines 2–3.

a lex Caecilia during his consulship, and the Livian epitomator mentions several praetors accused in 154 or 153 by their provinces of *avaritia*.[56] However, the removal of a causal link between the two events of 149 makes it far less certain that the attack on Galba was aimed at assisting the provincials, rather than, for instance, controlling the wayward activities of a holder of the *imperium*; and leaves open to discussion the question of the intention of the lex Calpurnia. This is not the place to examine this second matter,[57] but so far as the attitude of the senate to the Spanish governors is concerned, it is notable that in the years that follow, down to the fall of Numantia, there is no known case of a prosecution *de repetundis*, despite some remarkable examples of mis-government. The only commander said to have been brought before a court in Rome was C. Plautius, who went to Ulterior as praetor in 145, only to be defeated by Viriathus and retire into winter-quarters at midsummer. Diodorus records that, on his return to Rome, he was condemned on what appears to be a charge of *maiestas minuta*, and went into exile.[58] There is no indication here of any direct involvement of the senate, or anyone else at Rome, in the welfare of the provincials by means of the law-courts.

The senate and the attempts to end the wars

The senate was, however, far more involved with the series of attempts by consular governors, especially in Citerior, to end the war which they had inherited. At first sight senatorial attitudes towards such attempts seem consistent and extraordinary. Despite the expenditure of manpower and other resources, and the resistance to the levy which reached a climax in 151 and again in 138,[59] the senate repeatedly refused to ratify agreements reached between Roman commanders and their Spanish adversaries, thus prolonging the fighting until, in the case of Numantia, the enemy state was effectively eradicated. Some modern scholars have seen in this consistency the policy of Scipio Aemilianus, while others have

[56] Val. Max. 6.9.10; Livy, *per.* 47. Cf. A. H. M. Jones, *Criminal courts of the Roman republic and principate* (Oxford 1972) 48.

[57] I intend to argue elsewhere that Piso's primary intention was to protect *cives* rather than provincials.

[58] Appian, *Ib.* 69.269–272; Diodorus 33.2; cf. Mommsen, *StR* II³, 320–2, *Röm. Strafrecht* 555–6. R. Bauman's assertion (*The 'crimen maiestatis' in the Roman republic and early principate* (Johannesburg 1967) 22) that 'the procedure was that of *perduellio* – a capital trial in the *comitia centuriata*' has no support in Diodorus' notice. On the chronology of Plautius, see below Appendix II p. 186.   [59] Above n. 17.

ascribed it to an almost automatic response, learnt in the desperate days of the Hannibalic war, which led the senate to expect that Spain would be the scene of endless warfare until such time as their enemies had been obliterated.[60] It has perhaps been too little noticed that the senate's role in these questions is in itself a development from their apparent lack of concern about arrangements in Spain earlier in the century.

The first negotiations recorded in the sources are those conducted by M. Claudius Marcellus, who as consul in 152 succeeded Q. Fulvius Nobilior in Citerior. After some preliminary military successes, Marcellus managed to open negotiations with the alliance of Celtiberians, which had been formed in response to the Roman threat against Segeda the previous year. The allies, the Arevaci, the Belli and the Titthi, asked for leniency and a return to the terms established under the agreements made with Ti. Gracchus in the 170s; but because of objections by others living in the area, Marcellus decided to refer the matter to the senate. It is probable that these protests also came from members of the Belli and Titthi, who feared the dominance of the Arevaci.[61]

At the moment of the dispatch of the Spanish embassies to the senate, Marcellus appears to have been thinking in terms of a renewal of the Gracchan agreements, and in the speech which Polybius gives to the ambassadors of the Arevaci in the senate, reference is again made to these agreements.[62] However, despite Marcellus' urging of the case of the Arevaci through the envoys he himself had sent, the senate determined to continue the war, partly, according to Polybius, because of the fear shown by the loyal Belli and Titthi towards the Arevaci.[63] The embassies were dismissed without hearing the senate's decision, which they were to be given by Marcellus on their return. The fragment of Polybius only contains the debate in the senate, but Appian gives as the senate's reason that the Arevaci had not surrendered to Nobilior, and this may well have been the official formulation which Marcellus received from the envoys he had sent, and which he then communicated to the Celtiberians. The language which Appian uses indicates that what the Arevaci had not done was to make a formal *deditio*.[64]

[60] On Scipio, Ed. Meyer, *Kleine Schriften* I² (Halle 1924) 401–2; J. M. Blázquez, *Klio* 41 (1963) 167–86 (modified by Astin, *Scipio Aemilianus* 139–40 and 155–60). On the *Vernichtungskrieg*, Dahlheim, *Gewalt und Herrschaft* 77–110, esp. 95–102.

[61] Appian, *Ib.* 48.198–49.206. Cf. Polybius 35.2.1–3.9, who states that the two opposing embassies in Rome consisted of the Arevaci, as enemies of Rome, and the Belli and Titthi, as Roman allies (see further, below Appendix IV).

[62] Polybius 35.2.15.   [63] Polybius 34.3.1–4.

[64] Appian, *Ib.* 49.208: ὅτι μή, καθάπερ αὐτοὺς ἠξίου Νωβελίων, ὁ πρὸ Μαρκέλλου, 'Ρωμαίοις αὐτοὺς ἐπετετρόφεσαν. On ἐπιτρέπειν and its cognates, see Dahlheim, *Struktur und Entwicklung* 14.

Two points about the senate's attitude to the war emerge from this story: first, they wanted the war to continue, no doubt partly influenced by the arguments of the loyal ambassadors that the Romans should stay in the area, or at least make an example of the Arevaci if they intended to leave; but perhaps also by the presence in the senate of the newly installed consuls of 151, one of whom, L. Licinius Lucullus, is said by Appian to have been particularly eager for the glory and the money that he expected from his tenure of Hispania Citerior.[65] Second, the reason given for continuing the war was that the Celtiberians had not made a *deditio* to Fulvius Nobilior in 153. This is particularly important, for it was the first time that the senate had stated clearly that their acceptance of an end to hostilities was conditional on such a surrender. Over the next 20 years, this demand for a *deditio* was to play a vital part in the relations between Roman commanders and the Celtiberians, and between those same commanders and the senate. It is particularly fortunate therefore that the text of a *deditio*, dated 104 BC, has recently been found near Alcántara, in the province of Caceres, in the remains of a fortified native settlement, known as the Castro de Villavieja.[66] This records the surrender of a people, whose name is unfortunately incomplete, to the commander L. Caesius, who describes himself as *imperator*.

The new document makes explicit what had previously been deduced from the literary and legal tradition, that the surrender was made to the bearer of *imperium* on the spot, and that the conditions which were to apply to the newly surrendered peoples were determined by him after the *deditio* had been made. It also appears that the legal status of the people concerned, and the ownership of their property, was determined by the commander himself, although with the proviso, familiar from the decree of Aemilius Paulus in 189 and from the arrangements made by Ti. Gracchus in 179, that these arrangements were to be at the disposal of the senate and people of Rome.[67]

The application of these principles to the cases of Nobilior and Marcellus helps to clarify what the senate was demanding in 152. It is likely that Nobilior had made his demand for surrender when he had advanced on Numantia after his initial defeat by Karos, the leader of the allied forces, a demand which the Numantines might well have rejected.[68]

[65] Polybius 35.2.9–10, 3.7; Appian, *Ib.* 51.215.
[66] R. López Melero, J. L. Sánchez Abal and S. García Jiménez 'El bronce de Alcántara: una *deditio* del 104 a.c.', *Gerión* 2 (1984) 265–323; below Appendix v.
[67] See below Appendix v and above p. 118.
[68] Appian, *Ib.* 45.184–46.188. This is probably the context of the negotiations described by Diodorus 31.41 (Simon, *Roms Kriege* 26–7).

The agreement that Marcellus hoped to reach with the enemy was not and, in theory at least, could not have been a *deditio*, since this not only deprived those who had surrendered of their property but also deprived them of their legal existence as a community, and thus automatically annulled any arrangements previously made.[69] The senate clearly did not reject Marcellus' proposal without discussion, but the effect of their decision was to make it impossible for anything less than a *deditio* to be accepted in future.

Marcellus' subsequent action confirms this interpretation. He informed the Celtiberians that the war had been renewed, and returned the hostages he had taken from them before the ambassadors left for Rome. He then conferred privately with the leader of the embassy, and probably, as Appian says was later suspected, persuaded them to surrender to himself rather than wait for the arrival of Lucullus. At any rate, the Arevaci recaptured the town of Nergobriga, which Marcellus had taken the previous year. Marcellus himself advanced on Numantia, but, before he actually attacked the city, he was approached by the Numantine general, Litenno, who reported that the Belli, Titthi and Arevaci were surrendering to him. He, delighted, demanded hostages and money, and then set them free.[70]

Marcellus seems by this means to have used the senate's insistence on a *deditio* to circumvent their desire for the continuation of the war. By making the Celtiberians undergo the form of a technical surrender, but following it with relatively mild terms, he fulfilled the formal conditions stipulated by the senate, while ignoring the fears of the opponents of the Arevaci, which had been received with sympathy in Rome. From Marcellus' point of view, the advantage of the *deditio* was that its implementation was entirely in his own hands. All that was necessary was for him to ensure that those who asked to be allowed to surrender should be the representatives of a people *in sua potestate*, that they should hand over the state, its population, property and gods, and for him to reply 'at ego recipio'.[71] Indeed Marcellus was particularly careful to comply with the requirements, including the provision that the surrender should take place 'before the battering-ram touched the walls', a limitation which

---

[69] So H. Horn, *Foederati* (Frankfurt-am-Main 1930) 16–19; A. Heuss, *Klio* beiheft 31 (1933) 61–2; Dahlheim, *Struktur und Entwicklung* 12–13, 20–2, *contra* Mommsen, *StR* III, 56 n. 1 and E. Täubler, *Imperium Romanum* I (Berlin 1913) 14ff and 303ff.

[70] Appian, *Ib.* 50.211–12. The money was probably the 600 talents which Strabo, 3.4.13 (p. 162), citing Poseidonius, says Marcellus exacted from Celtiberia.

[71] Livy 1.38.1–3; Dahlheim, *Struktur und Entwicklung* 5ff. The argument of Heuss [n. 69] 60–1, that actual seizure of property was necessary to complete the *deditio* is not consonant either with the Livian *formula*, or with the evidence of actual cases (Dahlheim, *Struktur und Entwicklung* 23–5).

Cicero argued should be observed in spirit rather than to the letter.[72] Marcellus evidently did not take the risk. After all, if he could remain within the rules, not only the surrender of the Arevaci, but also the terms upon which they were declared free were his to decide.[73] There was much to be gained from attention to detail.

The absence of any mention of subsequent attacks on Marcellus in the senate indicates that both his acceptance of the *deditio* and his declaration that the Celtiberians were free were in fact not rejected by the senate, despite the flouting of their intentions. It may well be that the large quantity of silver which he brought back helped to quieten his critics.[74] But whatever the reason behind this apparent change of heart, and despite the failure of the senate's manoeuvres in early 151, their demand that the war in Citerior could only be concluded with a *deditio* and their rejection of other forms of settlement was the background against which the second phase of the Numantine war was enacted.[75]

The next negotiations recorded in the sources are those by which Q. Pompeius (*cos.* 141) attempted to end the war which had been stirred up by Viriathus among the northern tribes in 144. Pompeius took over the province from Metellus Macedonicus, probably late in 141, and his opening campaigns against Numantia and other towns in the northern *meseta* were notably unsuccessful. He made a final attempt against Numantia itself during the winter of 140/139, but the main sufferers were his own forces, who were affected both by disease and by the harsh climatic conditions.[76] Appian says that he was worried about the repercussions that might follow such a disastrous term,[77] and it seems that he had already misrepresented his situation to the senate before this. Certainly when additional troops had arrived in late 140, they had been accompanied by a senatorial commission, probably of ten *legati*, of the type which had regularly been sent out to assist victorious Roman commanders in the settlement of newly conquered areas ever since the

---

[72] Cic. *de off.* 1.11.35; Caesar, *BG* 2.32; E. Täubler, *Imperium Romanum* 1.21–2.

[73] Compare the case of L. Aemilius Regillus at Phocaea in 190 (Livy 37.32.10–14; Dahlheim, *Struktur und Entwicklung* 77).

[74] So Simon, *Roms Kriege* 45; Astin, *Scipio Aemilianus* 41–2.

[75] It was surely this, rather than, as Astin contends, a last-minute breach of agreed terms during Metellus Macedonicus' governship in 142, which led to the repeated demand for a *deditio* (Astin, *Scipio Aemilianus* 148, following E. Cavaignac, *Rev. Num.* 13 (1951) 132–3). The passage of Diodorus which refers to this breach (33.16) is of uncertain provenance, and in any case the first demand for a *deditio* pre-dates Macedonicus by a decade. In fact no source records Macedonicus as fighting against Numantia. Appian, *Ib.* 76.322 says he was sent against the Vaccaei, which Schweighaeuser emended to 'Arevaci', and only *de vir. ill.* 61.3 says he fought against the 'Arbaci'. Cf. Schulten [n. 19] 360 n. 1.

[76] Appian, *Ib.* 76.325–78.337; Livy, *per. Oxy.* 174ff, *per.* 54; Val. Max. 9.3.17; Diodorus 33.17; Dio fr. 77; Orosius 5.4.13; Simon, *Roms Kriege* 108ff.   [77] Appian, *Ib.* 79.338.

end of the first Punic war.[78] Pompeius needed to do something to end the war in a creditable fashion.

According to Appian, he undertook secret negotiations with the Numantines, who were themselves weary of the war, about bringing the fighting to an end. When they sent an embassy to Pompeius, he told them publicly to surrender themselves to the Romans, saying that he knew of no other form of treaty which would be fitting for the Romans; but he also gave them secret undertakings, which Appian does not specify. He then demanded and received hostages, prisoners and deserters, and in addition 30 talents of silver, part of which the Numantines brought, and part of which was to follow. By the time they came to deposit this second instalment, Pompeius' successor, M. Popillius Laenas, had arrived. Appian states that Pompeius was now no longer afraid of the war, and, knowing that his agreement was disgraceful and concluded without reference to Rome, denied that he had agreed with the Numantines. When the latter objected, they were supported by witnesses from among Pompeius' own staff, and from the senatorial commission, which had accompanied him into winter-quarters. Laenas transferred the dispute to Rome, where there followed a 'trial' in the senate, the Numantines and Pompeius contradicting one another, at the end of which the senate decided to continue the war.[79]

This account contains certain difficulties: it is not clear why Pompeius suddenly lost his fear of the war on the appearance of his successor, particularly as it had been dread of the accusations he might have to face on his return to Rome that had first driven him to open negotiations. Secondly it is difficult to see exactly what Pompeius was denying, particularly as it appears that the denial, although evidently false, was completely successful, the senate accepting that there were no grounds for ending the war. The other sources which refer to the debate, however, clarify the matter. They all describe him as having attempted to conclude a 'pax infirmata' or a 'pax ignobilis',[80] or alternatively a 'foedus', a formal treaty. The later writers, who could see nothing wrong in a *foedus* as such, talk of it as 'turpissima foedera' or 'infame foedus', but for Cicero, who mentions the case three times, it was sufficiently damning to state that he had made a *foedus* at all.[81] For him the issue had been settled decisively once the senate had realised that what Pompeius had

---

[78] Appian, *Ib.* 78.334; Mommsen *StR* II³, 642–4, 692–3; B. Schleussner, *Die Legaten der römischen Republik* (Munich 1978) 9–94.   [79] Appian, *Ib.* 79.338–44.
[80] Livy, *per.* 54; Eutropius 4.17.
[81] Vell. Pat. 2.1.3; Orosius 5.4.21; Cic. *de fin.* 2.17.54, *de off.* 3.30.109, *de rep.* 3.18.28.

done was to make a treaty, and Cicero distinguishes between this debate and that about Mancinus in 136 by noting that, whereas the latter admitted that he had concluded a *foedus*, the former denied it.

The importance of the *foedus* can be seen from a comparison with the events of 151, and Marcellus' negotiations then. A binding agreement could not be reached before a *deditio*, because the effect of this form of surrender was to deprive those who surrendered of any legal status, and thus they could not be party to any such treaty. A *foedus* could (and often did) follow a *deditio*, but only after the *dediticii* had been assigned a legal status by the commander or by the state to whom the surrender had been made.[82] There is a fundamental distinction between an agreement or a treaty and a surrender, a distinction which Appian did not recognise, for he makes Pompeius argue to the Numantines that *deditio* was the only fitting form of agreement, and then to deny, paradoxically, that any form of agreement had been reached.[83] What made the difference in 139 compared with 151 seems to have been the presence of Laenas and the members of the senatorial commission when the Numantines arrived with the second part of the silver, which was evidence for an agreement at a time when the surrender had not taken place.

The similarities in the two cases of Marcellus and Pompeius, and the very different outcome to their attempts to end the war, indicate a change of attitude at Rome in the intervening period. This cannot be attributed to any desire for 'fair treatment' of the Celtiberians, for both commanders were equally eager to bring hostilities to an end, and the demands made by Pompeius seem, at least in financial terms, to have been much lighter.[84] Pompeius, however, no doubt under greater pressure because of his poor showing hitherto, seems to have been much less careful about the details of the *deditio*, and also to have been under much closer senatorial scrutiny. Just as the absence of Lucullus from Spain in 151 when he finally accepted the surrender, and from Rome when the news of it reached the senate, will have helped Marcellus, the evidence of Laenas and the commissioners was fatal to Pompeius. Although, as has been seen, the acceptance of a *deditio* was the act of a Roman magistrate or pro-magistrate, and not of the senate, by 139 such action was more likely to be examined and rejected by the senate. Control of the commanders in Spain was closer than it had been even twelve years before. It is hardly surprising that, when three years later Mancinus capitulated to the

---

[82] See the discussion by Dahlheim, *Struktur und Entwicklung* 69–82.
[83] Appian, *Ib.* 79.340 and 342.
[84] That is, 30 talents, as opposed to 600 (Appian, *Ib.* 79.341; Strabo 3.162).

Numantines, and then made an agreement with them to end the war, the senate refused to ratify the *foedus*, and, in order to save face with the Numantines, handed Mancinus himself over to them.[85]

The wars against the Lusitanians in the province of Hispania Ulterior produced different reactions from the senate. There is no sign of the insistence on a *deditio* which was so marked a feature of the Celtiberian wars, and on at least two occasions agreements were made, by M. Atilius in 152 and by Q. Fabius Maximus Servilianus in 140. Neither lasted through the following year, but not, as in the examples from Citerior, because the senate refused to countenance anything but a surrender of the enemy.[86] Part of the reason for this difference probably lies in the very different nature of the Lusitanian peoples. In the north, both the Iberian and Celtiberian peoples seem to have been based on urban settlements, such as Indika, which Cato had found in the immediate vicinity of Emporion in 195, or indeed Numantia itself.[87] The Lusitanians by contrast were evidently semi-nomadic, supporting themselves in part by raids on their more settled neighbours in the Guadalquivir valley.[88] This distinction can be seen also in the terms which the Lusitanians sought in order to end the war, for on several occasions hostilities were suspended as the result of an offer of land for settlement, and, after the murder of Viriathus, the Lusitanians who had supported him were settled either by Caepio in 139 or by D. Iunius Brutus in 138.[89] The similarity between this method of achieving peace and the *deditio*, which had by this time become essential in the north, is that both were acts of the commander on the spot, and neither, in principle, involved the senate. As has been noted already, the senate apparently took no part in the provision of land or the setting up of communities, either for provincials or for Romans, unless a request was made directly to them. This was the case with Valentia, which probably consisted of Roman and Italian veterans and

---

[85] Sources, see Broughton, *MRR* I, 484, and especially Cic. *de off.* 3.30.109, *de rep.* 3.18.28, *de or.* 1.40.181, 56.238, 2.32.137, *Top.* 8.37, *de har. resp.* 20.43, *ad Att.* 12.5(b). Cf. Simon, *Roms Kriege* 149–59; Astin, *Scipio Aemilianus* 178–82. On the development of the tradition, M. H. Crawford, *PBSR* 41 (1973) 1–7.

[86] Atilius: Appian, *Ib.* 58.243–4. Fabius: Appian, *Ib.* 69.293–4; Livy, *per. Oxy.* 185–6, *per.* 54; Diodorus 33.13.

[87] On the towns of the Iberians in the north-east, see A. Arribas, *The Iberians* (London n.d.) 97–115, and the excellent brief account in *L'Arqueologia a Catalunya, avui* (Barcelona 1982) 93–107. On the Celtiberians, G. Fatás, *Caesaraugusta* 53–4. (1981) 212–25.

[88] Thus the description of Viriathus as shepherd and bandit-chief in Dio fr. 73.1–4, and of the raids of the Lusitanians (Strabo 3.3.5–6 (p. 154)). See A. Schulten, *Neue Jahrbücher* 39–40 (1917) 212.

[89] Galba in 151: Appian, *Ib.* 59.249–53. Vetilius in 146: Appian, *Ib.* 61.259. Fabius Servilianus in 140: Appian, *Ib.* 69.294. Caepio in 139: Appian, *Ib.* 75.321; Diodorus 33.1.4. Brutus in 138: Livy, *per.* 55. Compare Aemilius Paullus' action in 189 (above pp. 117–19).

which, although it had become a *colonia* of some sort by 60 BC, is described at its foundation in 138 as no more than an *oppidum*.[90] The *deditio*, however, of which the very formula (as preserved by Livy) specified the handing over of city, fields, water and boundaries, was scarcely applicable to a people who were not already settled, and it may be that this is why it did not form part of the diplomatic tradition of the Lusitanian wars.[91] In this respect the recently discovered *deditio* from Alcántara may be taken as the exception which proves the rule, since in that case the community involved did possess land, buildings and laws, as the inscription itself attests.[92] The commanders responsible for the war against the Lusitanians will have found very different conditions, which must have made such demands inappropriate.

Despite the considerable differences between the events in the two provinces, and the senate's attitude towards them, there is evidence of a similar concern that fighting should only be ended on grounds which the senate considered proper, and that the opinion of a particular commander's successor was of great importance in determining the acceptability of any attempt to come to a conclusion with the enemy. There were only two occasions on which a consul was assigned to Ulterior following the term of another consular, in 140/139, when Q. Servilius Caepio replaced Fabius Servilianus, and in 138 when Caepio himself was succeeded by D. Iunius Brutus.[93] On his arrival, Caepio wrote to the senate, urging them to reject the agreement which Fabius, his own brother, had reached with Viriathus, admittedly under duress, and, although the senate was unwilling to make a public retraction, they did encourage him to harass the Lusitanians and thus provoke them into making the first move.[94] There were also apparently objections to Caepio's handling of the closing stages of the struggle with Viriathus. When the three Lusitanians whom Caepio had bribed to murder their leader applied to the consul for their reward, immediately after having done the deed, he referred them to Rome. On their arrival there the following year, they were refused their prize.[95] Brutus did not appear to accept that the war was over, for he invaded the Lusitanians again, before settling the remains of Viriathus'

90 Livy, *per.* 55; *ILLRP* 385 (cf. Galsterer, *Untersuchungen* 12). For earlier instances see above pp. 117–20.

91 Livy 1.38.1–3 (cf. Dahlheim, *Struktur und Entwicklung* 5ff).

92 See R. López Melero *et al.* [n. 66] 288–95.

93 If L. Metellus (*cos.* 142) went to Ulterior, then he was replaced by Servilianus; but see below Appendix II.   94 Appian, *Ib.* 70.296–7.

95 Appian, *Ib.* 74.314; Livy, *per. Oxy.* 201–2; Orosius 5.4.14. Eutropius 4.16 has Caepio indignantly refusing a reward, but he is apparently unaware of Caepio's involvement in Viriathus' murder.

veterans, and when he eventually returned to Rome, celebrated a triumph not only over the Callaeci, whom he went on to fight, but also over the Lusitanians.[96]

Senatorial control of consular commanders: means and ends

Direct interference by the senate with the activities of the magistrates and pro-magistrates sent out to the Spanish *provinciae* occurred far more frequently in the second half of the century than at any point before this. Nor was such interference confined to the examination of treaties and agreements reached between Roman commanders and indigenous groups.

In 151 Lucullus arrived in Citerior to discover that the war he had been expecting to fight had been concluded by the rapid action of Marcellus in accepting the *deditio* of the Celtiberians. The consul, however, motivated according to Appian by ambition and financial greed, invaded the territory of the Vaccaei, even though there was no senatorial decree about the matter, nor had the Vaccaei fought against the Romans or done any harm to Lucullus. He crossed the Tagus and approached the Vaccaean city of Cauca. When asked by its inhabitants the reason for this hostility, he replied that they had wronged the Carpetani, whom he had come to assist.[97] Appian regards this as a mere excuse for an unjustified attack, but Lucullus' accusation may have had some truth in it. The Vaccaei lived in the central reaches of the valley of the Durius, west of the Arevaci and north of the Carpetani, whose territory covered the upper Tagus and Anas valleys. Cauca lay well south of the Durius, and thus towards the Carpetani. The Carpetani were to suffer several attacks from Viriathus during the 140s, which perhaps indicates an adherence to the Romans.[98] In any case Lucullus took advantage of the alleged difficulties of the Carpetani to indulge in a series of attacks on the Vaccaei, first at Cauca and then at Intercatia and Pallantia, during which he broke several promises and achieved only occasional success.[99] Certainly the campaign did not bring the rewards he had hoped for, but according to Appian he was fortunate to escape without trial, having started the war contrary to a decree of the Romans. Taken literally, this would certainly imply that

[96] Livy, *per. Oxy.* 212, *per.* 55. On Brutus' triumph, Plut. *Ti. Gracchus* 21.3; Eutropius 4.19.
[97] Appian, *Ib.* 51.215–16.
[98] Strabo 3.1.6 (p. 139) and 3.2.3 (p. 142); cf. E. Hübner, *RE* III, 1607–8. During the Sertorian wars, Segovia, south of Cauca, was also a Vaccaean town (Livy 91, fr. 22). On Viriathus in Carpetania, Appian, *Ib.* 64.269, 70.298.
[99] Appian, *Ib.* 51.215–55.233; Simon, *Roms Kriege* 46–56.

the senate actually forbade the prosecution of the war; however, in two other places Appian states that there was fighting without a decree, rather than contrary to one, and it may well be that the stronger version is merely a variation.[100] The reiteration of the claim that Lucullus was acting improperly suggests that he did face criticism for extending the fighting after the end of the war against the Arevaci, especially because what he did was not in fact unusual. The same pattern of war succeeding war without any obvious reason has already been observed earlier in the century, and Brutus' exploits against the Callaeci after the end of the Lusitanian war in 138 appear to be in the same tradition.[101]

A similar circumstance in 136 produced a more forceful intervention from the senate. M. Aemilius Lepidus (*cos.* 137) arrived in Citerior late in his consular year to replace his disgraced colleague, C. Hostilius Mancinus, after the notorious capitulation of the latter to the Numantines. Growing impatient of the delay caused by the senate's deliberations about the ratification of Mancinus' treaty, he accused the Vaccaei (falsely, according to Appian) of supplying the Numantines during the war, and attacked the town of Pallantia in conjunction with the consul D. Iunius Brutus, at that time in Ulterior. At this point two *legati*, named as Cinna and Caecilius by Appian, brought from Rome the message that the senate was astonished that, in the midst of such disasters in Spain, he should undertake another war, and handed over to him a decree ordering him to desist. Lepidus answered that the senate did not understand the situation, that the Vaccaei had supplied arms, provisions and manpower to the Numantines, that Brutus was collaborating with him, and that if the Romans remained inactive they might lose the whole peninsula. The envoys, having failed in their mission, carried this message back to the senate.[102]

It may be that Lepidus, like Lucullus before him, was right to be suspicious of the Vaccaei. His judgement appears to be confirmed two years later, when Scipio Aemilianus, before launching his assault on Numantia, first attacked Pallantia and Cauca, which he had last visited as *tribunus militum* in Lucullus' army in 151. Once again the reason given is that it was from the Vaccaei that the Numantines drew their supplies.[103] Lepidus, however, failed in an attempt to take Pallantia, though he was not defeated in open battle because a lunar eclipse caused the Vaccaei to

---

[100] Appian, *Ib.* 55.233; cf. 51.215, 59.247; Simon, *Roms Kriege* 49.
[101] Above Ch. 4. Brutus' expedition: Appian, *Ib.* 72.304–73.310.
[102] Appian, *Ib.* 80.349–81.352.
[103] Appian, *Ib.* 87.380–89.391. On Scipio in 151, Appian, *Ib.* 53.255–54.230; Livy, *per.* 48; Val. Max. 3.2.6; Florus 1.33.11; *de vir. ill.* 58.

abandon their pursuit. When the Romans heard what had happened, he was deprived of his command, recalled to Rome as a private citizen, and on his return subjected to a fine.[104]

The similarities between the cases of these two men emphasise the difference in their treatment: both are said to have been motivated by greed, and to have put forward inadequate reasons for going to war, both acted against the wishes of the senate.[105] This was of course by no means a unique occurrence. Galba's massacre and enslavement of large numbers of Lusitanians also roused the ineffectual wrath of members of the senate, probably in the same year that Lucullus returned home, and both these instances are reminiscent of the scandalous conduct of M. Popilius Laenas (*cos.* 173), who sold the Ligurian tribe of the Statellates into slavery, refused to reverse his action despite decrees from the senate, and only escaped punishment the following year because of the collusion of the consuls (one of whom was his brother) and the praetor in charge of the affair.[106] What is remarkable is the escalation in severity in the case of Lepidus. Although there had been threats during the Hannibalic war to abrogate the *imperium* of pro-magistrates, this was the first time that such a thing is recorded as actually happening, and never before had such a decision been taken in the absence of the man involved.[107]

The fate of Lepidus provides a further illustration of what has already been seen from the senate's handling of commanders' claims to have concluded Spanish wars, especially in Citerior. Not only was senatorial intervention far more pronounced in the 20 years which followed Fulvius Nobilior's first arrival in Citerior in 153 than it had been in the past half-century, but it seems to have increased considerably in severity during those two decades. The seriousness with which these wars, and especially the Numantine war, were regarded has also left its mark on the literary sources. Polybius comments on the length and bitterness of the fighting, and cites the Celtiberian war as the best example of a 'fiery' war, which is not brought to an end by a single decisive encounter.[108] For Cicero, however, it is not only the fierceness of the war which is remarkable, but the importance of the result. He describes Scipio

---

[104] Appian, *Ib.* 81.353–83.358. Appian wrongly states he was deprived of his command and his *consulship*. He was *pro consule* in 136 (P. Willems, *Le Sénat de la république romaine* II (Louvain 1883) 661 n. 2; cf. Mommsen, *StR* III, 1088 n. 3). The eclipse is probably that of 1 April 136 (so Schulten [n. 19] I, 365).

[105] Motives: Appian, *Ib.* 51.215, 54.230 (Lucullus); 80.349 (Lepidus). Reasons: Appian, *Ib.* 51.215–6 (Lucullus); 80.349 (Lepidus).

[106] Popilius: Livy 42.7.3–9.6, 10.9–11, 21.1–22.8.

[107] Marcellus in 209: Livy 27.20.21. Scipio in 204: Livy 29.19.6; Mommsen, *StR* I³, 629 n. 4.

[108] Polybius 35.1.1–6; cf. Diodorus 31.40.

Aemilianus as having destroyed two fearful threats to Roman imperial power, Carthage and Numantia; in the *de officiis* he goes still farther, singling out the wars with the Celtiberians and the Cimbri, which were fought to decide which of the two sides should survive, as opposed to those against the Latins, Sabines, Samnites, Carthaginians and Pyrrhus, which were struggles for supremacy.[109]

That such significance should be given to a war which, though long and bitter, was fought so far from Italy, and which seems to have had so little direct impact on the interests and power of the Romans outside the confines of the Iberian peninsula, is surprising. In particular, to compare the Celtiberian war to the threat posed to Italy by the Cimbric invasions, and to classify it as endangering the very existence of Rome, in a way in which the Hannibalic war did not, is sufficiently extraordinary to cast serious doubt on Cicero's historical judgement. What must have made this struggle in the north-eastern corner of the *meseta* seem of such importance even in Rome was the recurrent inability of Roman consuls, with consular armies, to bring it to a successful conclusion. As in the earlier part of the century, it was with the commanders that the senate dealt, and they only heard directly from the inhabitants of the area when a commander referred a disputed matter to them, as Marcellus did in 152/151 and Laenas in 139. There was no reason why the senate, having dispatched a consul to his *provincia*, should have anything more to do with it until the time came to renew his tenure or replace him the following year. This is the pattern which shaped the senate's relations with Spain earlier in the century, and which continued during the late 150s and early 140s. Then, as earlier, the matter of deciding whether or not a returning proconsul had been successful in bringing the war to an end was important because it affected the prestige of the man who was being replaced, and also the prospects of the newly assigned magistrate or pro-magistrate. Hence also the importance of the latter in the debates about the claims that the war had been ended, and hence also the arguments invariably presented by such men that their predecessors' claims were improper. It is likely therefore that the increased degree of senatorial attention devoted to these arguments in the 150s and early 140s derived not from the increased importance of the wars as such, but the increased prestige of the men involved, who were now no longer praetorians but consulars. In this context it must be remembered that the

---

[109] Cic. *pro Murena* 28.58: 'P. Africanus...duos terrores huius imperi, Carthaginem Numantiamque, deleverat'; *de off.* 1.12.38: 'cum Celtiberis, cum Cimbris bellum ut cum inimicis gerebatur, uter esset, non uter imperaret.' For a different assessment of Numantia, see Appian, *Ib.* 98.424–6.

major reason for sending consuls to Citerior in the first place seems to have been not the significance of Segeda and its attempts to draw together its neighbours into a single town, but the need to send consuls to an appropriate military *provincia*.

A further result of the increased prestige to be gained from, and thus of the increased attention paid to, the conclusion of the Spanish wars was that every failure of a consular commander attracted a far greater share of publicity than had been true in the 'praetorian' period. Consequently the credit which would accrue to the eventual victor grew as the difficulty of the task became more apparent. The anxiety of each succeeding consul to secure the prize for himself, and of the senate to ensure that each claim was properly made, seem to have grown *pari passu*. As had been the case with the debates about the award of triumphs to the praetorian governors of the first part of the century, the main consideration seems, so far as can be told from the admittedly inadequate accounts that survive, not the need for stability within the region in the long term, but that a returning governor should have fulfilled the rules laid down for the ending of the conflict. Both the Celtiberians, in 151 with Marcellus and in 140 with Pompeius, and the Lusitanians in 141 with Fabius Maximus Servilianus, had shown themselves willing to make peace on terms which recognised Roman dominance, and although in 151 the senate may well have been influenced by the protests of opponents of the Arevaci from the same area, Rome had shown in her treatment of erstwhile allies in the Greek world in the 190s and 160s that if she wished to make a settlement, the objections raised by local interests would not stand in her way.[110]

Although the attitude of the senate seems to have changed little, in that senators still saw themselves as the guardians of military propriety, the greater importance of the decisions they were making led them into matters in which they previously seem to have taken no interest. In particular, relations between the magistrate or pro-magistrate and the local communities, which appear to have been entirely at the disposal of the praetorian commanders of the earlier period, now fell within the oversight of the senate. This is especially clear in the arrangement of treaties, which, as has been seen, were subject to a markedly sceptical scrutiny; but the sending of a commission to Pompeius in 140 shows that the senate intended to be more closely involved with any settlement of the area than it had been hitherto. A similar commission of ten was sent

---

[110] Marcellus: Appian, *Ib.* 48.205–49.206. Pompeius: 79.340–1. Fabius: 69.294. Compare the treatment of the Aetolians in the 190s (E. Badian, *Foreign clientelae* (Oxford 1958) 72–3), and of Rhodes and Eumenes in the 160s (*ibid.* 98–105).

out after Scipio Aemilianus had finally forced the Numantines to surrender and had destroyed their city. These men are said by Appian, the only source to mention them, to have been given the task of setting in a peaceful order the places captured by Scipio, and also the arrangements made by Brutus, which therefore would include the settlement of Viriathus' former soldiers at Valentia, as well as his subsequent conquests further north.[111] It is uncertain what these ten did in the two provinces, as their work has left no discernible mark in the record of the development of the Roman presence in Spain, but the aftermath of the long wars will have left many disputes to adjudicate, not least the distribution of the territory of Numantia, which Scipio is said to have made in 133.[112] The mere fact of their presence, however, indicates greater attention being paid by the senate to the internal state of the areas controlled by the Romans than has been seen previously, an attention which seems to have its origin in the almost fortuitous presence of consuls in the peninsula.

The period in which Spain regularly provided *provinciae* for the consuls marked another stage in the development of attitudes towards the area, from its being seen in purely military and strategic terms, as a part of the world to which it was necessary to send Roman armies, and therefore a Roman commander, to its becoming a responsibility of the state; that is, not simply the *provinciae* of two holders of *imperium*, but provinces of a Roman empire. As before, and as was inevitable given the Roman constitution, such measures as were taken during this very disturbed 20 years were taken by the men sent out to Spain to command armies there. The establishment of towns at Corduba by Marcellus (if this took place during his wintering in Ulterior in 152, rather than during his praetorian term in 169/168), and of Valentia by Brutus may be taken as examples.[113] By the end of the period, however, there are clear signs of an increased senatorial concern and involvement with what such men were doing. It is entirely in keeping with what has been seen already of senatorial attitudes that this expanded interest appears to have its origin in a desire to control the activities of the commanders sent out by the senate, rather than any notion of responsibility for the area itself, or even a wish to further its systematic exploitation. It is part of the paradox of power that this use of consuls, who were in principle more self-sufficient in the authority their *imperium* gave them than their praetorian predecessors,

---

[111] Pompeius: Appian, *Ib.* 78.334, 79.338 and 343. Scipio and Brutus: 99.428.
[112] Appian, *Ib.* 98.427.
[113] Marcellus: see above p. 119; Brutus: Livy, *per.* 55.

necessitated a deeper involvement on the part of the senate. It was an inability to cope with the consequences of this paradox which over the next 100 years was to bring about the collapse of senatorial influence at Rome. For the time being, the presence of the consuls as commanders in Spain was enough to ensure the senate's attention.

CHAPTER 7

From *provinciae* to provinces: 133–82

The half-century which separated the tribunate of Ti. Gracchus in 133 from Sulla's return to Rome in 82 was of immense significance for the history of the Roman republic. In Spain the same period, beginning with Scipio Aemilianus' capture of Numantia and ending with the first phase of the Sertorian wars, has left almost no trace in the extant historical sources. Appian, whose account of Scipio's campaign alone covers eight pages of the Teubner text, deals with the next 50 years in just one page.[1] The disasters of the wars against Numantia and Viriathus, and the eventual defeat of both those enemies, had a glamour which was evidently lacking from the events which followed.

As a result of this silence, it is difficult to make any evaluation of the activity of the men sent to command in Spain, or of the policy of the senate which assigned them to the two *provinciae*. It is possible, however, by comparing such little information as survives with the clearer patterns of the earlier part of the second century, to trace elements both of continuity and of development in Roman attitudes to Spain. it is important that the attempt be made, because the end of this period marked an important stage in the gradual emergence of the idea of the province as part of a Roman empire. The codification and extension by Sulla in the legislation in the late 80s of the restrictions on the powers of provincial commanders drew together the occasional rulings of the senate and people into what for the first time might be called a corpus of 'imperial' law. In this, as in other fields, Sulla's laws were both the summation of previous experience and the beginning of a new chapter in the history of the republic.

The commanders in Spain, 133–82

The extent of the work of the ten commissioners sent to Spain by the senate in 133 after the defeat of Numantia is almost entirely unknown.

[1] Ed. Viereck and Roos, pp. 126–38, and pp. 138–9.

Although some scholars have envisaged them as undertaking a wholesale reorganisation of the administrative machinery of the two provinces, there is no sign of any such alteration in the years which follow. This lack of evidence is hardly surprising, as there is no record of any sort from the two provinces for 10 years after their arrival, but Appian, who alone mentions them, describes them as setting in order the conquests of Scipio and the arrangements made by D. Iunius Brutus, which may involve no more than the defeated Celtiberians of the upper Durius valley and the settlements of Viriathus' Lusitanians.[2]

After the departure of Scipio Aemilianus from Citerior in 133, and of Brutus from Ulterior, either in that year or some years earlier,[3] there is no interest in Spanish affairs either in the sources, or, so far as can be told, by the Romans of the time. Occasional references show what would in any case have been expected, that praetors continued to be sent out to the two *provinciae*, and served there probably for one or two years each.[4] The only exception was the campaign of Q. Caecilius Metellus (*cos.* 123) against the pirates of the Balearic Islands, and although he must have based his attack from Citerior, and subsequently drew 3,000 Romans from Spain to form settlements at Palma and Pollentia on Mallorca, it is not clear that he held the *provincia Hispania Citerior*.[5] Lack of interest in Spain is emphasised by Appian's note that Ser. Galba, whose praetorship in Ulterior is dated to 111, was sent without any troops, despite the rebellions faced by his predecessor, because of the shortage of manpower caused by the Cimbric invasions and the second Sicilian slave war.[6] Shortly after this, probably in 109, Cn. Cornelius Scipio was not permitted by the senate to go to the Spanish *provincia* allotted to him, because it was alleged, according to the story in Valerius Maximus, that

---

[2] Sutherland, *The Romans in Spain* (London, 1939) 88–91, who suggests that the commissioners may have spent several years at their task, and even that the ten ambassadors who were with T. Didius in the mid-90s may have belonged to the same commission. (Appian, *Ib.* 100.434). Appian says of the ten who were sent in 133 only that they brought into peaceful order those things which Scipio had taken and which Brutus before him had subdued or administered. Given the speed with which Gracchus had made his arrangements in 179/8, it is hard to believe that this took 30 years.

[3] Eutropius 4.19 places Brutus' triumph with Scipio's, after the death of Attalus of Pergamum. Degrassi (*Inscr. It.* 13.1.558) therefore dates it to 133, although his last recorded exploit appears in the Livian epitomators in 137/136 (Livy, *per.* 56; *per. Oxy.* 216–17).

[4] Q. Fabius Maximus in 123 (Plut. *C. Gracchus* 6.2 – province unknown); C. Marius in 114 (Plut. *Marius* 6 – Ulterior); L. Calpurnius Piso in 113 or 112 (Appian, *Ib.* 99.429; Cic. *II Verr.* 4.25.56 – in Ulterior); Ser. Galba in 111 (Appian, *Ib.* 99.430). See below Appendix III.

[5] Livy, *per.* 60; Florus 1.43; Orosius 5.13.1; Strabo 3.5.1–2 (pp. 167–8). M. G. Morgan, *CSCA* 2 (1969) 217–31, argues that these pirates had been driven out of southern Gaul and Liguria by Roman activity there. He also believes that Metellus held Citerior in 123–122 (*ibid.* 226–7 n. 43).

[6] Appian, *Ib.* 99.430. For the chronology, see below Appendix III.

his amorality unfitted him for the task.[7] The accuracy of this report, with its strongly moralising tone, may be doubted, but, if true, it may reflect a gradual change in the senate's attitude to the *provinciae* at this period.

In the last decade of the second century reports of activity, at least in Ulterior, become more frequent. Q. Servilius Caepio, who in 105 was to be partly responsible for the disastrous Roman defeat by the Cimbri and the Teutones at Arausio, was praetor in Ulterior in 109, and returned to triumph over the Lusitanians in 107.[8] Brief notices in Obsequens record varying Roman fortunes through the remainder of the decade, and Appian mentions in passing the successes of M. Marius, presumably the brother of the great Marius, against the Lusitanians in about 102. It was presumably in the context of such activity that L. Caesius received the surrender of the *populus* which occupied the settlement at Villavieja, near Alcántara, in 104, which is recorded on the *tabula Alcantarensis*.[9] At the very end of the century L. Cornelius Dolabella secured a sufficient victory for him to be allowed to triumph over the Lusitanians in 98.[10] Citerior, in the mean time, had seen the irruption of the Cimbri in 104, and a successful campaign by C. Coelius Caldus, probably in 100–99.[11]

The absence of the consuls from this fighting is not difficult to explain. The period of renewed successful warfare, from 109 to 99, coincided with the latter stages of the Jugurthine war and the struggle against the Cimbri and the Teutones. It was only after these major preoccupations of the consuls had come to an end that they would have had the leisure, and the need, to seek other fields. It is not surprising therefore that in the early 90s T. Didius (*cos.* 98) and P. Licinius Crassus (*cos.* 97) took the *provinciae* of Citerior and Ulterior respectively. Didius is recorded as having killed 10,000 of the Arevaci, and moved the town of Termesos (perhaps to be identified with Termantia) from high ground to an unfortified position in the plain. He also spent nine months besieging an unknown town, called Kolenda by Appian, and subsequently slaughtered a settlement of Celtiberians made only five years previously by M. Marius. Didius disliked their indulging in brigandage to support themselves on the poor land they had been given, and tricked them into believing they

---

[7] Val. Max. 6.3.3. For the date, Munzer, *RE* IV, 1427. This man was probably the great-grandson of Cn. Scipio, who died in Spain in 211.

[8] Val. Max. 6.9.13; Eutropius 4.27.5; *Inscr. It.* 13.1.85 and 561.

[9] See below Appendix V.

[10] Obsequens 42 (105 BC), 44a (101 BC), 46 (99 BC); Appian, *Ib.* 100.433; *Inscr. It.* 13.1.85 and 562.

[11] Cimbri: Livy, *per.* 67; Obsequens 43; Plut. *Marius* 14. Caldus' campaign is known only from the coin series commemorating his career, issued in 51, one of which depicts a standard with the letters 'HIS' (Crawford, *RRC* no. 437.2a).

would receive some of the Kolendians' land. Once he had them in a convenient defile, he massacred them all, men, women and children.[12] Of Crassus' activities, nothing is known, except that he is said to have crossed to the Cassiterides, the famous 'tin islands', which may mean either the small islands off Cape Finisterre or, perhaps more probably, the Scillies. It may also be he who ordered the Bletonenses not to conduct human sacrifice. Neither of these actions can be responsible for the triumph which he celebrated in 93 over the Lusitanians, just three days after Didius' triumph over the Celtiberians which presupposes a major, but otherwise unknown, military success.[13] Once again, as in the 150s, the factor which decided whether or not consuls went to Spain was whether or not there were other wars, more important, closer at hand, or both, which might occupy them.

Crassus and Didius were both in Spain for an unusually long period by the standards of the second century as a whole, the latter being in Citerior for between five and six years, the former in Ulterior for perhaps four. Since the first sending of praetors to Spain in 197, only two men had held command there for comparable lengths of time, C. Flaminius, sent to Citerior as praetor in 193 and not replaced until 189, and D. Iunius Brutus, who went as consul to Ulterior in 138, returning at some point between 136 and 133. It is difficult to imagine why either Crassus or Didius did not come back to Rome earlier, but even their extended terms cannot be compared with what followed. In Ulterior, Crassus was succeeded by P. Scipio Nasica, praetor probably in 93, the length of whose tenure is unknown, but Didius' replacement was C. Valerius Flaccus, *cos.* 93, who did not return to Rome until his triumph in 81.[14] This was by far the longest period spent in Spain by any Roman commander since the Romans arrived there. Further, he was also responsible for Transalpine Gaul for at least the later part of his command, for Cicero describes him as being there in 83, and his triumph in 81 is recorded by Granius Licinianus as being from Celtiberia and Gaul.[15] The reason for this accumulation of responsibility was the

---

[12] Appian, *Ib.* 99.431–100.436; Livy, *per.* 70; Obsequens 47 and 48; Frontinus 1.8.5, 2.10.1; Sall. *Hist.* 1.88 (M); Plut. *Sert.* 3; *Inscr. It.* 13.1.85 and 562–3.

[13] Cassiterides: Strabo 3.5.11 (p. 176); cf. R. Dion, *Latomus* 11 (1952) 306–14. Human sacrifice: Plut. *quaest. Rom.* 83; C. Cichorius, *Römisches Studien* (Berlin 1922) 7–12. The Bletonenses are probably from Bletisa, near Salamanca (*CIL* 11, 858–9). Triumph: *Schol. Bob.* p. 131 (St); Ascon. 14C; *Inscr. It.* 13.1.85 and 563.

[14] P. Scipio Nasica is recorded by Obsequens, 51, as punishing rebellious chieftains and destroying their towns in 94 BC. As both Crassus and Didius triumphed in June 93, it is probable that Nasica went to Spain in that year. Flaccus was in Citerior (Appian, *Ib.* 100.436–7), so Nasica must have been in Ulterior. On Flaccus' triumph in 81, Granius Licinianus 36 (p. 31–2 F) (cf. Degrassi, *Inscr. It.* 13.1.563). [15] Cic. *Quinct.* 6.24 and 7.28. For triumph, see last note.

disruption in provincial arrangements, caused by the Social War and its aftermath. As in the second century, an unusual extension of the length and scope of a Spanish command resulted from the pressure of wars elsewhere.[16]

The administrative responsibilities of Roman commanders

In this, as in every period we have considered, the sources give the overwhelming impression that the primary concern of the Roman commanders in Spain was with warfare, and such was undoubtedly the case. It was, however, by no means their only activity. Some of the area which they controlled had, by the time of Sulla, experienced a Roman military presence for almost a century and a half, and concerns which had arisen from the need to feed and maintain an army, and to establish relationships with local communities had begun to take on a more institutionalised shape.

The *stipendium* (in the sense of fixed tax) and the levy of 5 per cent on corn, which were probably introduced by Ti. Gracchus in 179, would, by the early first century, be collected on a wider geographical base. Even though the work of the ten senatorial commissioners sent to Spain in 133, and of the similar body which worked with T. Didius in the 90s, may have been restricted to the areas subdued by Scipio, Brutus and Didius, at least in those areas fiscal contributions will have been laid on the inhabitants. Cicero's later remarks about the use of the fixed *stipendium* in Spain suggest that this was the form of tax imposed.[17] That corn was still levied is indicated by the action taken by C. Gracchus against Q. Fabius Maximus, described by Plutarch as propraetor (*antistrategos*) in Spain in 123. Fabius had sent grain to Rome which Gracchus insisted should be sold, and the money sent back to the 'cities'. He also persuaded the senate to censure Fabius for making the government of the province hated and insupportable.[18] Both Fabius' offence and Gracchus' response, through an appeal to the senate, recall the trials of the three former governors from Spain in 171.[19] Although there is too little detail in Plutarch to be at all certain, it may well be that C. Gracchus' accusation in 123 was of a breaking of the agreements made by his father, Ti. Gracchus, in 179.

[16] On the state of provincial allotments at this time, see E. Badian, *Studies in Greek and Roman history* (Oxford 1964) 71–104; and on Flaccus in particular, *ibid.* 88–96, G. Fatás, *Contrebia Belaisca II: Tabula Contrebiensis* (Zaragoza 1980), 111–23. Compare above pp. 132–7.

[17] Cic. *II Verr.* 3.6.12.

[18] Plut. *C. Gracchus* 6.2. [19] Above pp. 114–15.

In addition to the *stipendium* and the half-tithe on corn, there were doubtless other forms of income for the occupying Roman forces. Polybius' account of the silver mines near Cartagena, already examined,[20] provides one clear instance, and there may well have been others which have left still less trace in the sources. Cato's interest in iron and in salt[21] probably resulted in a regular income to the Roman state through the second century, though the amount collected and the means of collection must remain pure speculation. It is likely, as argued above for the early and middle part of the second century, that the money was paid to the quaestor in the province, rather than direct to the *aerarium* in Rome or to a *societas publicanorum*.

By the beginning of the first century BC, Rome had made her presence felt in Spain not only through her military activity and the collection of taxes, but also by alterations to the pattern of settlement. Once again the close relationship between individual commanders and the townships settled by them and the lack of involvement or of recognition by the governing bodies of the state in Rome are observable in the late second and early first centuries. Neither Valentia nor Brutobriga, both founded by D. Iunius Brutus, in about 138 (perhaps the former being for Roman and Italian veterans, the latter for Lusitanians) seem to have been accorded any official status at the time.[22] Similarly Palma and Pollentia, which, although not on the mainland of Spain, were settled by Q. Metellus in 123 or 122 with people whom Strabo calls Romans, are described by Pliny as *oppida civium Romanorum*, which suggests that they were not given the privileged status of colonies when they were founded.[23] Perhaps the most striking case of the gap between the actions of commanders in Spain with regard to recognition and status of Spanish communities and the attitude of the senate is found on the famous decree of Cn. Pompeius Strabo, by which in 89 BC he granted citizenship under the lex Julia to a squadron of Spanish horsemen from the Ebro valley, who had served

---

[20] Above pp. 120–1.

[21] Above pp. 90–1.

[22] D. Fletcher Valls, *Arch. preh. Lev.* 10 (1963) 197–9 believes that Livy, *per.* 55, who states that Brutus gave lands and a town to those 'qui sub Viriatho militaverant' refers to soldiers serving 'in the time of Viriathus' but this is improbable (see R. Wiegels, *Chiron* 4 (1974) 162–3). For the status of Valentia and Brutobriga see Galsterer, *Untersuchungen* 12 and 15; Knapp, *Aspects* 125–31; R. Wiegels, *op. cit.* 153–76.

[23] Pliny, *NH* 3.5.77. Strabo 3.5.42 (pp. 167–8); Wilson, *Emigration* 22; Galsterer, *Untersuchungen*, 10. Knapp, *Aspects*, 131–9, believes that Palma and Pollentia were citizen colonies, but cf. Pliny, *NH* 3.3.18, where he explicitly distinguishes *oppida civium Romanorum* from *coloniae*, cities with the old Latin right, towns with a *foedus* and those paying *stipendium*. This also undermines the argument of A. Balil, *IX Congreso Nacional de Arqueologia* (Zaragoza 1966) 312–14, 318–19, that the towns were *coloniae*. For the meaning of *oppida CR* in Pliny, see A. N. Sherwin-White, *The Roman citizenship*[2] (Oxford 1973) 344–50.

with him at Asculum.[24] Whereas most of the Spaniards listed are called by their own native names, three from Ilerda have Latin names, although the names of their fathers are native. This must mean that Ilerda had some status, otherwise unknown, which separated it from the other towns of the region, and that they had therefore adopted Roman names, even though they were not Roman citizens. It has been suggested that they might already have had Latin rights, but if this is the case it is the only instance of Latin rights being given to such a community. It is more probable that their use of the names resulted from a status given not by Rome but by a Roman commander.[25]

The use of such Roman and Italian names depended not on the introduction of Roman institutions, such as colonies or grants of citizenship but on the fact that Romans and Italians were in Spain, and there acquired clients. As often, the prolonged presence of an army led to contacts with the native population, which had already resulted in the group of 4,000 people, the offspring of Roman soldiers and Spanish women, who in 171 petitioned the senate for a place in which to live.[26] This cannot have been the entire number of such people, since the extent of their organisation, which made it possible for the embassy to be sent to Rome, indicates that they were drawn from a fairly cohesive group. It is likely that they were all from Ulterior, as they were settled at Carteia in the extreme south. There must have been similar products of Romano-Spanish relations in Citerior also. Secondly, it is likely that the four thousand comprised the males within the group. Not only must there have been therefore a substantial number of such people in Spain in the 170s, but the circumstances which had produced them did not alter over the next 90 years. The continued presence of Roman and Italian soldiers, who, at least in the middle of the second century had to spend as long as six years in Spain before returning to Italy, is bound to have increased the number of Romano-Spanish *hybridae*.[27]

---

[24] *ILLRP* 515.

[25] Degrassi, *ILLRP* 515; N. Criniti, *L'epigrafe di Asculum di Gn. Pompeo Strabone* (Milan 1970) 189–91. The only community known to have Latin rights at this date is Carteia, whose situation was unique (see above p. 119). The Ilerdenses may have been acting as Roman citizens with no legal right, as did the Anauni and others in the region of Tridentum before Claudius granted them citizenship in AD 46 (*ILS* 206). For a similar explanation of this inscription, and other instances see E. Badian, *Foreign clientelae* 256–7. On the spread of Roman *nomina* in Spain during the republic, R. C. Knapp, *Ancient Society* 9 (1978) 187–222; S. L. Dyson, *Ancient Society* 11/12 (1980/1981) 257–99.

[26] Livy 43.1.1–4.

[27] Appian, *Ib.* 78.334 (140 BC). E. Gabba, *Republican Rome: the army and the allies* (Oxford 1976) 23, believes that this is a reduction in the period of service, but points out that in Spain the service was continuous rather than annual (cf. R. E. Smith, *Service in the post-Marian army* (Manchester 1958) 7).

In addition to military personnel and their offspring, there will also have been Roman and Italian civilians. The numbers of such men is a matter of controversy. Diodorus speaks of a multitude of Italians arriving to exploit the silver resources,[28] and Strabo mentions 3,000 'Romans' taken by Q. Metellus in 123/122 from Spain to the Balearic Islands.[29] We cannot be certain exactly who these last were, and the unlikelihood of there being so many Roman civilians available and willing to colonise Mallorca from the mainland at this date has led to them being identified as veteran settlers, as Romano-Spanish *hybridae* and even as Italians who had intended to go to C. Gracchus' overseas *coloniae* and been transferred to the Balearics when Gracchus' scheme failed.[30] There is no way to tell precisely what Strabo meant, still less whether he was right. Certainly Sertorius was to find a number of Roman residents ready to join him when he came to build up his forces in 82 just after his arrival.[31] These, unlike the 2,600 men, whom, according to Plutarch, he 'called Romans', and who joined him in 80,[32] were not driven out of Italy by Sulla's return and presumably had already settled in the area. Similarly the Roman residents in both provinces played an important part in the wars between Pompey and Caesar.[33] Unfortunately, numbers for the early first century simply do not exist, nor does the evidence on which to base an intelligent estimate. It is notable, though hardly surprising, that those individuals with Roman names who appear from among the civilian population from time to time are almost always from cities known to have been settled by the Romans.[34] More importantly, recent surveys of the inscriptional evidence from Spain have illustrated a widespread assumption of Roman names by native Spaniards during the republican period. As already noted, this suggests that in Spain, Roman nomenclature did not necessarily imply the possession of Roman citizenship, and that the privileged status that the use of such a name conferred was a gift not of the Roman senate and people, but of individual Romans present in the area and, pre-eminently, of the proconsul himself.[35] In the reign of the emperor Claudius a prohibition had to be issued to prevent the use by non-citizens

---

[28] Diodorus 5.36.
[29] Strabo 3.5.1–2 (pp. 167–8). Above n. 23.
[30] Wilson, *Emigration* 22; Knapp, *Aspects* 136–8; A. Balil [n. 23] 310–12.
[31] Plut. *Sertorius* 6.9.   [32] Plut. *Sertorius* 12.2.
[33] Wilson, *Emigration* 32–40.
[34] Thus, in this period, C. Marcius, a Spaniard from Italica in 143 (Appian, *Ib.* 66.282) and the three cavalrymen from Ilerda (above nn. 24 and 25). The oddly named Curius and Appuleius, two robber chieftans in Ulterior in 141, do not conform to this pattern (Appian, *Ib.* 68.289). For later instances, see Knapp, *Aspects* 154–6.
[35] See the articles by Knapp and Dyson, [n. 25].

of Roman names, and particularly of the names of Roman families, but an edict of Claudius himself in AD 46 shows that in northern Italy the assumption of the privileges of citizenship, including Roman names, by non-citizens was going on, and, in the case recorded at least, led to the official grant of citizenship by the emperor.[36]

Although the characteristic lack of concern by the senate which underlies this situation makes any attempt to identify and distinguish Romanised Spaniards from native Romans and Italians resident in Spain difficult, the distribution of such names does imply fairly widespread acceptance of Roman ideas in the valleys of the Ebro and the Baetis, at least to the extent of adopting Roman names.[37] Once again, the shaping of the Roman provinces in Spain proves to be the result of the activities of Roman commanders, not the policy of the senate.

The other area in which the Spanish governors of the late second and early first centuries must have had contact with the non-Roman inhabitants of the areas assigned to them was in the legal and juridical sphere. Indeed it is from this period that the first substantive evidence has survived of proconsuls involved with such activities in Spain. Cicero tells the story of L. Calpurnius Piso Frugi, known to have been governor in Ulterior *c.* 113/112, who broke his gold ring, and had a replacement made publicly by a goldsmith before his official seat in the forum at Corduba, from gold weighed out by the workman on the spot.[38] Although this has been related by some scholars to the requirements of the *lex de repetundis*, there is nothing in Cicero's story to suggest this.[39] Piso seems simply to be making a demonstration of his own probity in a deliberately public and judicial setting. However, that he used such a setting itself implies that he was called upon to act as a source of law. A recently discovered bronze tablet from Botorrita, in the Ebro valley, some 20 kilometres south of Zaragoza, shows a Roman commander at work in just such a legal context. In 87 BC C. Valerius Flaccus set up a judgement to be made by the 'senate' of the town Contrebia Balaisca over a claim by a people called the Salluienses to have the right to construct a watercourse through the land of a people, called the Sosinestani, despite the opposition of yet a third group, the Allavonenses. The case is set out on the bronze

---

[36] Suetonius, *Div. Claud.* 25; *ILS* 206 (note esp. lines 35–6; nominaque ea, quae habuerunt antea tamquam cives Romani ita habere permittam); Mommsen, *StR* III, 213.

[37] Dyson [n. 25] 296. On Romans and Italians in Spain during this period, see Wilson, *Emigration* 22–7 and 29–42; E. Gabba, *Athenaeum* nos. 32 (1954) 289–99 (= *Republican Rome, the army and the allies* (Oxford 1976) 105–8; Brunt, *Italian manpower* Ch. 14.

[38] Cic. *II Verr.* 4.25.56–7. On the chronology, see below Appendix III.

[39] As pointed out, in a different context, by A. W. Lintott, *ZSS* 98 (1981) 176 n. 63.

in a form clearly derived from the formulary procedure of the praetor's court in Rome, despite the fact that none of the parties to the case held Roman citizenship, and that such forms were therefore not required.[40] Once again the proconsul was free to choose the means most acceptable to himself, apparently unhampered by restrictions imposed on him from Rome. It was the decision of the local commander which shaped both the relationships between the Romans and the provincial communities, and the institutions which gradually became the basis of those relationships. There was a long way to go before the situation was reached which Strabo describes, in which the governor of the *provincia Tarraconensis* under Augustus resided on the coast during the winter, dispensing justice particularly in Tarraco and Nova Carthago, and spent his summers travelling the interior, looking to see what needed to be put right.[41] Flaccus had indeed been 'putting things right' in his province, but this had included, a year or two previously, killing some 10,000 rebellious Celtiberians (if Appian's figures are to be trusted) and executing the ringleaders of a group among the populace of the city of Belgeda, who had burnt their own senators in their senate house, because they had been slow to join the uprising.[42] Although the commanders of the early first century were still essentially military commanders at war, the new inscription shows the attention paid to juridical matters. No doubt these were not unconnected with military requirements. The Salluienses, who were successful in the action recorded, were the same who gave their name to the squadron of horsemen enfranchised for their valour by Cn. Pompeius Strabo in 89.[43]

There is no evidence that the board of 10 commissioners who seem to have been active in Spain in 133 and again in the mid-90s[44] attempted to lay down regulations even of the provisional and only quasi-legal sort known as a *lex provinciae*.[45] Indeed the only limitation in law upon the Spanish governors was the possibility of their being tried for *repetundae* or for *maiestas* on their return. This does not relate, except incidentally, to the juridical role of the governors.

The work of the Roman commanders in Spain had thus grown with the geographical extension of Roman control, and with the inevitable

[40] G. Fatás, *Contrebia Belaisca II: Tabula Contrebiensis* (Zaragoza 1980); J. S. Richardson, *JRS* 73 (1983) 33–41 (where further bibliography is cited); P. Birks, A. Rodger and J. S. Richardson, *JRS* 74 (1984) 45–73.

[41] Strabo 3.4.20 (p. 167).   [42] Appian, *Ib.* 100.436–7.

[43] *ILLRP* 515.   [44] Appian, *Ib.* 94.428, 100.434.

[45] On the *lex provinciae* in general, see B. D. Hoyos, *Antichthon* 7 (1973) 47–53; A. W. Lintott, *G & R* 28 (1981) 58–61.

effects of a prolonged Roman presence in the peninsula. The raising of money and other levies, which seems to have begun with the need to feed, clothe and pay an army, had become formalised and institutionalised. The number of Spaniards who looked to the commander, whether for protection or for a favourable verdict, had increased immensely since Cn. Scipio had first made contact with peoples north of the Ebro in 218. Even in the conditions of warfare which dominate the accounts of the activities of the Spanish governors in the 90s and 80s, they were engaged also in work recognisably similar to that of a provincial governor of the age of Cicero or Augustus. The defining of the boundaries of this work, and the creation of the institutional machinery to carry it out, seem to have been left entirely in the hands of the men to whom the senate had assigned the *provinciae*.

Senatorial attitudes and responsibilities

It would not be accurate to say, however, that the senate had no concern whatever for what was going on in the Iberian peninsula in the half-century before the return of Sulla in 82. There are indeed some signs that in this period the senate took a more responsible view of the *provinciae*.

On matters within the areas themselves, M. Marius is said to have received senatorial approval for the settlement of his Celtiberian allies in or about 102, though this may mean no more than the formal clause, found as early as L. Aemilius Paullus' decree of 189, that the senate and people could revoke a grant.[46] As noted above, this clause suggests rather non-involvement by the senate than any active role.[47] Appian's mention of the senate suggests, however, a more active participation in the arrangements made by a commander than has been seen hitherto. Also in this period comes the first indication of road-building in the west. In Spain itself a pair of milestones record the work of Q. Fabius Q. f. Labeo *pro consule*, near Lerida, and another three, one from north of Barcelona towards Caldas de Montbuy and two near Vich, give the name of M'. Sergius M'. f., also *pro consule*.[48] Fabius' road probably ran from the

---

[46] Appian, *Ib.* 100.433; cf. *ILLRP* 514, lines 6–7, and *tab. Alcantarensis*, lines 10–11 (below Appendix v).

[47] Above p. 118.

[48] *ILLRP* 461 (Fabius) and 462 (Sergius); A. Balil, *Fasti Archeologici* 14 (1959) (1962) no. 4042 (Sergius). For Sergius' milestones, see now G. Fabre, M. Mayer and I. Rodà, *Inscriptions romaines de Catalogne* I (Paris 1984) nos. 175, 176 and 181.

Mediterranean coast, westwards up the Ebro valley, Sergius' also from the coastline, perhaps at Badalona (Roman Baetulo) or Mataró (Iluro), at both of which there are traces of Roman settlement from the very beginning of the first century BC, northwards towards Vich, the centre for the Ausetani.[49] There is no certainty about the date of the roads, but epigraphic and prosopographic considerations and the building of other Roman roads outside Italy in the last thirty years of the second century, including the *via Domitia*, the land link from Italy to Spain (*c.* 120–118 BC), have suggested a date towards the end of the century.[50] Almost certainly expenditure on road-building meant the expenditure of public money, and it is likely that this would require senatorial approval. Although their construction was intended for military purposes, these roads may also indicate a more immediate senatorial concern for the state of affairs in Spain. The oddly disconnected location of these roads, if this is not merely a result of the fragmentary state of our knowledge, perhaps shows that the interests and needs of particular Roman commanders dictated their building, rather than any idea of a coherent pattern of routes throughout the peninsula; but this also might be expected given the relationship already observed between the senate and the men being sent to Spain through the second century.

Two other anecdotes reveal senatorial concern with the behaviour of the proconsuls. The reprimand issued on the motion of C. Gracchus to Fabius, who sent corn to Rome from Spain in 123, because of the extent to which he had made his government of the area insupportable to the local inhabitants, was action taken directly by the authorities in Rome, apparently without the need for the investigatory procedure which had been used in 171.[51] Moreover the communities from which Fabius obtained the corn did receive financial recompense for it, at least if the senate's decree was obeyed, which does not seem to have happened in 171.

The second story is that recorded in Valerius Maximus of Cn. Cornelius Scipio who, probably in the last decade of the second century, was forbidden by the senate to go to the Spanish *provincia* which had been assigned to him, on the grounds that he did not know how to behave with propriety.[52] Although Valerius is hardly the most reliable source, he at

---

[49] The distances on Fabius' milestones provide no obvious terminus for his road (it cannot be the Pyrenees, as suggested by Hübner, *CIL* II, p. 651, which are too far distant). On Sergius' road, see the suggestion of Balil, that it ran to Mataró. On Badalona, see J. Cuyas Tolosa, *VII Congr. Nacional de Arqueología* (Zaragoza 1962) 358ff; J. Guitart Duran, *Baetulo* (Badalona 1976).

[50] Munzer, *RE* VI, 775; cf. T. P. Wiseman, *PBSR* 38 (1970) 140 n. 150.

[51] Plut. *C. Gracchus* 6.2. On 171, see above p. 114.

[52] Val. Max. 6.3.3: 'Nam cum ei Hispania provincia sorte obvenisset, ne illuc iret decrevit [*sc.* senatus], adiecta causa, quod recte facere nesciret.'

least believed that the senate took this action in order to avoid the depredations that the Spaniards would suffer if Scipio went to his *provincia*, for he comments that Scipio received his condemnation without serving in the provinces and without the use of the *lex repetundarum*. If this at all reflects the feeling of the senate at the time, it indicates that the possibility that an offence against the provisions of the *repetundae* legislation might occur could be used as an argument in advance of any such offence being committed. This shows that the expectations that the senate had of a governor at this period included propriety over financial dealings with the inhabitants of the provinces.

These two incidents, separated though they are from any context which might help in their interpretation, suggest that the senate was acquiring a sense of responsibility towards the inhabitants of the areas within which it stationed the armies and magistrates of Rome, even to the extent of being prepared to take pre-emptive action against a magistrate who might disturb the security of his *provincia* by excessive greed. This attitude is also exemplified by the great *lex repetundarum* of the *tabula Bembina*, identified with the law proposed by C. Gracchus in 123.[53] Although it is clear that some senators were opposed to Gracchus' bill, the sources agree in ascribing to the senate as a whole a sense of disquiet at the activities of provincial commanders, and an acknowledgement that some action should be taken to restrain them.[54]

Legislation on provincial commanders and Roman experience in Spain

Gracchus' law is perhaps the best-known instance of legislation aimed at such provincial commanders; it is by no means the only one from the later years of the second century. The recently discovered fragments of a law regulating Roman foreign policy in the eastern Mediterranean, found at Cnidos,[55] and almost certainly the same law as that inscribed on the monument of L. Aemilius Paullus at Delphi, reveal two such enactments. A lex Porcia, proposed by a praetor, M. Porcius Cato, in February of the same year as the Delphi/Cnidos law itself was passed (i.e. either 100 or 101 BC) and cited on the inscription, forbade a commander to raise troops

---

[53] On the content of the *tabula Bembina*, see most recently Lintott [n. 39] 177–81; A. N. Sherwin-White, *JRS* 72 (1981) 18–31.

[54] Plut. *C. Gracchus* 5.2–6.1; Appian, BC 1.22.92.

[55] Published by M. Hassall, M. H. Crawford and J. Reynolds, *JRS* 64 (1974) 195–220.

outside his *provincia*, to lead troops out of his *provincia*, or even (though the text is uncertain here) to be outside his *provincia* at all with ill intent.[56] The lex Antonia *de Termessibus*, dated probably to 68 BC, forbade commanders to billet troops on Termessus, or to demand that they be supplied with anything other than what was allowed by the lex Porcia.[57] Secondly the Delphi/Cnidos law itself enlarged on the lex Porcia by specifying that a commander appointed by the law should not leave the *provincia* to which he was assigned without the permission of the senate, and that he should restrain those with him, presumably his own staff.[58] Far more specific instructions are given to the magistrate or pro-magistrate who, as a result of the law itself, or by senatorial decree, was assigned to the *provincia* of Macedonia. He was to go to the Caeneic Chersonnese, recently seized by T. Didius, as rapidly as possible, collect public revenues there and protect the friends and allies of the Roman people, and was explicitly instructed to spend at least 60 days each year in the area until he was replaced.[59] Although this law shows every sign of originating from the group of 'populares' of whom Glaucia and Saturninus are the best known,[60] such control of Roman commanders abroad and of the details of their activity is very much of a piece with what has already been noted in Spain in this same period.

The most substantial body of legislation on the provinces did not appear for another twenty years. L. Cornelius Sulla, in 81 BC in the course of his dictatorship, drafted a *lex de maiestate* which seems, for the first time, to have brought together a number of offences which might be committed by provincial commanders.[61] Cicero instances leaving the *provincia*, leading an army out from the *provincia*, conducting a war on one's own initiative and attacking a foreign kingdom without instructions from the Roman people or the senate, as having been forbidden by several earlier laws, and explicitly by the lex Cornelia *de maiestate* and the lex Iulia *de pecuniis repetundis*.[62] When in 51 Cicero reminded his predecessor as proconsul in Cilicia, Appius Claudius Pulcher, that he had to leave the area within thirty days of his successor's arrival, he cites a lex Cornelia

---

[56] Cnidos III, 11.4–9 (*JRS* 64 (1974) 202), with fresh readings communicated by Michael Crawford and Joyce Reynolds. The date of Cato's law is now read as πρὸ ἡμέρων γ' τῶν Φηραλίων, i.e. 19 February. For the year, see J-L. Ferrary, *MEFRA* 89 (1977) 619–60, Lintott [n. 39] 191–2. On the lex Porcia, see Lintott [n. 39] 191–7.

[57] *FIRA* I. No. 11, 11.13–17.   [58] Cnidos III, 11.9–15.

[59] Cnidos V, 11.6–31.

[60] Hassall, Crawford and Reynolds [n. 55] 218–19; Ferrary [n. 56] 654–60; *contra* A. Giovannini and E. Grzybek, *Mus. Helv.* 35 (1978) 33–47.

[61] On the lex Cornelia *de maiestate* see Mommsen, *Strafrecht* 557–8; R. Bauman, *The 'crimen maiestatis' in the Roman republic and Augustan principate* (Johannesburg 1977) 68–87. For the sources, see Broughton, *MRR* II, 75.   [62] Cic. *Pis.* 21.50.

as the relevant statute, and the fact that this matter was later covered by
the lex Iulia *maiestatis* indicates that Cicero's reference was to Sulla's
maiestas law.[63] A little later in his correspondence with Appius, Cicero
again cites a lex Cornelia, which forbade excessive expenditure made by
provincial communities in sending embassies to Rome to congratulate and
thank a commander who had already left the province, and this may also
belong to the *lex de maiestate*.[64] Indeed it would appear that Sulla's law
was, so far as our information goes, concerned entirely with the activities
of holders of *imperium* in the provinces, and it is also likely that this was
the only law be proposed which dealt in this sort of detail with such
men.[65]

Clearly Sulla was drawing on the provisions of earlier laws when he
drafted his *lex de maiestate*. Not only is this indicated by Cicero, but the
epigraphic references to the lex Porcia discussed above indicate that it
covered some of the same ground. However, behind the lex Porcia and
whatever other laws were used by Sulla in 81, lay the experience of the
senate over the previous century in dealing with provincial commanders.
Inevitably much of that experience came from Spain, since there was
more fighting in Spain through the second century than anywhere else.
The problems of controlling the extension of warfare beyond provincial
boundaries arose early in Spain, where there were in any case no clear
divisions on the ground, whatever the senate might think. The order to
the first praetors, sent to the peninsula in 197, to fix the boundary between
Hispania Citerior and Hispania Ulterior, the refusal to grant M. Helvius
a triumph in 195 and the apparent disregard of any such provincial *termini*
shown by Cato in 195/4 and by C. Flaminius and M. Fulvius Nobilior
in 193–191[66] instance the difficulties of restraining a commander operating
so far from Rome, and the senate's desire that *provinciae* should be
delimited. Similarly the need to clarify the process of transfer of a
provincia on the arrival of a new commander was recognised in the first
half of the second century. Cato is known to have spoken on the subject,
and, on at least one occasion, when in 180 Ti. Gracchus replaced

[63] Cic. *ad fam.* 3.6.3; D. 48.4.2 and 3.

[64] Cic. *ad fam.* 3.10.6 – not, as Bauman [n. 61] 79 a restriction on expenditure by Appius' own
staff.

[65] Bauman [n. 61] 80–3. Lintott [n. 39] 193–7 suggests that the *leges repetundarum* also contained
provisions on this type from Servilius Glaucia's law onwards (as the lex Iulia of 59 BC certainly did),
but there is nothing in the evidence to compel such an interpretation, and the lack of explicit citation
of particular delicts by Cicero in the Verrines suggests that the *crimen repetundarum* remained
unspecific until Caesar. This may also explain Cicero's placing of the two laws side by side as
containing explicit exclusions at *Pis.* 21.50.

[66] On the order to fix boundaries see above pp. 77–8; Helvius, p. 89; Cato, pp. 85–9; Flaminius
and Nobilior, pp. 97–8.

Q. Fulvius Flaccus in Citerior, a situation arose which might have caused concern.[67] The more serious matter of initiating war without the permission of the senate and people also occurred in Spain. Indeed it is most improbable that any official declaration of war by senate and people was made for any of the Spanish wars, and the different treatment meted out to Lucullus in 149 and to Aemilius Lepidus Porcina in 136 seems to show that the senate only gradually became aware of the dangers involved.[68] In his legislation about the *provinciae*, as in so much else, Sulla was attempting to solve the problems of the previous century.

[67] Cato fr. 223 (Malc.). On Flaccus and Gracchus, Livy 40.39–40.
[68] See Rich, *Declaring war* 15, and my remarks in *JRS* 69 (1979) 159. On Lucullus and Lepidus, see above pp. 149–51.

CHAPTER 8

Rome, Spain and imperialism

The Spain from which C. Valerius Flaccus returned to Rome in 81, at the end of his protracted term in Hispania Citerior and Transalpine Gaul, was from the Roman viewpoint a very different area from that to which P. Scipio had been sent in 218. Scipio went to his *provincia* to fight the Carthaginians and it is likely that most members of the senate at that time had rather less interest in Spain as such than the average member of the British House of Commons had in the Sahara desert in 1942, at the time of the battle of El Alamein. By the 80s BC the two *provinciae* contained substantial numbers of Romans and Italians, both military and civilian, and many of the indigenous communities had developed close links with these representatives of the Roman power.

Apart from the army itself, this Roman presence must have been most obvious in the settlements of Roman origin, both those such as Valentia (modern Valencia) which appear to have been founded on previously unoccupied sites, and those in which an already existing indigenous population was either replaced or absorbed.[1] Most of these settlements seem to belong to this second category, and it is possible that at Italica and Corduba, two separate communities, Iberian and Italian, lived in distinct quarters.[2] Of the archaeological remains discovered so far, there is little to suggest that these towns would have displayed very much 'Romanness' in the grandeur of their buildings,[3] but by the early years of the first century the influence of Hellenised Roman architecture was already being seen in at least some indigenous communities. In the Celtiberian town of Contrebia Belaisca (modern Botorrita) there existed, probably by the end of the second century, a large two-storey building, fronted with columns in stucco. The purpose of this building is as yet

---

[1] See the useful survey by M. Jose Pena Gimeno, 'Apuntes y observaciones sobre las primeras fundaciones romanas en Hispania', *Estudios de la antigüedad* 1 (1984) 47–85.

[2] Italica: R. Corzo Sánchez, 'Organizacion de territorio y evolucion urbana en Italica', in *Italica: actas de las primeras journadas sobre excavaciones en Italica* (Excavaciones arqueologicas en España 121, 1982) 299–319, esp. 306–10. Corduba: A. M. Vicent, 'Ultimos hallazgos romanos en Corduba' *XII Congr. nacional de arqueológia* (Zaragoza 1973) 676–9; R. C. Knapp, *Roman Corduba* (California Univ. Class. Studies 30, 1983) 13.   [3] Pena Gimeno [n. 1] 82.

unknown, and its plan is certainly not 'classical', but it is clearly influenced in its details by the Greek architectural styles adopted by the Romans. The masons who constructed the columns were not, however, either Greek or Roman, for they marked the capitals and bases of the columns with Iberian letters.[4] It was, in all probability, to this building that the Latin inscription recording the decision of the 'senatus Contrebiensis' in the case of the watercourse dispute between the Allavonenses and the Salluienses was affixed.[5] The presence of this inscription and the nature of the building indicate the influence of a Graeco-Roman style of urbanisation, at least in this site on the southern edge of the middle Ebro valley. The same is likely to have been true of those native settlements founded by the Romans, such as Gracchurris, further up the Ebro, and the *colonia Latina libertinorum* at Carteia, in the extreme south.

By the early years of the first century there were also Romans and Italians in certain areas of Spain, living in villas in the countryside around some urban settlements. This is particularly true of the rich lands of modern Catalonia in the north-east. A recent survey of an area of 210 square kilometres around Badalona (Roman Baetulo), near Barcelona, reveals some 260 sites, which are certain or possible locations of villas, of which the majority originated in the late second and early first centuries BC. The heaviest density of such sites is along the coastal strip, and many seem, from the evidence of the pottery found there, to have been flourishing and wealthy establishments at an early date.[6] The relative proximity to Italy, the fertility of the land and the increase in Roman military control inland will have made this area an attractive proposition. The same period, as has been noted, saw the founding of several other towns, including Baetulo itself, and also increased activity at already established sites, such as Italica.[7]

Economic links from Spain to Italy and the eastern Mediterranean had grown considerably by the first century. At Nova Carthago, pottery from the Aegean area in substantial quantities indicates contacts between the last third of the second century and the first third of the first, which no doubt resulted from the role of the port as a centre for the export of the

---

[4] A. Beltrán and A. Tovar, *Contrebia Belaisca I: el bronce de Botorrita* (Zaragoza 1982) 23–31.
[5] See above p. 164.
[6] Marta Prevosti Monclús, *Cronologia i poblament a l'area rural de Baetulo* (Badalona 1981).
[7] Above pp. 161–4. Italica: Pena Gimeno [n. 1] 50–3. Though the conclusions of J. M. Luzon, *Excavationes en Italica* (Excavaciones arqueologicas en España 78, 1973), that there was no distinction in culture between the inhabitants of Italica and the surrounding Iberians until the end of the second century, are now in doubt in the light of subsequent excavations, there is evidence of greater 'Romanization' at that date (M. Bendala Galán, 'Excavaciones en el cerro de los Palacios', in *Italica: actas de las primeras journadas* [*op. cit.* n. 2 above] 29–73; R. Corzo Sanchez, *ibid.* 306–11.

production of the silver/lead mines both of the immediate vicinity and of the Castulo region, at the head of the valley of the Guadalquivir.[8] There must also have been a considerable trade in agricultural produce and fish products, for which Spain was famous.[9] The export of wine from Italy probably never reached the enormous proportions of the trade into Gaul, but Dressel 1 amphorae, which were used for the shipment of wine in the late second and first centuries BC are found in both Roman and Iberian sites, especially down the east coast and in the valleys of the Ebro and the Guadalquivir.[10] One, from a pre-Roman village near Barcelona, carries the consular date of 119 BC.[11] Even more significant, as an indication of Roman influence and Roman settlement in Spain, is the production on the Catalan coast of local imitations of Dressel 1 amphorae.[12] These were no doubt used before the end of the first century BC by the occupants of the villas which had begun to be established in Catalonia at the end of the second century for the shipment of their own produce. A similar concentration of activity in these areas is apparent from the coin hoards from this period, which show Roman denarii (as opposed to the locally produced Iberian type), minted in the last two decades of the second and the first decade of the first centuries, in contexts which suggest that they have been brought from Italy by private individuals. The regions in which these hoards have been found are almost exclusively Catalonia, the eastern coast, and the Guadalquivir valley.[13]

This picture of the Roman involvement in Spain in the early first century, brief and partial though it is (and, because of the paucity of evidence, is bound to be), illustrates clearly that at that date Spain had become far more a part of the Roman world than it had been in the last decades of the third century. Roman taxation, Roman law and Roman soldiers, to say nothing of the considerable numbers of Roman and Italian civilians, were all to be found in the two *provinciae*, and although the influence of geography on the spread of the Roman presence meant that these phenomena were concentrated on the eastern coast, from Catalonia

---

[8] J. Perez Ballester, 'Ceramicas helenisticas del mediterraneo oriental en Cartagena', *XVI Congr. nacional de arqueológia* (Zaragoza 1983) 519–32.

[9] For a general survey of the economy of the republican period, see J. M. Blazquez Martinez, *Historia de España* (2nd ed., Madrid 1982) 295–332.

[10] Gaul: A. Tchernia, 'Italian wine in Gaul', in P. Garnsey, K. Hopkins and C. R. Whittaker (eds), *Trade in the ancient economy* (London 1983) 85–104. Spain: M. Beltrán Lloris, *Las anforas romanas en España* (Zaragoza 1970) 317–29.

[11] J. M. Nolla, *Cypsela* 2 (1977) 221–2.

[12] R. Pascual Guasch, 'Centros de produccion y difusion geografica en un tipo de anfora', *VII Congr. nacional de arqueológia* (Zaragoza 1962) 334–45.

[13] M. H. Crawford, *Coinage and money under the Roman republic* (London 1985) 97–8.

to Cartagena, and in the valley of the Guadalquivir, this must have affected the view of Spain from Rome. Although there was still a long way to go before reaching the complex organisation described by Pliny (which probably belongs to the period of Augustus),[14] *Hispania* was, by the time of Sulla, more than the name of a battlefield.

As the nature of the Roman presence in Spain changed through the second century, so inevitably did the senate's role with regard to the two *provinciae*. While the Hannibalic war was being fought, and through the first half of the second century, the main functions of the senate were to allot the two *provinciae* as areas of military responsibility, to provide the necessary resources to the magistrates and pro-magistrates who held that responsibility, and to reward military success by the award of triumphs and *ovationes*. During the wars in Lusitania and Celtiberia in the second half of the century, senatorial involvement in such matters as the relations between Roman commanders and the inhabitants of Spain began to intrude in areas which had previously been left entirely to the holder of the *provincia* concerned, and this involvement was to begin to take legislative form in the 50 years which led up to Sulla's *lex de maiestate*.

Although this development constituted a weakening of the autonomy of the magistrates and pro-magistrates sent out to the *provinciae*, nevertheless the form taken by such control of the provinces reveals how central that autonomy was to Roman political practice. All the provisions of which we have evidence, the *leges repetundarum*, the lex Porcia, the law from Delphi and Cnidos, Sulla's enactments, as well as the occasional stories of senatorial intervention from the literary sources, all these consist of attempts not to influence or direct the affairs of the provinces, but to circumscribe the actions of the provincial commanders. The method employed to effect the will and policy of the senate and people overseas was not the establishment of a Colonial Office, or some institution in Rome to keep a watch on the implementation of senatorial policy, but a series of courts to administer *ex post facto* punishment to those men who had overstepped the boundaries placed by statute on their otherwise unlimited powers.

This understanding of what the *provinciae* were has important consequences for the practice of Roman imperialism through the second century. First it meant that the shaping of Roman policy in Spain and of the institutions which embodied that policy was in the hands of the individual commanders in the two *provinciae*. Decisions about relations with local tribes, about the administration of justice or about the starting

[14] Pliny, *NH* 3.6–30; 4.113–18. Above pp. 3–4.

and ending of wars were all of this type, and there must have been many more instances of this which have left no trace in the literary or archaeological record. The recently discovered *deditio*, received by L. Caesius in 104, and the *formulae* approved by C. Valerius Flaccus for the settlement of a water dispute on the *tabula Contrebiensis* illustrate the work of such men, and also the paucity of our knowledge about that work.[15] Although there may well have been occasions when the senate was involved in events in Spain, the examples of representations from the peninsula which have survived in the literary record[16] and the complete absence of epigraphic evidence (though it must be admitted that very few inscriptions of any kind have survived from this period) suggest that the importance of senatorial involvement cannot be compared with that of the men the senate placed in command of the *provinciae*. The changes in the nature of the Roman presence in Spain between the late third and early first centuries are largely the result of particular decisions taken in response to circumstances which confronted particular Roman commanders or (as with the growth of Italian and Roman settlement in the late second and first centuries) the consequences of those decisions.

The lack of any state direction of trade and exploitation of natural resources by private individuals, which is not particularly surprising in the context of the ancient world, is very striking indeed in comparison with the policy of imperial powers of more recent times. Even at the beginning of European expansion in the early modern period, almost the first act of the Spanish crown, in response to the discovery of the New World, was to institute the Casa de Contratacion in 1503, to control shipping and license trade with the colonies, and the Portuguese had already set up their Casa da Mina to fulfil a similar purpose in the middle of the fifteenth century.[17] This is not to say that Roman senators in the second century had no interest or involvement in trade, still less that members of the Roman nobility were disinclined to profit from the presence of Roman armies around the Mediterranean. Despite the reticence of the literary sources, and the ambiguity of attitude among the Roman upper classes which is itself responsible for that reticence, there are clear indications of investment by members of the senatorial order in

---

[15] *Deditio*: see above p. 158 and below Appendix v. *Tabula Contrebiensis*: above pp. 164–5.

[16] For instance, the embassy of the Saguntines in 205; the embassies of 171; and the embassy of the Belli, Titthi and Arevaci in 151.

[17] C. H. Haring, *The Spanish empire in America* (New York 1947) 317–30; B. W. Diffie and G. D. Winius, *Foundations of the Portuguese empire 1415–1580* (Minneapolis/Oxford 1977) 316–17; J. Serrão, *Dicionário de História de Portugal* (Lisbon, 1963–71) III, 64–8.

commercial enterprise.[18] However, as has been seen in the case of the Spanish provinces, there is no more action from the senate to promote such activity than in any other aspect of the creation of those provinces. The mines certainly had some form of fiscal levy imposed upon them, but there is no indication in that case or, for example, in the case of villa-settlement in Catalonia, that there was any encouragement or supervision of the individuals undertaking such enterprises. Indeed, if the comparison is made with military and diplomatic activity, it is from the holder of the *provincia* rather than from Rome that assistance or control might be expected.

The pattern which this suggests is not one of a senatorial policy of the exploitation and organisation of overseas possessions, but rather of local developments, stemming from decisions taken in Rome about the placing of Roman armies and their commanders. To borrow a concept from historians of modern empires, it is a picture of 'peripheral imperialism'. To quote from D. K. Fieldhouse, writing of the period 1870–1945:

> 'It was an almost invariable rule that those Europeans sent to take control of new colonies felt that their own reputations and careers would be enhanced by success in expanding the effective authority of their parent state. Soldiers, in particular, could hope for promotion only if they could demonstrate their ability and bravery. Their activities were often unauthorized or even forbidden by the authorities in Europe, but their achievements were irreversible. To a large extent the character of the modern colonial empires was formed by 'the men on the spot', for personal motives.[19]

This could almost be a description of the way in which Roman Spain emerged from the *provincia* allotted to Publius Scipio in 218 BC. Repeatedly the decisions which were to prove crucial to the eventual shape of the Spanish provinces were taken by the men to whom the task had been entrusted of commanding the armed forces which the senate had sent to the peninsula. Inevitably, because of the independence of action which was given to and expected of a holder of *imperium*, and the physical

[18] Discussed by G. Clemente, 'Lo sviluppo degli atteggiamenti economici della classe dirigente fra il III e il II sec. a.C.', in W. V. Harris (ed.), *The imperialism of mid-republican Rome* (Papers and monographs of the American Academy in Rome 29, 1984) 165–83. On the same topic see the contributions of D. Musti and E. S. Gruen to the same volume, and the discussion of those papers, especially by J. Linderski, E. Gabba and F. Coarelli. Also I. Shatzman, *Senatorial wealth and Roman politics* (Brussels 1975); Harris, *War and imperialism* 54–104.

[19] D. K. Fieldhouse, *Colonialism 1870–1945* (London 1981) 23.

distance between Rome and Spain, these decisions were not and could not be made by the senate. Imperialism in the second century, just as much as in the period of Caesar and Pompey, was the product of individual initiative *in situ*.

There is another curiosity about the remarkable expansion of Roman power in the second century which becomes less perplexing once the nature of the *provincia* is understood. So long as the assignment of a *provincia* is seen as a territorial claim on the area in which it is situated, there appears to be an anomaly between Roman policy in the east, where there was no 'annexed territory' in this sense until *c.* 148, and the west, where Sicily, Sardinia/Corsica and Spain were 'annexed'. The question of 'annexation' or the lack of it lies at the root of the recent debate on the nature of Roman imperialism. Supporters of Mommsen's view, that Roman expansion was the result of the necessity of self-protection against external threats, real or imagined, stress this apparent reluctance to acquire territory as evidence of a fundamentally defensive attitude.[20] Their opponents argue that annexation was the normal and natural outcome of Roman aggression, and was only delayed on occasion because some greater advantage could be gained by so doing.[21]

In the case of the Spanish *provinciae*, however, the language of annexation or non-annexation hardly seems appropriate. The first sending of Publius Scipio was not a territorial claim, even though in some sense the very presence of a Roman army might be held to violate the autonomy of the Spanish tribes, through whose lands it moved. Once an army and a commander were in the peninsula, once *provinciae* were located there, it is very difficult indeed to determine at what point any decision to annex the area was made. For a long period fiscal exploitation and civilian administration were rudimentary, even compared with that of other states in the Mediterranean world, and seem to have been of little or no concern to the senate in Rome. Although there can be no doubt that, by the time of Sulla, Spain had become an integral part of the Roman empire, this had come about gradually, and as a consequence of the Roman military presence, rather than as a deliberate and specific act of policy.

The assignment of a *provincia* marked out an area of military responsibility, and as such was not an act of annexation but an act of war. Following Clausewitz' famous dictum that war is merely an extension of policy by other means,[22] it may be seen that what the Romans were doing

---

[20] See above, Ch. 1, n. 4. [21] So Harris, *War and imperialism* esp. Ch. 4.
[22] K. von Clausewitz, *Vom Kriege* Ch. 1, Sect. 24: 'Der Krieg ist ein blosse Fortsetzung der Politik mit andern Mitteln.'

in Spain was essentially the same as what they were doing in the Greek east, that is using all means available to ensure that the peoples of the Mediterranean did what the Romans wanted them to do. To Polybius at least this is precisely what *archē* (empire) meant, but it was a very different conception of empire from that of the ever-present control administered by proconsuls and *legati Augusti* in the first century A.D.[23] The difference between the treatment of Macedonia and Spain was that, in the opinion of the senate, the latter required constant warfare in order to achieve this end, whereas the former could be controlled by a combination of continuous diplomacy and occasional open war.[24] Consequently in the case of Macedonia, as with the rest of the eastern Mediterranean, the senate was deeply involved in receiving and making decisions about a never-ending stream of embassies from the kings and cities of the Greek world through the first half of the second century, while they had relatively little to do with Spain. In both areas, they seem intent on maintaining control, to which end both diplomacy and war were appropriate means. The assignment of a *provincia* was a part of implementing such a foreign policy.

The common purpose behind these two patterns of imperialism, eastern and western, can be seen most easily by comparing the situation in Spain with that of the one region in the west in which something like the eastern pattern was used. The coastal strip of southern France, between the Pyrenees and the Alps, was clearly of strategic importance to the Romans, both because of the land-route to Spain, and because of the access to northern Italy through the Alpine passes. Moreover the Greek colony of Massilia (modern Marseilles) provided a major trading link with the hinterland, for goods moving in both directions.[25] However, with the exception of military action against Ligurian tribes at the eastern end of the strip in 154, it was not until 125 that the Romans began to send commanders and armies to the area.[26] Significantly on both occasions, Roman intervention followed an appeal from Massilia. The reason for the comparatively slow arrival of the Romans in this crucial area, and the lack of any sign of 'provincial' organisation which followed it,[27] lies surely in the presence of Massilia itself, which could be used as

---

[23] P. S. Derow, 'Polybius, Rome and the east', *JRS* 69 (1979) 1–15; J. S. Richardson, 'Polybius' view of the Roman empire', *PBSR* 47 (1979) 1–11.

[24] Macedonia was a *provincia* from 209 to 206, from 200 to 194, from 171 to 167, and then not until 149 (see Broughton, *MRR* I, *sub annis*).

[25] G. Clemente, *I Romani nella Gallia meridionale* (Bologna 1974) 12–71; S. L. Dyson, *The creation of the Roman frontier* (Princeton 1985) 126–47; Ch. Ebel, *Transalpine Gaul* (Leiden 1976) 26–40.   [26] 154: Polybius 33.8.1–10.14. 125: Livy, *per.* 60; Vell. Pat. 2.6.4.

[27] Ch. Ebel [n. 25] 75–95.

a means of control, not unlike Rome's allies in the east. The absence of any comparable ally in Spain, especially in the critical situation created by Hannibal's invasion, made direct military activity the only practicable method of ensuring Roman control.

Both these methods, by which Rome sought to extend her power throughout the Mediterranean, brought financial, strategic and political advantages to the Roman state, which no doubt were of great interest to members of the Roman upper classes. Neither was in origin a form of annexation. Of the two, it might reasonably have been assumed in the middle of the second century, as Polybius did, that the eastern form was more significant for the growth of Roman power. Roman foreign policy continued for many years to be conducted through overseas 'friends and allies', whether within Roman military areas or beyond them; but it was those military areas, the *provinciae*, which were to develop to form the framework of the Roman empire. The permanent presence of Roman armed forces and the increased contact with and responsibilities for the inhabitants of the *provinciae* created the institutions of law, taxation and urban settlement which turned *provinciae* into provinces; and it was the west, and in particular Spain, which provided the conditions within which this gradual transformation took place, and which, in the period between the war with Hannibal and the dictatorship of Sulla, formed the matrix of the Roman empire.

Praetors and *provinciae* 197–195

The account in Livy of the Spanish provinces for the years 197 to 195 is confused in its allocation of magistrates to provinces, and the confusion is worse compounded by uncertainties in the geographical location of the activities which he ascribes to these men. Various attempts have been made recently to clarify the position, particularly by G. V. Sumner and by Robert Develin,[1] but, given the importance of these years in the development of the senate's attitude to the Spanish provinces, Livy's evidence will be examined first before considering either of these solutions.

The annual lists of *provinciae* and *imperia* which Livy provides, if taken by themselves, are clear enough.

Citerior	*Ulterior*
197 C. Sempronius Tuditanus	M. Helvius (Livy 32.28.2)
196 Q. Minucius Thermus	Q. Fabius Buteo (Livy 33.26.1)
195 M. Porcius Cato (consul)	Ap. Claudius Nero (Livy 33.43.5)
P. Manlius (praetor)	

However, various other pieces of information given by Livy seem to place Minucius in Ulterior rather than in Citerior. First he states that Helvius, who had been delayed in his province by a severe illness, and eventually returned to Rome in 195, celebrated an *ovatio* only two months before Minucius returned to a triumph; and that Minucius was Helvius' successor in the same *provincia*.[2] Secondly, when earlier in 195 Minucius wrote to tell of his victory, the battle is said to have taken place 'ad Turdam oppidum', a name which it is natural to connect with the Turdetani, of whom at least the greater part lived in Ulterior.[3] Lastly, although Minucius' successor is said to be P. Manlius, Manlius himself is reported, at the time of his second praetorship in 182, to have held Ulterior, rather than Citerior, during his first praetorship.[4]

It is not possible to reconcile these passages, but some of the discrepancies are explicable. The precise location of Turda is unknown, but it is certain that the senate believed it to be within his *provincia*, for, as Fraccaro pointed out long

[1] G. V. Sumner, 'Proconsuls and provinciae in Spain, 218/17–196/5 BC', *Arethusa* 3 (1970) 85–102; R. Develin, 'The Roman command structure in Spain', *Klio* 62 (1980) 355–67.

[2] Livy 34.10.6. Unfortunately both the *Fasti Triumphales Capitolini* and the *Fasti Urbisalvienses* have lacunae in their records of these celebrations.

[3] Livy 33.44.4; cf. Strabo 3.1.6 (p. 139), and above pp. 85–6. [4] Livy 34.17.1; 40.16.7.

Appendix I

ago, he could not have celebrated a triumph on his return, if he had won his victory in someone else's province.[5] As it happens, the case which best illustrates this principle is that of Helvius. Ap. Claudius Nero, on his arrival in Ulterior in 195, equipped Helvius, now restored to health, with a *praesidium* of 6,000 men to accompany him through Spain on his journey back to Rome. At the town of Iliturgi, Helvius met and defeated a large force of Celtiberians, whence he marched to Cato's camp, presumably at Emporion on the coast. On reaching Rome he was allowed to celebrate an *ovatio*, but was refused a triumph, 'quod alieno auspicio et in aliena provincia pugnasset'.[6] Unfortunately there are at least two towns in Spain called Iliturgi by the sources, one on the Baetis in Ulterior, the other in Citerior, south of the Ebro.[7] Livy's account suggests that Helvius' victory helped to make the area of Cato's camp safe from enemy attack. This together with the objection to his claim for a triumph, that the battle took place *in aliena provincia*, indicates that he was fighting in Citerior. This suggests that Helvius' province was Ulterior, and also that, if Minucius was indeed assigned to Citerior, that his battle 'ad Turdam' was believed to have taken place within his own *provincia*. It is quite likely that Minucius' report was in fact of a victory over the Turdetani, who were at this time in alliance with the Celtiberian tribes to the north of their own area.[8]

The difficulties posed by the reference to Minucius as Helvius' successor are twofold. First, according to the annual lists in Livy, C. Sempronius Tuditanus was in Citerior in 197; and secondly, it was Q. Fabius Buteo who was the praetor in Ulterior in 196. The first problem is more easily resolved, as Livy states that Tuditanus dies of wounds following the rout of his army.[9] In such circumstances Helvius will have taken responsibility for the area, even though it is most improbable that it was added to his *provincia* by the senate.[10] In this sense, Minucius was *de facto* Helvius' successor. It is not surprising therefore that Livy, recording the return of Helvius and Minucius to Rome within two months of one another should have omitted to mention Fabius Buteo, who took over Ulterior from Helvius. Sumner, unnecessarily disturbed by the lack of information about Fabius' tenure of his *provincia*, suggests that he died before leaving Rome. If this had happened, it is difficult to see why Ap. Nero, who was allotted the *provincia* in 195, should have been given command of the forces 'which Fabius had had'.[11] It is easier to suppose, with Develin, that the reason we hear little of Fabius is that he did little.[12]

---

[5] P. Fraccaro, *Opuscula* I (Pavia 1956) 224 n. 15 (originally published in *Studi storici per l'antichità classica* 3 (1910) 199 n. 15). [6] Livy 34.10.1–5.

[7] A. Schulten, *Hermes* 63 (1928) 297; Fraccaro [n. 5].

[8] Livy 34.17.1–4. [9] Livy 33.25.8–9; 33.42.5.

[10] Develin [n. 1] 365–7 assumes, in an attempt to save Livy's account intact, the Helvius' assumption of responsibility would have entailed that Tuditanus' area of command would have become part of his *provincia*. As the naming of *provinciae* was the senate's prerogative, Develin's argument cannot stand.

[11] Sumner [n. 1] 95–7. Livy 33.43.7: 'legionem quam Q. Fabius habuerat'.

[12] Develin [n. 1] 365–6.

The confusion over P. Manlius' *provinciae* in his two praetorships probably occurred for reasons similar to those which cause problems with Helvius. As Cato's lieutenant, Manlius was probably active in the Baetis valley, even though this was not part of his *provincia* of Citerior.[13] When in 182 he was assigned to Ulterior, this will be what was remembered of his previous experience in Spain.

The lists of *imperia* and *provinciae* which Livy gives for these years are probably accurate in their allotments of praetors to the two provinces in Spain; nor are there any grounds here for the deduction, made by Sumner, that the geographical division between the two did not exist, at least in the minds of the senators. The other information which Livy gives, although not entirely compatible with the lists, can be seen to confirm them, once it is recognised that the provincial boundaries were of far greater importance to those who assigned *provinciae* and triumphs in Rome than to the proconsuls fighting in Spain. That the boundaries were regarded seriously in Rome at this date is well illustrated by the charge that Helvius had fought 'alieno auspicio' and 'in aliena provincia'.[14] This allegation has caused some puzzlement, especially as Helvius is shown by a tiny fragment of the *Fasti Urbisalvienses* to have been *pro consule* when he celebrated his *ovatio* in 195.[15] If, as suggested above, he won his victory over the Celtiberians both with forces lent to him for his protection (but under the command of Ap. Nero), and in an area other than that assigned to him in 197, then the charge was well-founded. That it was made at all illustrates the importance for the senate of the limits of a commander's competence.

[13] Livy 34.17.1–4; 19.1.
[14] Livy 44.10.5.
[15] Degrassi, *Inscr. It.* XIII. 1, 338–9. Sumner [n. 1] 95; Develin [n. 1] 367, treats *alieno auspicio* and *in aliena provincia* as 'practically equivalent' (n. 88).

The chronology of the Spanish *provinciae* 155–133

	Citerior	Ulterior
155	?	(M'.) Manilius *pr.* 155
154	?	(L.) Calpurnius Piso (Caesoninus) *pr.* 154
153	Q. Fulvius Nobilior *cos.* 153	L. Mummius *pr.* 153
152	M. Claudius Marcellus *cos.* 152	M. Atilius (Serranus) *pr.* 152
151	L. Licinius Lucullus *cos.* 151	Ser. Sulpicius Galba *pr.* 151
150	L. Licinius Lucullus *cos.* 151	Ser. Sulpicius Galba *pr.* 151
149	?	?
148	?	?
147	?	?
146	?	C. Vetilius *pr.* 146
145	Claudius Unimanus *pr.* 145	C. Plautius *pr.* 145
	C. Laelius *pr.* 145	Q. Fabius Maximus Aemilianus *cos.* 145
144	C. Laelius or C. Nigidius *pr.* 145 or 144	Q. Fabius Maximus Aemilianus *cos.* 145
143	Q. Caecilius Metellus Macedonicus *cos.* 143	?Quinctius/Q. Pompeius ?*pr.* 143
142	Q. Caecilius Metellus Macedonicus *cos.* 143	?Quinctius/Q. Pompeius ?*pr.* 143
141	Q. Pom⁓ ⸳s. 141	Q. Fabius Maximus Servilianus *cos.* 142
140	Q. Pompeius *cos.* 141	Q. Servilius Caepio *cos.* 140
139	M. Popilius Laenas *cos.* 139	Q. Servilius Caepio *cos.* 140
138	M. Popilius Laenas *cos.* 139	D. Iunius Brutus *cos.* 138
137	C. Hostilius Mancinus *cos.* 137	D. Iunius Brutus *cos.* 138
	M. Aemilius Lepidus Porcina *cos.* 137	
136	L. Furius Philus *cos.* 136	D. Iunius Brutus *cos.* 138
135	Q. Calpurnius Piso *cos.* 135	D. Iunius Brutus *cos.* 138
134	P. Cornelius Scipio Aemilianus *cos.* 134	D. Iunius Brutus *cos.* 138
133	P. Cornelius Scipio Aemilianus *cos.* 134	D. Iunius Brutus *cos.* 138

Notes on particular chronological problems

(a) Manilius and Calpurnius Piso

These two men are mentioned only by Appian, in a passage which follows his account of events in Citerior from 153 to 150, and is followed by the narration of the war in Ulterior down to the death of Viriathus.[1] The language used by Appian and the fact that they are described as fighting against the Lusitanians indicate that they were praetors in Ulterior.[2] Counting back from the praetorship of Galba, which the Livian epitomator dates to 151, Manilius would have been in the province in 155 and Piso in 154.[3]

Simon, pointing out that Appian gives only one casualty figure for the campaigns of both men, argues that the two praetors were in Spain simultaneously, were assigned to the two provinces, but combined together to fight against the Lusitanians in 154.[4] It would be surprising if so substantial a defeat resulted in the sending of another praetor to Ulterior in 153, especially as it was in this year that the consul, Fulvius Nobilior, was assigned to Citerior to deal with the relatively minor difficulty at Segeda.[5] Appian is only giving a summary at this point of the position in Ulterior before the arrival of Mummius, and it is unwise to place too much reliance on his use of only one figure, which may represent a total of the men lost by both praetors, or may have appeared in the source he was using attached to just one or other of the two names, and simply been appended by him to his account of both.[6]

(b) The chronology of both provinciae 148–143

After his account of Galba's outrages against the Lusitanians, and subsequent events in Rome, Appian describes the war against Viriathus as beginning 'not much later'. This unhelpful phrase can elsewhere mean a matter of a few days or as much as fifteen years.[7] He then records three commanders, C. Vetilius, C. Plautius and Q. Fabius Maximus Aemilianus.[8] Fabius was consul in 145 and seems to have arrived in Spain in that year. This is confirmed by a story in Valerius Maximus in which Scipio Aemilianus objects to either of the consuls of 144 being sent to Spain. This must have been at the allocation of *provinciae*

---

[1] Appian, *Ib.* 56.234. On the division of Appian's account by provinces, see Simon, *Roms Kriege* 13 n. 6 and 79 n. 6.

[2] Appian calls them τοὺς στρατηγοῦντας [*sc.* τῶν Ῥωμαίων].

[3] Livy, *per.* 48. So D. Wilsdorf, *Fasti Hispaniarum provinciarum* (Leipzig 1878) 95–6; Broughton, *MRR* I, 488, 450 and 451 n. 1.

[4] Simon, *Roms Kriege* 13 n. 6.

[5] Above pp. 132–4.

[6] L. Castiglioni, *Descisa forficibus* (Milan 1959) 52–3 would read ⟨ἐς⟩ ἑξακισχιλίους, which might indicate an overall total, but the parallels on which his argument is based undoubtedly refer to single instances.

[7] Appian, *Ib.* 61.256: οὐ πολύ...ὕστερον. Compare Appian *Ib.* 49.210, where Scipio in 151 is described as capturing Carthage and Numantia 'not much later'.

[8] Appian, *Ib.* 61.256–66.282.

early in the year, and is best understood as an attempt to replace Fabius, rather than to frustrate his being sent for the first time. Appian gives him two winters in his province, and these were probably 145/4 and 144/3.[9]

Livy seems to have placed Vetilius' period in Ulterior in 146, and Orosius, who was probably drawing on the Livian tradition, states that the troubles with Viriathus, of which the first was the defeat of 'Vecilius', began in the same year as the sack of Corinth, that is 146.[10] Simon argues that this must be incorrect because Polybius, reporting the embassy of Sex. Iulius Caesar to the Achaeans at Aegion in 147, says that the latter believed the Romans were occupied not only with the war against Carthage but also with affairs in Spain. This, according to Simon, cannot refer to the Celtiberians, with whom there was peace at this time, and therefore implies that the Lusitanian war had already begun before this date.[11] This is not, however, decisive for the dating of Vetilius' praetorship. It is probable that here, as in a similar passager earlier in his work in which he discusses the factors that persuaded Demetrius of Pharos to ignore Roman wishes in 220, Polybius is talking about the general situation rather than any specific incident.[12] In any case it appears from Appian that there had been disturbances of some sort before Vetilius' arrival, and the Oxyrhyncus epitome of Livy notes under the year 147 the repression of a Lusitanian uprising.[13]

If the dating given by Livy and Orosius for the governorship of Vetilius is correct, his successor, Plautius, must have been in Ulterior in the same year in which the consul, Fabius Aemilianus, arrived there, that is 145. Plautius is said by Appian to have gone into winter-quarters at midsummer after his defeat by Viriathus, while Fabius managed to do no more in his first year, before withdrawing for the winter, than train his forces. This would be expected if he had been sent out to replace the praetor after a serious deterioration of the position in Ulterior, which is indeed suggested by the Livian epitomator's note.[14]

One other piece of information given by the sources which might help to fix the chronology of the early years of the Viriathic war is its total length. Unfortunately there seem to have been at least three separate traditions. Appian records a duration of 8 years, which would accord with a war that started in 146 and ended in 139; Velleius and Justin give the length as 10 years, while Livy, as reported by the epitomator and followed by Florus and Orosius, gives 14.[15] It is possible to explain these different figures by relating them to different

---

[9] Livy, *per Oxy.* 151, *per.* 52; Val. Max. 6.4.2 (cf. Astin, *Scipio Aemilianus* 103–4); Appian, *Ib.* 65.278.

[10] Livy, *per.* 52 (with the praenomen 'Marcus'); Orosius 5.4.1–2.

[11] Polybius 38.10.10; Simon, *Roms Kriege* 76; Walbank, *Commentary* III, 701–2.

[12] Polybius 3.16.2, where Demetrius is represented as believing that the Romans were occupied with the Gauls and Carthaginians (cf. Walbank, *Commentary* I, 325).

[13] Appian, *Ib.* 61.256–7; Livy, *per. Oxy.* 136. Astin, *Scipio Aemilianus* 343–4, for reasons which are not clear, favours 146 as the year for Plautius.

[14] Appian, *Ib.* 64.271, 65.275–7; Livy, *per.* 52 (quoted above, Ch. 6 n. 32).

[15] Appian, *Ib.* 71.319 (and 63.265, with Schweighaeuser's emendation: the MS gives τρια!); Vell. Pat. 2.90.3; Justin 44.2.7; Livy, *per.* 54; Florus 1.33.15; Orosius 5.4.14.

starting-points for the war – thus 153/2 might count as the outbreak of serious warfare, and 150/49 as the breaking of his oath by Galba, which led to Viriathus' assumption of the command, with the ten-year period being a rounding-up (or down) of one of these figures.[16] This is hardly satisfactory, as all the sources claim to be describing the same period, that in which the Lusitanians successfully fought against the Romans under the leadership of Viriathus. Indeed one other author, Diodorus, gives yet another figure for the time the Lusitanians were led by Viriathus, rather than fighting under him, that of eleven years, and this could reasonably be counted from the date of their escape from Galba after the latter's treachery in 150/49[17] It seems likely that the source used for the description of Viriathus' character, which seems to be distinct from that used for the narrative of the war, contained a wrong figure, and that Appian either used a different source, or altered the number to fit his own account.[18] In either case, it would be unwise to rely on these various estimates of the length of Viriathus' career to establish the *fasti* of the Roman commanders in Ulterior.

Although the outline given by Appian provides a continuous succession of magistrates in the province from 146 to 143, three other men are mentioned in other sources as having met Viriathus in the field in the early stages of his leadership. The best documented of these is C. Laelius, said by Cicero to have defeated Viriathus while praetor, an office which he held in 145.[19] Claudius Unimanus is said to have been defeated by Viriathus in a passage of Florus, who places this before the defeat of Viriathus by 'Fabius Maximus'. Florus, however, may well have conflated Fabius Aemilianus with Fabius Servilianus, since he gives as his successor Popilius, the consul of 139. Though Popilius was in Citerior, he may well have reached Spain not long after the departure of Servilianus. Orosius attributes a disaster very similar to that described by Florus to 'Claudius Unimammus', presumably the same man, and dates it after the defeat of Plautius and before the consulship of Ap. Claudius and Q. Caecilius Metellus in 143. The third man is mentioned in only one source, the *de viris illustribus*, which merely records that Viriathus overpowered the *imperator* Claudius Unimanus, and then C. Nigidius.[20]

The first question with regard to these three men is why, if they fought against Viriathus, they are not mentioned by Appian. The most likely explanation is that they were not in Ulterior. Appian's work, as previously noted, is subdivided by *provinciae*.[21] It is clear that Viriathus did not confine himself to one province, so that his activities are not best covered by this neat arrangement. Appian and other sources make it plain that he often wandered north, both to stir up others against the Romans,

[16] Simon, *Roms Kriege* 135 n. 68.
[17] Diodorus 33.21a.
[18] On the distinction between accounts of the war and those of the character of Viriathus, see Simon, *Roms Kriege* 135–8 n. 69.
[19] Cic. *de off.* 2.11.40. For the date of this praetorship, Cic. *de amicit.* 25.96.
[20] Claudius Unimanus: Florus 1.33.15; Orosius 5.4.3. Nigidius: *de vir. ill.* 71.1. Cf. Astin, *Scipio Aemilianus* 344.   [21] Above p. 126 and n. 2.

Appendix II

and in the course of his own campaigning.[22] It is probable therefore that the exploits of Laelius, Claudius Unimanus and Nigidius took place in Citerior. If so, a *terminus ante quem* for their commands there, assuming them to all have been praetorian governors, is given by the consulship of Q. Metellus Macedonicus in 143. This marks the beginning not only of Appian's relation of events in Citerior, but also of the sequence of consular commanders, which continues down to the fall of Numantia in 133, six years after the death of Viriathus. Although it is possible that a praetor was assigned to the area as well as a consul, as had happened during Cato's tenure of Citerior in 195/4, there is no indication that this pattern was followed at this time, or indeed ever, apart from the single instance in Cato's consulship.[23] The following chronology for the careers of these three men in Spain has therefore been adopted above.

(i) *Claudius Unimanus*

If Laelius was in Citerior in his praetorian year, and if Orosius is correct in placing Viriathus' defeat of Unimanus after that of Plautius, which seems to have taken place in the early summer of 145, then it is probable that Unimanus was beaten in the middle or latter part of the summer of 145, and came to the province as praetor in either 146 or 145. His replacement by Laelius late in the year would then be parallel to Plautius' being succeeded by the consul of 145, Q. Fabius Aemilianus.

(ii) *C. Laelius*

If he was sent out to replace Claudius Unimanus in late 145, this would appear to be part of a concerted attempt by the senate to restore the military position in both provinces. That he did not go out immediately is suggested by his leading the opposition to the bill of the tribune C. Licinius Crassus on the priesthoods, presumably before departing for Spain.[24] It is probable that, if he did not reach his *provincia* until late in 145, he remained there at least for the early months of the following year.

(iii) *C. Nigidius*

The only suggestion that Nigidius held *imperium* in Spain at all is the uncertain implication of the bare mention of his defeat in the *de viris illustribus*, where he is linked with Unimanus, who is described as an *imperator*.[25] Although this is not a source which inspires much confidence, it is difficult to see why even *de vir. ill.* should mention him if he were not involved in some way. Kornemann suggested that he was the unnamed lieutenant of Fabius Aemilianus, left in charge when the latter went to Cadiz late in 145, and defeated by Viriathus.[26] In this case, he probably did not hold *imperium*. However, it is likely that there

---

[22] Appian, *Ib.* 66.279–281, 76.322; Florus 1.33.15; Orosius 5.4.1–2. On the nature of the Lusitanian war, see above pp. 147–8.   [23] Above p. 79–94.   [24] Cic. *de amicit.* 25.96.
[25] *De vir. ill.* 71.1: [Viriathus] imperatorem Claudium Unimanum, dein C. Nigidium oppressit.
[26] Appian, *Ib.* 65.275–6. E. Kornemann, *Klio* beiheft 2 (1904) 99, followed by Astin, *Scipio Aemilianus* 344.

was a defeat of some kind in Citerior in 144, since the sending of the consul Q. Metellus Macedonicus would be more justified if it came after a disaster such as that attributed to Nigidius, rather than after the victory of Laelius, even though this may have been exaggerated by Cicero. Laelius' success is confirmed by a note in Appian, which must have come from his source, as it cannot be deduced from his own narrative, that Fabius Aemilianus' success against Viriathus in 144 was the second which the Romans achieved against the Lusitanian leader. If Nigidius is excluded as a commander with *imperium* in Citerior, it would still be possible to place Unimanus' tenure *after* that of Laelius, so that the sending of Metellus resulted from *his* defeat. This solution would, however, cause difficulties for Kornemann's hypothesis, as it would ignore the clear chronological relationship of Unimanus and Nigidius in *de vir. ill.*, the only source to mention the latter at all.

(c) The governors of Ulterior 143–141

The *fasti* of these years are beset by problems with the text of Appian's *Ibērikē*, the textual tradition of which depends on one manuscript alone, Vaticanus gr. 141. According to this, Fabius Maximus Aemilianus, after his second year in Ulterior (i.e. 144), was replaced by a praetor called Κοΐντιος, who was himself replaced in the following year by Fabius Servilianus.[27] The matter is complicated by the appearance shortly after this in the text of a short passage in the middle of Appian's account of Servilianus which refers to Q. Pompeius, son of Aulus, and to Maximus Aemilianus (68.291). This is clearly out of place, and Schweighaeuser suggested that it should be transferred to the end of 65.278, where, after some emendation, it would identify the 'Quintius' of the following section with Q. Pompeius. Schweighaeuser pointed out that the words καὶ ἐχείμαϑε occur at both 65.278 and 68.291, and ascribes the error not to Appian but to the copyists.[28]

Among recent scholars, this proposal has received little support,[29] but it is confirmed by the evidence of an alternative tradition to that of Vaticanus gr. 141, which has not been previously isolated and is now only represented, so far as I can discover, by two early translations. One of these, a Latin translation by Caelius Secundus Curio, published by Froben in Basle in 1554, has long been known. The other, in Italian and appended to the Aldine edition of Alessandro Braccio's version of Appian published in Venice in 1545, is certainly the Italian translation by 'Manutius', of which Mendelssohn had heard, but which he was unable to trace.[30] Both these translations appeared before the publication of the

[27] Appian, *Ib.* 66.281–67.283.
[28] J. Schweighaeuser, *Appiani Historiae Romanae* (Leipzig 1785) 3.282 and 286–9.
[29] Simon, *Roms Kriege* 82–6; Astin, *Historia* 13 (1964) 246 n. 4. Viereck and Roos, in the Teubner edition of Appian (ed. ster., with additional notes by E. Gabba, Leipzig 1962) 111 and 113, simply bracket the intrusive passage at 68.291.
[30] L. Mendelssohn's Teubner text of Appian, Vol. 1 (Leipzig 1879) xi. On the Latin and Italian translations of Appian, see E. Gabba, *Appiani bellorum civilium liber primus*[2] (Florence 1967) xxxix–xli.

editio princeps of the *Ibērikē* by H. Stephanus in 1557. This is not the place for a full investigation of the relationship between this tradition and that of Vaticanus gr. 141, but it is clear, as Viereck and Roos saw for Curio's version, that they are taken from some other source, whereas Stephanus used only the Vaticanus.[31] It is therefore worth noting that, although they do not indicate a lacuna at 65.278, both translators give the name Q. Pompeius where Vat. gr. 141 has Κοϊντίος at 66.281.[32]

Simon raises two other objections to Schweighaeuser's proposal. First, if Q. Pompeius were the successor to Fabius Aemilianus, it would have been difficult for him to have been back in Rome in time for the consular elections of 142, in which he was elected consul for the following year. Secondly, the reference to the relatively obscure Pompeius by his praenomen alone is unlike Appian's normal usage, and contrary to the principles he himself laid down in his *proemium*.[33] Neither of these objectives is decisive. There is no certainty about the exact date at which Servilianus reached his province, although he is not known to have undertaken any action in 142; and earlier in the *Ibērikē* Appian used praenomina for the various members of the Scipio family, once they have been identified by a fuller reference, as would be the case of Pompeius here, if Schweighaeuser's transposition is correct.[34] Moreover, if a defeat had been suffered by Pompeius in Ulterior in 143, this would explain a mysterious notice in a fragment of the historian Charax of Pergamum, that Quintus, the general of the Romans, was defeated by Viriathus in both Spains and made a treaty with him, which may be a confused reminiscence of both Pompeius' defeat by Viriathus and his notorious *foedus* with the Numantines.[35] On the other hand, if the passage at 68.291 is simply rejected as an inexplicable insertion into the text of Appian, then Quinctius will have been in Ulterior from early in 143, when he succeeded Fabius Aemilianus, until late in 142 or early in 141, when Fabius Aemilianus arrived.[36]

Simon's own reconstruction of these years is in fact different again. He believes that Quinctius was in Ulterior in 143, but was replaced by L. Caecilius Metellus, *cos.* 142, in the following year. This is based on an entry in the Oxyrhyncus epitome of Livy for the year 142, that the consul Metellus was harassed by the Lusitanians.[37] The obvious interpretation of this, adopted by Simon, raises

---

[31] Viereck and Roos [n. 29] ix and xiii.

[32] Curio, p. 477; Aldine translation, p. 26 verso.

[33] Simon, *Roms Kriege* 82–6. Cf. Appian, *proem.* 13.51ff.

[34] Publius and Cnaeus: Appian, *Ib.* 15.57–16.63. Lucius: 29.114.

[35] Charax, *FGH* 103 F27. For another interpretation of this fragment, see Simon, *Roms Kriege* 69–71.

[36] A. Schulten, *Neue Jahrbücher* 39–40 (1917) 222 and n. 2, places Pompeius in Ulterior and Quinctius in Citerior, fighting on 'Aphrodite's mountain', and wintering in Corduba, as Lucullus and Marcellus, both in charge of Citerior, had done before. Pompeius is then replaced by Servilianus, Quinctius by Metellus. This is difficult, for Appian elsewhere does not deal in detail with events in Citerior in a section about Ulterior (Simon, *Roms Kriege* 79 n. 6); and the Quinctius/Quintus replaced by Servilianus is the same man who fought on Aphrodite's mountain (Appian, *Ib.* 67.283).

[37] Livy, *per. Oxy.* 167; Simon, *Roms Kriege* 80–1, 118.

several problems.[38] To include L. Metellus in the list of commanders in Spain is to reject the account given by Appian, and supported by other sources, dependent on Livy, such as Orosius.[39] Further, if Metellus did go to Ulterior in 142, he would have been replaced either in that same year, or early the next, by Fabius Servilianus, his colleague as consul of 142. Such an event would be virtually unprecedented at this date, and when five years later the consul of 137, C. Hostilius Mancinus, was replaced by his colleague, M. Aemilius Lepidus Porcina, this was the immediate result of Mancinus' defeat and his ignominious conclusion of a treaty.[40] In the case of Metellus, there is nothing in the sources to suggest that he had been responsible for a major disaster, even if he was in Spain, for the little that is said of Ulterior indicates rather inconclusive fighting.[41]

It is difficult to believe that L. Metellus held Hispania Ulterior as his consular *provincia*, and the passage in the Oxyrhyncus epitome is better explained, as Astin has done, by assuming that 'procos' should be read for 'cos' as the description of Metellus, the reference being not to L. Metellus, but to Q. Metellus (*cos.* 143), who was in Citerior in 142 and might well in that capacity have fought with the Lusitanians.[42] This is confirmed by a comparison of the Oxyrhyncus epitome with the fuller Livian epitome found in the manuscripts. The relevant fragment of the former begins with a description of Q. Occius' duel with Tyresius (or 'Pyresius') while serving with Q. Metellus in Citerior, continues with the notice about the harassment of 'Metellus cos.' and a reference to the return of L. Mummius with booty from Corinth, and ends the summary of book 53 with the consular date for 141 and Fabius Servilianus' initial success against Viriathus. The parallel passage in the latter records Q. Metellus' attack on the Celtiberians, follows with Fabius' action in Lusitania, and concludes the book with a reference to the Greek *annales* of Acilius. Although of course the manuscript epitome may have omitted a section in the original about L. Metellus in Ulterior, the comparison would suggest that the Oxyrhyncus sentence about 'Metellus cos.' is in fact a concluding remark about the activities of Q. Metellus.

If L. Metellus did not go to Spain at all, the best reconstruction of the *fasti* of Ulterior during these years is that the *provincia* was held by a praetorian governor, either Q. Pompeius or Quinctius, during 143 and 142, who was succeeded by Q. Fabius Servilianus, either late in 142 or early in 141.

[38] Best discussed by Astin [n. 29] 245–54.
[39] Orosius 5.4.8 and 12.
[40] See above p. 131.
[41] Apart from the remark in Livy, *per. Oxy.* 167, Obsequens 22 notes that in this year a Roman army 'adversus Viriathum dubie dimicavit'.
[42] Astin [n. 29] 245–54.

The chronology of the Spanish *provinciae* 133–81

	Citerior	*Ulterior*	*Unknown*
123			Q. Fabius Maximus (*pr.*)
123–122	?Q. Caecilius Metellus (*cos.* 123)		
114		C. Marius (*pr.* 115)	
113/112		L. Calpurnius Piso Frugi (*pr.* 113 or 112)	
111		Ser. Sulpicius Galba (*pr.* prob. 111)	
109–107		Q. Servilius Caepio (*pr.* 109)	
104		L. Caesius C. f.	
c. 102			M. Marius (*?pr.*)
c. 100–98		L. Cornelius Dolabella (pr. ?100)	
c. 98			C. Coelius Caldus (*pr.*)
98–93	T. Didius (*cos.* 98)		
97–93		P. Licinius Crassus (*cos.* 97)	
93	C. Valerius Flaccus (*cos.* 93) returned to triumph ?81	P. Cornelius Scipio Nasica (*pr.* ?93)	

For the careers of these men, see above Chapter 7 pp. 157–60. On the chronology adopted in this table, the following should also be noted.

(1) C. Marius is said by Plutarch, *Marius* 6.1, to have gone to further Spain in the year after his praetorship. A. Passerini (*Ath.* 12 (1934) 17) rejects this account on the grounds that this pattern is post-Sullan. He also points out that the inclusion by Cicero of Marius in a list of those who held *provinciae* and purchased corn (*II Verr.* 3.90.209) does not necessarily refer to his tenure of a Spanish *provincia*; in addition, there is no mention of such a tenure in Marius' *elogium* (*II* 13.3.83). However, it is hard to believe that Plutarch invented Marius' time in Spain, and not all steps in a career are recorded in *elogia* (Broughton, *MRR* I, 535 n. 3).

(2) The first commanders in Spain mentioned by Appian, after his note about the ten commissioners sent after the fall of Numantia, are Calpurnius Piso and his successor Servius Galba (*Ib.* 99.429–30). Cicero also mentions Piso, telling the story of the public making of his gold ring in the forum at Corduba, and

recording that he was killed in his *provincia* (*II Verr.* 4.25.56). Galba was consul in 108, so 111 is the latest date for his praetorship under the *lex Villia*. If this is the date at which he went to Spain, Piso's tenure will have been from 113 or 112.

(3) Rufius Festus (*brev.* 5.1) says that D. Brutus suppressed the Lusitani, and that 'Sylla' was then sent out; and that the younger P. Scipio conquered the Celtiberians. This has been thought to be a reference to Silanus (i.e. M. Iunius Silanus, *cos.* 109, and probably praetor therefore in 113 or 112), who has been inserted into the praetors in Ulterior as a result (so Wilsdorf, *Fasti* 110 ('D. Iunius Silanus'); Münzer, *RE* x (1917) 1094, with some uncertainty; Broughton, *MRR* I, 535, 537 n. 2, 538). However, it has now been demonstrated by J. W. Eadie, *The breviarium of Festus* (London 1967) 37, that 'Sylla' is not a manuscript corruption for 'Silanus', and is probably a simple error on the part of Festus.

(4) L. Caesius C.f. is now attested by the *tabula Alcantarensis* as present in Ulterior in 104 (see below Appendix v). He is described as 'imperator', which suggests that he was *pro consule*, and had probably been praetor in 105.

(5) C. Coelius Caldus is known to have been in Spain only from a series of coins issued by a descendant of his in the 50s BC, one of which shows a *vexillum* with the letters 'HIS' (Crawford, *RRC* no. 437, 2a). If he was in Citerior (as Schulten, *FHA* IV, 149 and Broughton, *MRR* II, 3 n. 2), he must precede Didius, and his praetorship should be dated to 101, 100, or 99; if in Ulterior, he should be placed between Dolabella, who triumphed in January 98, and the arrival in Spain of P. Licinius Crassus.

The sources of Appian's *Ibērikē*, with special reference to the events of 152–151

In 1896 Ed. Schwartz, in what remains the best survey of the sources of Appian's histories,[1] remarked that for the period between the end of the second Punic war and the end of Polybius' histories Appian's account is so close to that of Polybius as to indicate a use of the latter by the former, either directly or through an intermediate source. A closer examination, he argued, revealed sufficient discrepancies to suggest that there was an intermediary, and Schwartz believed this to be an annalist of the Sullan period, but not Valerius Antias. The passages on which he based this analysis were *Lib.* 67.302–135.643, the fragments of the *Makedonikē*, *Syr.* 1.2–47.244 and *Mithr.* 2.3–7.23. He also added, though with less certainty, *Ib.* 39.158–60.255. The problems of this section of the *Ibērikē* and the identification of its sources were complicated by Livy's use of annalistic rather than Polybian material for his account of events in Spain. At any rate Appian does not seem to be using Livy or Livy's sources, as is shown by a comparison of their accounts of Ti. Gracchus in 180–179.[2]

In 1911 Adolf Schulten, in a discussion of the writings of Polybius and Poseidonius on the Iberians,[3] argued that the work of these two historians survived in the accounts of Appian and Diodorus respectively. He pointed out in particular the precision of Appian's placing and description of the camps with which Scipio surrounded Numantia, as revealed in his own excavations, and suggested that this could only have come from Polybius' monograph on the Numantine war.[4] There are, however, other possible explanations of Appian's accuracy. For instance, he may have gained the information from the memoirs of Rutilius Rufus, who was on Scipio's staff at the time, and is described by Appian himself as the historian of these events.[5] Further, there are some indications that Poseidonius used Rutilius, so that he might be the source of Appian's account.[6] To confuse matters further, Poseidonius, as Schulten himself points out, used Polybius to a considerable extent, so that it is difficult to determine how much of Appian's Polybian material comes directly from Polybius and how much from Appian.

[1] *RE* II, 219–22 (*s.v.* Appianus).
[2] Livy 40.39.1–40.15, 47.1–50.5; Appian, *Ib.* 43.175–44.183.
[3] *Hermes* 46 (1911) 568–607.
[4] Schulten [n. 3] 570–1. On Polybius' monograph: Cic. *ad fam.* 5.12.2; P. Pédech, *La Méthode historique de Polybe* (Paris 1964) 580.
[5] Appian, *Ib.* 88.382.
[6] H. Peter, *Historiarum Romanorum reliquiae* I² (Leipzig 1914) CCLX.

It is certain that some of Diodorus' information comes from Poseidonius. A passage on the Iberian silver mines, cited by Strabo from Poseidonius, contains many similarities to a similar account in Diodorus.[7] Both mention that a private individual could make a Euboeic talent of silver in three days; both claim that there was so much silver in Spain that during forest fires the metal boiled out of the ground; both report in this context the joke of Demetrius of Phaleron about the Attic mining contractors exploiting the mines at Laureion, which is also attributed by Athenaeus to Poseidonius.[8] However, if Diodorus does depend for his Spanish material on Poseidonius, then the apparently simple answer to the problem of Appian's source, that he was using Poseidonius, who himself used Polybius and probably Rutilius, will not solve the difficulty. In several places where an incident is related both by Diodorus and by Appian, there are discrepancies over names and details which show clearly that they are not both derived from the same source.[9]

Fortunately there is one place where a direct comparison can be made between Appian and Polybius. Polybius 35.2.1–4.14 (preserved in Constantine Porphyrogenitus' collection of excerpts on foreign embassies to the Romans) and Appian, *Ib.* 49.206–10, both contain accounts of the reception given at Rome to the envoys sent by Marcellus early in 151. As Simon notes, this is a key place for the examination of the relationship between Polybius and Appian, and he points out that despite the very great similarity between the two, there are important differences. Polybius treats Marcellus with much greater hostility, ascribing the difficulties over the levy in 151 as being caused by Marcellus' evident cowardice (35.4.14), while Appian, in so far as he adopts any position at all, seems to favour Marcellus' attempts to reach a settlement with the enemy. This Simon ascribes to Polybius' use of Scipio Aemilianus as a source, for Aemilianus was clearly supporting the demand of the consul Lucullus that the war should be continued. He therefore cites with approval the *dictum* of Schwartz that Appian's account is basically Polybian, with discrepancies introduced by an intermediary.[10]

All that Simon says is quite unexceptionable, and, so far as it goes, may well be true. However, neither he nor Schwartz have appreciated the extent of the differences between the two accounts, nor the significance of these differences. Thus Appian describes the background to the negotiations in terms of a move by Marcellus against the Nergobriges. It is only when they ask for terms that he insists that all the Arevaci, Belli and Titthi, against whom his predecessor Fulvius Nobilior, had been fighting, should also make peace.[11] Polybius states that *after* he had made peace with the tribes, he marched against the Lusitanians,

---

[7] Strabo 3.2.9 (pp. 146–7); Diodorus 5.35–7.   [8] Athenaeus 6.233e.

[9] Appian, *Ib.* 42.172–4, Diodorus 29.28; Appian, *Ib.* 44.180–45.185, Diodorus 31.39; Appian, *Ib.* 77.329, Diodorus 33.17.

[10] Simon, *Roms Kriege* 36–7 n. 41. On Scipio as Polybius' source, see M. Gelzer, *Sb. Heidelberg* 1956, 14–16 (= *Kleine Schriften* (Weisbaden 1964) 173–80); Walbank, *Commentary* I, 4.

[11] Appian, *Ib.* 48.204.

and, having taken the town of Erkobrika, wintered at Corduba.[12] Schweighaeuser emended Polybius to read 'Nerkobrika', and this emendation has found universal acceptance.[13] The difficulty with this identification of the towns in Appian and Polybius is that while Polybius' town is in or near Lusitania, and thus in the south of Spain (and, incidentally, in the *provincia Hispania ulterior*), Appian's Nergobriga is in or near the territory of the Arevaci (as is shown again in the events with follow the failure of the negotiations in Rome[14]) and thus in the valley of the Duero, and in Citerior.

Curiously the reaction of most modern scholars has been to posit the existence of two towns called Nergobriga, both attacked by Marcellus, and to identify one, that of Appian, with a town in the valley of the Jalón, probably on the site of the modern Calatorao, and a second, that of Polybius, in the province of Badajoz, in or near ancient Lusitania.[15] The methodology of these identifications is extremely unsound, for, as Schweighaeuser made plain in his note on the passage, the reason for emending the text of Polybius was the similarity of the two accounts of Marcellus' campaign. If in fact the two places are geographically distinct, two options are open. Either Schweighaeuser's emendation should be rejected, in which case Marcellus first used his attack on Nergobriga in order to achieve the peace negotiations, and then moved south to take a second town called Ercobrica;[16] or, as the similarity of the names would suggest, Schweighaeuser was right, the towns are one and the same, and either Polybius or Appian has misplaced it geographically. If Appian has made the mistake this is not merely an insignificant slip on his part, for the location of Nergobriga is of considerable importance for his account of the situation in Citerior immediately before the negotiations, and recurs in Marcellus' probably feigned attack on the Arevaci, which then led to the *deditio* of the three tribes.[17] Appian's version of the events surrounding the negotiations was clearly different from that of Polybius.

The details of the reception of the embassies in Rome reveal a still more remarkable divergence. One of the similarities which has attracted the attention of scholars is the mention that both authors made of the Roman practice of lodging embassies from friendly powers on the city side of the Tiber, while those hostile to Rome were kept on the far side. This detail of diplomatic protocol is mentioned by other writers referring to other similar occasions.[18] However, whereas Appian's two sets of embassies consist of the Belli, Titthi and Arevaci,

---

[12] Polybius 35.2.2.
[13] Vol. IV (Leipzig 1790) 659 and Vol. VIII.[1] (Leipzig 1794) 124.
[14] Appian, *Ib.* 50.213, where Nergobriga is a town of the Arevaci.
[15] A. Schulten, *RE* XVII, 54–5; Simon, *Roms Kriege* 32–5.
[16] A town called Ercavica in Lusitania seems to be too far north or too far west to be Polybius' town (see E. Hübner, *RE* VI, 397–8).
[17] Appian, *Ib.* 48.198–205, 50.211–14.
[18] Polybius 35.2.3–4; Appian, *Ib.* 49.207. Cf. Dio frs. 42.27, 79.1; Appian, *lib.* 31.13; Mommsen, *StR* III, 1152 n. 5. On Polybius and Appian, see Schulten, *FHA* IV, 19–20; Simon, *Roms Kriege* 36–7, n. 41.

who would be outside the city, and the representatives of 'certain indigenous peoples against whom the Arevaci had made war', who were within, Polybius' division is between 'those from the Belli and the Titthi, such as supported the Romans' and 'those from the Arevaci'.[19] This difference appears again when the two sides are introduced into the senate. In Polybius' version, the Belli and Titthi ask that the Roman troops should stay in Spain, that a consul should be sent out each year, and that they should be protected from the depredations of the Arevaci. In reply the Arevaci suggested that it was only by chance that they had been beaten at all, and that, though they were prepared to accept a fixed penalty, they demanded for the future a return to the agreement made with Ti. Gracchus.[20] Appian on the other hand represents one side as consisting of representatives of all three tribes, the other as unnamed natives of northern Spain.

One possible explanation of these two accounts might be that there was a division between those of the Belli and Titthi who supported Rome and those who sided with the Arevaci. Such a distinction would explain Polybius' description of the ambassadors who made the first speech in the senate as 'those of the Belli and Titthi who were allied to the Romans', on the assumption that there were some who were not so allied.[21] In this case Appian's unnamed natives would be the pro-Roman factions among those tribes. However, even if this expedient is adopted, it still does not explain Appian's account. Not only are the Belli and Titthi represented by him as the peoples who began the war with the Romans (an interpretation which is also found in Diodorus) and who then asked the Arevaci for assistance, but Marcellus' demand after his attack on Nergobriga was that all the Arevaci, Belli and Titthi should ask for terms.[22] Another explanation, adopted by Shuckburgh,[23] that the Belli and the Titthi became allies of Rome and that the Arevaci at least thought it worth asking for a truce, also presents problems. The argument of the former in Polybius' account is based upon the obligation of the Romans to protect their allies, and this surely implies more than a last-minute conversion.

The accounts of Appian and Polybius about this matter are inconsistent and irreconcilable. Moreover this implies that the two writers had fundamentally different pictures of the outbreak of the war and its conduct in the early years. No doubt this is in part due to Polybius' pro-Scipionic and thus pro-Lucullan attitude, which has already been noted in his attitude to Marcellus. The request of the envoys of the Belli and Titthi for a consul to be sent out each year to protect the allies is clearly an argument for sending Lucullus to succeed Marcellus, despite the claim of the latter to have ended the war. Whatever the reason for the discrepancy, it indicates a major difference between the accounts of Polybius and Appian.

[19] Appian, *Ib.* 48.205; Polybius 35.2.2–4.
[20] Polybius 35.2.6–15.   [21] Polybius 35.2.11.
[22] Appian, *Ib.* 44.180–45.185, 48.204; Diodorus 31.39.
[23] In his translation, *The histories of Polybius* (London 1889) II, 493.

Thus the simple distinction urged by Schulten between the Polybian account of Appian and the Poseidonian version of Diodorus requires considerable modification.[24] Appian, or Appian's source, is using Polybian material, as is shown by the similarities in the two passages examined above; but he is embodying it in a different framework, evident in the contrasting views on the outbreak and early stages of the Celtiberian war. Again, although Appian shows signs of some material shared with Diodorus, the discrepancies are too numerous to support the assumption that both are using Poseidonius exclusively. It may well be, as Schwartz suggested, that Appian is using an intermediary who drew on both Polybius and Poseidonius, but if that is so either Appian or his source has reused that material to present a coherent account different from either.

[24] Note also Appian's stress on the divine pretensions of Scipio Africanus (*Ib.* 23.88–9), which is unlikely to have come from Polybius (cf. Polybius 10.2.1–13).

The Tabula Alcantarensis

This bronze, the left-hand section of a tablet, and including the upper, lower and left edges, was discovered in the course of the excavation of a hill-top site known as Villavieja, near Alcántara, in the province of Caceres, on the southern side of the river Tagus towards the frontier with Portugal. It was first published by R. López Melero, J. L. Sánchez Abal and S. García Jiménez in *Gerión* 2 (1984) 265–323.

The bronze contains virtually the whole of the text of a record of the *deditio* of a people, whose name is partially lost at the break at the end of line 2, to L. Caesius, presumably the moneyer of 112 or 111 BC (Crawford, *RRC* no. 298), but previously unknown as a magistrate or pro-magistrate in Spain. It is unlikely that there was a second column of text, since the indenting of the names of the consuls in the first line suggests that the consul-date was centred with respect to the inscription as a whole; even if the word CONSVLIBUS appeared in full, the tablet would still be insufficiently wide for a further column.

The text which follows is based on the reading of the first editors, with supplements of my own.

1   C. Mario *vac* C. Flavio *vac* [cos
2 L. Caesio C. f. imperatore populus SEANOC[...se
3   dedit. L. Caesius C. f. imperator postquam[eos in deditionem
4   accepit ad consilium retolit quid eis im[perandum
5   censerent. De consili sententia imperav[it ut omnes
6   captivos, equos, equas quas cepisent [traderent. Haec
7   omnia dederunt. Deinde eos L. Caesius C.[f. imperator liberos
8   esse iussit. Agros et aedificia leges cete[ra omnia
9   quae sua fuissent pridie quam se dedid[erunt quae tum
10   extarent eis redidit dum populus[senatusque
11   Roomanus vellet; deque ea re eos[qui aderunt...
12   eire iussit *vac* legatos Cren[us (?)...f.
13   Arco Cantoni f. *vac*. legates [

l. 1   [COS should be read, as the only republican examples of the omission of 'consulibus' in a date are *tesserae nummulariae* (*ILLRP* 987–1063), and a solitary instance on a roof tile (*ILLRP* 1163).
l. 2   Last letter C, G, O or Q.

Appendix V

l. 3   or [DEDITIONEM; or [EOS IN FIDEM.

l. 4   The first editors suggested IM[PERARE.

l. 7   Cf. *ILLRP* 514, line 4.

l .10 Surely SENATVSQVE; cf. *ILLRP* 514, lines 6–7.

l .11 There should also be some indication of the destination of those whom Caesius ordered to go, to complete the sense.

l. 12 The syntax of LEGATOS is unclear, and may be an engraver's error, though the rest of the inscription shows no sign of such mistakes.

l. 13 Perhaps [ACTVM IN CASTRIS, and a date (cf. *ILLRP* 514, line 7).

Translation
In the consulship of C. Marius and C. Flavius. The people of SEANO... surrendered themselves to L. Caesius, son of Gaius, *imperator*. L. Caesius, son of Gaius, *imperator*, after he accepted their surrender, referred to his advisory council what demands they considered ought to be imposed upon them. On the advice of the council, he ordered that they hand over all captives, horses, mares which they had captured. All these they surrendered. Then L. Caesius, son of Gaius, *imperator*, ordered that they be free. He handed back to them such lands and buildings, laws and all other things which were theirs on the day before they surrendered, which were in existence at that date, for so long as it pleased the people and senate of Rome. With regard to this matter, he ordered those present to go..... Crenus, son of...and Arco, son of Cantonus, were the ambassadors.

Notes
The line length which I have used (maximum *c.* 49 letters) is several letter-spaces longer than that assumed by the original editors. There are two points at which such a line-length seems to be indicated: (a) at line 10, the supplement SENATVSQVE is surely inevitable, especially given the similar formulation in Aemilius Paullus' decree from Lascuta (*ILLRP* 514); (b) at line 7, the name and filiation of Caesius should be followed by IMPERATOR, as in lines 2 and 3. Furthermore, the supplements in lines 7 and 8 must establish the legal status of the *dediticii*, since without this it is not possible for them to be assigned their property, as happens in lines 8 to 10. Hence the alternatives to LIBEROS suggested by the original editors (SALVOS, IN FIDE, IN DICIONE or IN POTESTATE, p. 278) will not do. For the formula of the *deditio*, see above pp. 143–4.

It is possible that the supplement for line 11 should be ROMAM, in which case the legates listed here would have been sent to the senate to obtain confirmation of the *deditio*, or of the terms granted following the *deditio*. There is however no parallel for such an embassy, except in cases, such as that of Pompeius in 139 (above, p. 146), where an objection was raised.

The spelling of this document shows the variation in single and double consonants and vowels typical of the late second and early first century. The third declension dative singular in *e* (*imperatore*, l. 2) is found regularly in inscriptions of the earlier republic (Degrassi, *ILLRP* ii, p. 497), but is somewhat surprising at this date. The second declension nominative plural in -*es* (*legates*, l. 13) is frequent in later republican texts (Degrassi, *ibid.*).

Bibliography

The works included in this list are those cited in the footnotes, with the addition of some others which have been used in the preparation of this book, but are not so cited. Articles in Pauly–Wissowa have not been listed individually.

Afzelius, A. *Die römische Kriegsmacht* (Acta Jutlandica 17, Copenhagen 1944)
  'Zur Definition der römischen Nobilitat vor der Zeit Ciceros', *Classica et Mediaevalia* 7 (1945) 150–200
Albertini, E. *Les Divisions administratives d'Espagne romaine* (Paris 1923)
Almagro, M. *Las fuentes escritas referentes a Ampurias* (Barcelona 1951)
  Ampurias (2nd edition, Barcelona 1951)
  Origen y formacion del pueblo hispano (Barcelona 1954)
  Ampurias: history of the city and guide to the excavations (Barcelona 1956)
Amoros, J. 'Argentum oscense', *Numario Hispanico* 6 (1957) 51–71
Arribas, A. *The Iberians* (London n.d.)
Astin, A. E. 'The lex annalis before Sulla: I', *Latomus* 16 (1957) 588–613
  'The lex annalis before Sulla: II', *Latomus* 17 (1958) 49–64
  'The Roman commander in Hispania Ulterior in 142 BC', *Historia* 13 (1964) 245–54
  Scipio Aemilianus (Oxford 1967)
  'Saguntum and the origins of the second Punic war', *Latomus* 26 (1967) 577–96
  Cato the Censor (Oxford 1978)
Aymard, A. 'Polybe, Scipion et le titre de roi', *Revue du Nord* 36 (1954) 121–8
Badian, E. 'Notes on Roman policy in Illyria', *Papers of the British School at Rome* 20 (1952) 72–93
  'The prefect at Gades', *Classical Philology* 49 (1954) 250–2
  'Caepio and Norbanus', *Historia* 6 (1957) 318–46
  Foreign clientelae (264–70 BC) (Oxford 1958)
  'Mam. Scaurus cites precedent', *Classical Review* 72 (1958) 216–20
  Studies in Greek and Roman history (Oxford 1964)
  Roman imperialism in the late republic (Oxford 1968)
  T. Quinctius Flamininus (Cincinatti 1970)
  Publicans and sinners (Oxford 1972)
Balil, A. Report on a republican milestone, no. 4042, *Fasti Archeologici* 14 (1959) (1962)

Bibliography

'Notas sobre las baleares romanas', in *IX Congreso Nacional de Arqueològia* (Zaragoza 1966) 310–19

Balsdon, J. P. V. D. 'The history of the extortion court at Rome, 123–70 BC', *Papers of the British School at Rome* 14 (1938) 98–114

'Consular provinces under the late republic', *Journal of Roman Studies* 29 (1939) 58–73

Barbieri, G. 'Iaccetani, Lacetani e Laeetani', *Athenaeum* N.S. 21 (1943) 113–21

Bauman, R. *The 'crimen maiestatis' in the Roman republic and early principate* (Johannesburg 1967)

Beloch, K. J. 'Polybios' Quellen im dritten Buch', *Hermes* 50 (1915) 357–72

Beltrán Lloris, M. *Las anforas romanas en Espana* (Zaragoza 1970)

Beltrán, A. and Tovar, A. *Contrebia Belaisca I: el bronce de Botorrita* (Zaragoza 1982)

Bendala Galán, M. *La necropolis romana de Carmona* (*Sevilla*) (Seville 1976)

'Excavaciones en el cerro de los Palacios', in *Italica: actas de las primeras journadas sobre excavaciones en Italica* (Excavaciones arqueologicas en España 121, 1982) 29–73

Bernhardt, R. 'Die Entwicklung römischer Amici et Socii zu Civitates Liberae in Spanien', *Historia* 24 (1975) 411–24

Bickerman, E. J. *The chronology of the ancient world* (London 1968)

Birks, P., Rodger, A. and Richardson, J. S. 'Further aspects of the tabula Contrebiensis', *Journal of Roman Studies* 74 (1985) 45–73

Blanco, A. and La Chica, G. 'Die situ Iliturgis', *Archivo Español de Arqueológia* 33 (1960) 193–6

Blázquez, J. M. 'El impacto de la conquista de Hispania en Roma (154–83 a. C.)', *Klio* 41 (1963) 167–86

Article on the economy of Roman Spain under the republic, in *Historia de España* 11. 1 (2nd edition, Madrid 1982) 295–332

Boardman, J. *The Greeks overseas* (2nd edition, Harmondsworth 1973)

Bosch-Gimpera, P. *El poblamento antiguo y la formacion de los pueblos de España* (Mexico 1944)

Botsford, G. W. *The Roman assemblies* (New York 1909)

Braudel, F. *The Mediterranean and the Mediterranean world in the age of Philip II*, 2 vols. (2nd edition, London 1972)

Braun, F. *Die Entwicklung der spanischen Provinzialgrenzen* (Berlin 1909)

Briscoe, John *A commentary on Livy, books XXXI–XXXIII* (Oxford 1973)

A commentary on Livy, books XXXIV–XXXVII (Oxford 1981)

Broughton, T. R. S. *The magistrates of the Roman republic*, 2 vols. and supplement (New York 1951, 1952 and 1960)

Brunt, P. A. 'The equites in the late republic', in R. Seager (ed.), *The crisis of the Roman republic* (Cambridge 1962) 83–115

Italian manpower, 225 BC–AD 14 (Oxford 1971)

'Laus imperii', in P. A. Garnsey and C. R. Whittaker (eds.), *Imperialism in the ancient world* (Cambridge 1978) 158–91

Bibliography

Buckland, W. W. 'Civil proceedings against ex-magistrates in the republic', *Journal of Roman Studies* 27 (1927) 37–47

Calboli, G. M. *Porci Catonis oratio pro Rhodensibus* (Bologna 1978)

Carcopino, J. *Les Etapes de l'impérialisme romaine* (2nd edition, Paris 1961)

Cary, M. *The geographic background of Greek and Roman history* (Oxford 1949)

Castiglioni, L. *Descisa forficibus* (Milan 1959)

Cavaignac, E. *Histoire de l'antiquité*, 4 vols. (Paris 1913–20)

Cavaignac, E. 'A propos des monnaies de Tryphon: l'ambassade de Scipion', *Revue Numismatique* ser. 5 13 (1951) 131–8

Caven, B. *The Punic wars* (London 1980)

Chic Garcia, G. 'La actuacion politico-militar cartaginesa en la peninsula iberica entre les años 237 y 218', *Habis* 9 (1978) 233–42

Cichorius, C. *Römische Studien* (Berlin 1922)

Cimma, M. R. *Ricerche sulle societa di publicani* (Milan 1981)

Clemente, G. *I Romani nella Gallia meridionale* (Bologna 1974)

'Lo sviluppo degli atteggiamenti economici della classe dirigente fra il III e il II sec. a. C.', in W. V. Harris (ed.), *The imperialism of mid-republican Rome* (*Papers and monographs of the American Academy in Rome* 29, 1984) 165–83

Coarelli, F. 'La porta trionfale e la via dei trionfi' *Dialoghi di Archeologia* 2 (1968) 55–103

Combès, R. *Imperator* (Paris 1966)

Corzo Sanchez, R. 'La secunda guerra punica en la Betica', *Habis* 6 (1975) 213–40

'Organizacion de territorio y evolucion urbana en italica', in *Italica: actas de las primeras journadas sobre excavaciones en Italica* (Excavaciones arqueologicas en España 121, 1982) 299–319

Crawford, M. H. 'The financial organisation of republican Spain', *Numismatic Chronicle* 9 (1969) 79–93

Roman coin hoards (London 1969)

'Money and exchange in the Roman world', *Journal of Roman Studies* 60 (1970) 40–8

'Foedus and sponsio', *Papers of the British School at Rome* 41 (1973) 1–7

Roman republican coinage, 2 vols. (Cambridge 1974)

'Rome and the Greek world: economic relationships', *Economic History Review* 30 (1977) 42–52

Coinage and money under the Roman republic (London 1985)

Criniti, N. *L'epigrafe di Asculum di Gn. Pompeo Strabone* (Milan 1970)

Cuff, P. J. 'Polybius 3.30.3:a note', *Rivista storica dell' antichita* 3 (1973) 163–70

Cuyas Tolosa, J. 'Origines de la romana Baetulo', in *VII Congreso Nacional de Arqueológia* (Zaragoza 1962) 358–60

D'Ors, A. *Epigrafia juridica de la España romana* (Madrid 1953)

Bibliography

Dahlheim, Werner. *Struktur und Entwicklung des römischen Völkerrechts im dritten und zweiten jahrhundert v. Chr.* (Munich 1968)
Gewalt und Herrschaft: das provinziale Herrschaftssystem der römischen Republik (Berlin 1977)
Davies, O. *Roman mines in Europe* (Oxford 1935)
Degrassi, A. *Fasti consulares et triumphales (Inscriptiones Italiae* XIII.1, Rome 1947)
Scritti vari di antichità, Vol. 3 (Venezia/Trieste 1967)
Deman, A. 'La date julienne de *ILS* 15', *Latomus* 35 (1976) 805–7
Derow, P. S. 'The Roman calendar, 190–168 BC', *Phoenix* 27 (1973) 345–56
Derow, P. 'The Roman calendar, 218–191 BC', *Phoenix* 30 (1976) 265–81
'Polybius, Rome and the east', *Journal of Roman Studies* 69 (1979) 1–15
Develin, R. 'Tradition and development of triumphal regulations at Rome', *Klio* 60 (1978) 429–38
'The Roman command structure in Spain', *Klio* 62 (1980) 355–67
Diffie, B. W. and Winius, G. D. *Foundations of the Portuguese empire* (Minneapolis/Oxford 1977)
Dion, R. 'La problème des Cassiterides', *Latomus* 11 (1952) 306–14
Dorey, T. A. 'The treaty with Saguntum', *Humanitas* 11–12 (1959–60) 1–10
Droysen, H. 'Zu Polybius', *Rheinisches Museum* 30 (1875) 62–7
'Die polybianische Beschreibung der zweiten Schlacht bei Baecula, 548', *Rheinisches Museum* 30 (1875) 281–4
Dyson, S. L. 'The distribution of Roman republican family names in the Iberian peninsula', *Ancient Society* 11–12 (1980/81) 257–99
The creation of the Roman frontier (Princeton 1985)
Earl, D. C. '"Calpurnii Pisones" in the second century BC', *Athenaeum* N.S. 38 (1960) 283–98
Ebel, Ch. *Transalpine Gaul* (Leiden 1976)
Eckhel, J. M. *Doctrina nummorum*, 2 vols. (Vienna 1792–8)
Eder, W. *Das vorsullanische Repetundenverfahren* (Munich 1969)
Errington, R. M. 'Rome and Spain before the second Punic war', *Latomus* 29 (1970) 25–57
Etienne, R. *La Culte impériale dans la péninsule ibérique d'Auguste à Dioclétien* (Bibl. des écoles françaises d'Athènes et de Rome 191, 1958)
Fabre, G., Mayer, M. and Rodà, I. *Inscriptions romaines de Catalogne* I (Paris 1984)
Fatás, G. 'Sobre Suessetanos y Sedetanos', *Archivo Español de Arqueologia* 44 (1971) 109–25
Contrebia Belaisca II: Tabula Contrebiensis (Zaragoza 1980)
'Romanos y celtiberos citeriores en el siglo I a. C.', *Caesaraugusta* 53–4 (1981) 195–234
Ferguson, W. S. 'The lex Calpurnia of 149 BC', *Journal of Roman Studies* 11 (1921) 86–100

Bibliography

Ferrary, J.-L. 'Recherches sur la législation de Saturninus et de Glaucia', *Mélanges de l'école française de Rome (Antiquité)* 89 (1977) 619–60

Fieldhouse, D. K. *Colonialism 1870–1945* (London 1981)

Florez, E. *Medallas de las colonias, municipios y pueblos antiguos de España*, 3 vols. (Madrid 1757–73)

Fraccaro, P. *Opuscula*, 4 vols. (Pavia 1956–57)

Frantz, J. *Die Kriege der Scipionen in Spanien 536–548 a.u.c.* (Munich 1883)

Friedersdorff, F. *Livius et Polybius Scipionis rerum scriptores* (Göttingen 1869)

Gabba, E. 'Le origini della guerra sociale e la vita politica romana dopo l'89 a. C.', *Athenaeum* N.S. 32 (1954) 193–345

Appiani bellorum civilium liber primus (2nd edition, Florence 1967)

Republican Rome: the army and the allies (Oxford 1976)

Galsterer, Hartmut *Untersuchungen zum römischen Stadtwesen auf der iberischen Halbinsel* (Berlin 1971)

García y Bellido, A. *Fenicos y Carthaginenses en occidente* (Madrid 1942)

Hispania Graeca, 2 vols. (Barcelona 1948)

Gast, K. *Die zensorischen Bauberichte bei Livius und die röm. Bauinschriften* (Göttingen 1965)

Gauthier, P. 'L'Ebre et Sagonte: défense de Polybe', *Revue de Philologie* 42 (1968) 91–100

Gelzer, M. *Kleine Schriften*, 3 vols. (Wiesbaden 1964)

Giovannini, A. and Gryzbek, E. 'La lex de piratis persequendis', *Museum Helveticum* 35 (1978) 33–47

Gonzalez, J. 'Italica, municipium iuris Latini', *Mélanges de la Casa de Velasquez* 20 (1984) 17–44

Gotzfried, K. *Annalen der römischen Provinzen beider Spanien* (Erlangen 1907)

Griffin, M. 'The elder Seneca and Spain', *Journal of Roman Studies* 62 (1972) 257–81

Gruen, E. *Roman politics and the criminal courts* (Harvard 1968)

Gsell, S. *Histoire ancienne de l'Afrique du nord*, 4 vols. (Paris 1913–20)

Guadan y Lascaris, A. M. de. *Numismatica iberica e ibero-romana* (Madrid 1969)

La moneda iberica (Madrid 1980)

Guarducci, M. 'Hora Quirini', *Bulletino della Commissione archeologica communale di Roma* 64 (1936) 31–6

Guitart Duran, J. *Baetulo* (Monografias Badalonesas 1, Badalona 1976)

Gurt i Araceli Martin, J. M. (dir.) *L'arqueologia a Catalunya, avui* (Barcelona 1982)

Hampl, F. 'Zur Vorgeschichte des ersten und zweiten Punischen Krieges', in *ANRW* 1.1 (Berlin/New York 1972) 412–41

Haring, C. *The Spanish empire in America* (New York 1947)

Harris, W. V. *War and imperialism in republican Rome 327–70 BC* (Oxford 1979)

Hassall, M., Crawford, M. H. and Reynolds, J. 'Rome and the eastern provinces

Bibliography

at the end of the second century BC', *Journal of Roman Studies* 64 (1974) 195–220

Henderson, M. I. 'Julius Caesar and Latium in Spain', *Journal of Roman Studies* 32 (1942) 1–13

Heuss, A. *Die völkrechtlichen Grundlagen der röm. Aussenpolitik (Klio* Beiheft 31, 1933)

Hildebrandt, H. J. 'Die Römerlager von Numantia', *Madrider Mitteilungen* 20 (1979) 238–71

Hill, G. F. *Notes on the ancient coinage of Hispania Citerior* (New York 1931)

Holleaux, M. *Rome, la Grèce et les monarchies hellénistiques* (Paris 1921)

Horn, H. *Foederati* (Frankfurt-am-Main 1930)

Hoyos, B. D. 'Lex provinciae and governor's edict', *Antichthon* 7 (1973) 47–53

Hübner, E. 'Tarraco und seine Denkmäler', *Hermes* 1 (1866) 77–127
'Drei hispanische Völkerschaften', *Hermes* 1 (1866) 337–42
Monumenta linguae Ibericae (Berlin 1893)

Humbert, M. 'Libertas id est civitas', *Mélanges de l'école française de Rome* (Antiquité) 88 (1976) 221–42

Jashemski, W. F. *The origins and history of the proconsular and propraetorian imperium* (Chicago 1950)

Jones, A. H. M. *Criminal courts of the Roman republic and principate* (Oxford 1972)

Jumpertz, M. *Der römisch-karthaginische Krieg in Spanien 211–206* (Berlin 1892)

Kahrstedt, U. *Die Annalistik von Livius, B. XXXI–XLV* (Berlin 1913)
Geschichte der Karthager III (Berlin 1913)

Kajanto, I. *The Latin cognomina* (Helsinki 1965)

Kienast, D. *Cato der Zenzor* (Heidelberg 1954)
'Imperator', *Zeitschrift der Savigny-Stiftung (röm. Abt.)* 78 (1961) 403–21
'Entstehung und Aufbau des römischen Reiches', *Zeitschrift der Savigny-Stiftung (röm. Abt.)* 85 (1968) 330–67

Klein, J. *The Mesta: a study in Spanish economic history, 1273–1836* (Cambridge, Mass. 1920)

Klotz, A. 'Zu den Quellen der vierten und fünften Dekade des Livius', *Hermes* 50 (1915) 481–536
Appians Darstellung des zweiten punischen Krieg (Paderborn 1936)
Livius und seine Vorgänger (Berlin/Leipzig 1940–41)
'Studien zu Polybios', *Hermes* 80 (1952) 325–43

Knapp, R. C. *Aspects of the Roman experience in Iberia 206–100 BC* (Vallodolid 1977)
'The date and purpose of the Iberian denarii', *Numismatic Chronicle* 17 (1977) 1–18
'The origins of provincial prosopography in the west', *Ancient Society* 9 (1978) 187–222

Bibliography

'Cato in Spain', in C. Deroux (ed.), *Studies in Latin literature and Roman history* II (Brussels 1980) 21–54

Roman Corduba (California University Studies 30, 1983)

Kramer, F. J. 'Massiliote diplomacy before the second Punic war', *American Journal of Philology* 69 (1948) 1–26

Lange, L. *Römische Alterthümer*, 3 vols. (3rd edition, Berlin 1876–9)

Lazenby, J. F. *Hannibal's war* (Warminster 1978)

Lehmann, G. A. 'Polybios und die altere und zeitgenossische griechische Geschichtsschreibung', *Fondation Hardt Entretiens* 20 (1973) 175–82

Linderski, J. 'Si vis pacem, para bellum: concepts of defensive imperialism', in W. V. Harris (ed.), *The imperialism of mid-republican Rome, Papers and monographs of the American Academy in Rome* 29 (1984) 133–64

Lintott, A. W. 'What was the imperium Romanum?', *Greece and Rome* 28 (1981) 53–67

'The leges de repetundis and associate measures under the republic', *Zeitschrift der Savigny-Stiftung (röm. Abt.)* 98 (1981) 162–212

Lopez Melero, R., Sanchez Abal, J. L. and Garcia Jimenez, S. 'El bronce de Alcantara: una deditio del 104 a. C', *Gerión* 2 (1984) 265–323

Lovejoy, J. 'The tides of New Carthage', *Classical Philology* 67 (1972) 110–11

Luzon, J. M. *Excavaciones en Italica* (Excavaciones arqueologicas en España 78, 1973)

McDonald, A. H. Review of T.R.S. Broughton, *The magistrates of the Roman republic*, in *Journal of Roman Studies* 43 (1953) 142–5

Mackie, Nicola. Review of R. C. Knapp, *Aspects of the Roman experience in Iberia, 206–100 BC, Journal of Roman Studies* 71 (1981) 187

Local administration in Roman Spain (BAR International Series 172, 1983)

Malaquer de Motes, J. 'Los pueblos de la España celtica', in R. Menendez Pidal (ed.), *Historia de España* 1.3 (Madrid 1954) 5–194

Marchetti, P. 'La marche du calendrier romain de 203 à 190', *Antiquité Classique* 42 (1973) 473–96

'La marche du calendrier romain et la chronologie à l'époque de la bataille de Pydna', *Bulletin de Correspondance Hellénique* 100 (1976) 473–96

Marquardt, J. *Römische Staatsverwaltung*, 3 vols. (2nd edition, Leipzig 1881–85)

Martin Valls, R. 'La circulacion monetaria iberica', *Boletin de seminario de estudios des arte y arqueologia (Valladolid)* 32 (1966)

Martinez Gasquez, J. 'La sucesion de los magistrados romanos en Hispania en el ano 196 a.d. C.', *Pyrenae* 10 (1974) 173–9

Mata Carriazo, J. de. *Tartessos y El Carambolo* (Madrid 1973)

Meltzer, O. *Geschichte der Karthager*, 2 vols. (Berlin 1879–96)

Mendelssohn, L. *Appiani Historia Romana*, 2 vols. (Leipzig 1879–81)

Menendez Pidal, G. *Los caminos en la historia de España* (Madrid 1951)

Meyer, E. *Römischer Staat und Staatsgedanke* (3rd edition, Zurich 1964)

Meyer, Ed. *Kleine Schriften*, 2 vols. (Halle 1924)

Bibliography

Michels, A. K. *The calendar of the Roman republic* (Princeton 1967)

Mommsen, Th. *Die römische Chronologie bis auf Caesar* (2nd edition, Berlin 1852)
'Bemerkungen zum Decret des Paulus', *Hermes* 3 (1869) 261–7
Römisches Staatsrecht, 3 vols. (Leipzig 1887–9)
Römisches Strafrecht (Leipzig 1899)
Römische Geschichte, 3 vols. (11th edition, Berlin 1912–19)

Morales, Ambrosio de. *La coronica general de España*, 3 vols. (Alcala 1574–86)
Antiguedades de España (Alcala 1575)

Morgan, M. G. 'The Roman conquest of the Balearic Isles', *California Studies in Classical Antiquity* 2 (1969) 217–31

Münzer, F. *Römische Adelsparteien und Adelsfamilien* (Stuttgart 1920)

Musti, D. *Polibio e l'imperialismo romano* (Naples 1978)

Nissen, H. *Kritische Untersuchungen uber die Quellen der vierten und fünften Dekade der Livius* (Berlin 1863)

Nolla, J. M. 'Una produccio caracteristica: les amfores "DB"'. *Cypsela* 2 (1977) 201–30

Nostrand, J. J. van. 'Roman Spain', in T. Frank (ed.), *An economic survey of ancient Rome* III (Baltimore 1937)

Oliva Prat, M. 'Las fortificaciones de la cuidad preromana de Ullastret, Gerona, España', in *Atti de VI congresso int. delle scienze preistoriche e protoistoriche* (Rome 1966) III, 23–8
Ullastret: Guia de las excavaciones y su museo (Gerona 1967)

Pais, E. *Fasti triumphales populi Romani* (Rome 1920)

Pascual Guasch, R. 'Centros de produccion y difusion geografica en un tipo de anfora', in *VII Congreso Nacional de Arqueologia* (Zaragoza 1962) 334–45

Pedech, P. *La Méthode historique de Polybe* (Paris 1964)

Pellicer, M., Hurtado, V. and La Bandera, M. L. 'Corte estratigrafico de la Casa de Venus', in *Italica: actas de las primeras journadas sobre excavaciones en Italica* (Excavaciones arqueologicas in España 121, 1982) 29–73

Pena Gimeno, M. J. 'Apuntes y observaciones sobre las primeras fundaciones romanas en Hispania', *Estudios de la antiguedad* 1 (1984) 47–85

Perez Ballester, J. 'Ceramicas helenisticas del mediterraneo oriental en Cartagena', in *XVI Congreso Nacional de Arqueologia* (Zaragoza 1983) 519–32

Perl, G. *Kritische Untersuchungen zu Diodors römische Jahrzahlung* (Berlin 1957)

Peter, H. *Historicorum Romanorum Reliquiae*, 2 vols. (2nd and 1st editions, Leipzig 1914 and 1906)

Prevosti Monclús, M. *Cronologia i poblament a l'area rural de Baetulo* (Monografias Badalonesas 3, Badalona 1981)

Pritchard, R. T. 'Gaius Verres and the Sicilian farmers', *Historia* 20 (1971) 224–38

Reid, J. S. 'Problems of the second Punic war', *Journal of Roman Studies* 3 (1913) 197–204

Rich, J. W. *Declaring war in the Roman republic in the period of transmarine expansion* (Brussels 1976)

Richard, J. C. M. and Villaronga, L. 'Recherches sur les étalons monétaires en Espagne et en Gaule du sud antérieurement à l'époque d'Auguste', *Mélanges de la Casa de Velasquez* 9 (1973) 81–131

Richardson, J. S. 'The triumph, the praetors and the senate in the early second century BC', *Journal of Roman Studies* 65 (1975) 50–63
   'The Spanish mines and the development of provincial taxation in the second century BC', *Journal of Roman Studies* 66 (1976) 139–52
   'Ea quae fiunt in provinciis', *Journal of Roman Studies* 69 (1979) 156–61
   'Polybius' view of the Roman empire', *Papers of the British School at Rome* 47 (1979) 1–11
   'The tabula Contrebiensis', *Journal of Roman Studies* 73 (1983) 33–41

Rickard, T. A. 'The mining of the Romans in Spain', *Journal of Roman Studies* 18 (1928) 129–43

Robinson, E. S. G. 'Punic coins in Spain, and their bearing on the Roman republican series', in R. A. G. Carson and C. H. Sutherland (eds.), *Essays in Roman coinage presented to Harold Mattingly* (Oxford 1956) 34–53

Rögler, G. 'Die Lex Villia Annalis', *Klio* 40 (1962) 76–123

Rotondi, G. *Leges publicae populi Romani* (Milan 1912)

Rougé, J. 'La navigation hivernale sous l'empire romain', *Revue des Etudes Anciennes* 54 (1952) 316–25

Sanctis, G. de. *Storia dei romani*, 4 vols. (Turin/Florence 1907–64)

Saumagne, Ch. 'Une colonie latine d'affranchis: Carteia', *Revue Historique* 40 (1962) 135–52

Schlag, U. *Regnum in senatu* (Stuttgart 1968)

Schleussner, B. *Die Legaten der römischen Republik* (Munich 1978)

Schmitt, H. H. *Die Staatsverträge des Altertums*, vol. III (Munich 1969)

Schuckburgh, E. (tr.) *The histories of Polybius*, 2 vols. (London 1889)

Schulten, A. 'Polybius und Poseidonius über Iberien und die iberischen Kriege', *Hermes* 46 (1911) 568–607
   Numantia, 4 vols. (Munich 1914–29)
   'Viriatus', *Neue Jahrbücher* 39–40 (1917) 209–37
   'Iliturgi', *Hermes* 63 (1928) 288–301
   'Segeda' in *Homenagen a Martins Sarmento* (Guimaraes 1933) 373–5
   Fontes Hispaniae Antiquae III and IV (Barcelona 1935, 1937)
   Tartessos (2nd edition, Hamburg 1950)
   Iberische Landeskunde, 2 vols. (Strasbourg 1955 and 1957)

Schumpeter, J. A. *Imperialism and social classes* (Oxford 1951)

Schweighaeuser, J. *Appiani Historiae Romanae*, 3 vols. (Leipzig 1785)
   Polybii Historiae, 8 vols. (Leipzig 1789–95)

Scullard, H. H. *Scipio Africanus in the second Punic war* (Cambridge 1930)

Bibliography

Roman politics 220–150 BC (2nd edition, Oxford 1973)

Festivals and ceremonies of the Roman Republic (London 1981)

Szádeczky-Kardoss, S. 'Nouveau fragment de Polybe sur l'activité d'un proconsul romain, distributeur de terres en Hispanie', *Oikumene* I (1976) 99–107

Serrão, J. *Dicionário de História de Portugal*, 4 vols. (Lisbon 1963–71)

Shatzman, I. *Senatorial wealth and Roman politics* (Brussels 1975)

Sherwin-White, A. N. *The Roman citizenship* (2nd edition, Oxford 1973)

'The lex repetundarum and the political ideas of Gaius Gracchus', *Journal of Roman Studies* 72 (1982) 18–31

Simon, H. *Roms Kriege in Spanien 154–133 v. Chr.* (Frankfurt 1962)

Smith, R. E. *Service in the post-Marian army* (Manchester 1958)

Soltau, W. 'Zur Chronologie der hispanischen Feldzüge 212–206 v. Chr.', *Hermes* 26 (1891) 408–39

Spranger, P. P. 'Zu Lokalisierung der Stadt Castulo und das Saltus Castulonensis', *Historia* 7 (1958) 95–112

'Die Namengebung der römischen Provinz Hispania', *Madrider Mitteilungen* 1 (1960) 128–41

Strachan-Davidson, J. L. *Problems of the Roman criminal law*, 2 vols. (Oxford 1912)

Sumner, G. V. 'A new reading in the Fasti Capitolini', *Phoenix* 19 (1965) 95–101

'Roman policy in Spain before the Hannibalic war', *Harvard Studies in Classical Philology* 72 (1967) 204–46

'Proconsuls and provinciae in Spain 218/17–196/5 BC', *Arethusa* 3 (1970) 85–102

'Rome, Spain and the outbreak of the second Punic war', *Latomus* 31 (1972) 469–80

Sutherland, C. H. V. *The Romans in Spain* (London 1939)

Taracena, B. 'Los pueblos celtibericos', in R. Menendez Pidal (ed.), *Historia de España*, I.3 (Madrid 1954) 197–299

Tartessos y sus problemas (V Symposium internacional de prehistoria peninsular) (Barcelona 1969)

Täubler, E. *Imperium Romanum* I (Berlin 1913)

Taylor, L. R. 'The forerunners of the Gracchi', *Journal of Roman Studies* 52 (1962) 19–27

Tchernia, A. 'Italian wine in Gaul', in Garnsey, P., Hopkins, K. and Whittaker, C. R. (eds.), *Trade in the ancient economy* (London 1983) 85–104

Thiel, J. H. *A history of Roman sea-power before the second Punic war* (Amsterdam 1954)

Tovar, A. and Blázquez Martinez, J. M. 'Forschungsbericht zur Geschichte des röm. Hispanien', in *ANRW* II.3 (Berlin/New York 1975) 428–51

Toynbee, A. J. *Hannibal's legacy*, 2 vols. (Oxford 1965)

Tränkle, H. Review of A. H. MacDonald (ed.), *Titi Livi Ab urbe condita 31–35*, *Gnomon* 39 (1967) 365–80

Bibliography

Tyrell, R. Y. and Purser, L. C. *The correspondence of Cicero*, 7 vols. (2nd and 3rd editions, Dublin 1904–33)

Ukert, F. A. *Geographie der Griechen und Römer*, 3 vols. (Weimar 1819–46)

Vallejo, J. 'Questiones hispanicas en las fuentes griegas y latinas', *Emerita* 11 (1943) 142–79

Tito Livio libro XXI (Madrid 1946)

Venturini, C. *Studi sul 'crimen repetundarum' nell'età repubblicana* (Pisa 1979)

Veyne, P. 'Y-a-t-il eu un impérialisme romain?', *Mélanges de l'école française de Rome (Antiquité)* 87 (1975) 795–855

Vicent, A. 'Ultimos hallazgos romanos en Corduba', in *XII Congreso Nacional de Arqueologia* (Zaragoza 1973) 676–9

Viereck, P. and Roos, A. G. *Appiani Historia Romana* I (ed. ster., with notes by E Gabba, Leipzig 1962)

Vives y Escudero, A. *La moneda hispánica* (Madrid 1926)

Walbank, F. W. *A historical commentary on Polybius*, 3 vols. (Oxford 1957, 1967, 1979)

Walsh, P. G. *Livy, his historical aims and methods* (Cambridge 1961)

Warmington, B. H. *Carthage* (2nd edition, London 1969)

Way, Ruth and Simmons, Margaret. *A geography of Spain and Portugal* (London 1962)

Weissenborn, W. and Müller, H. J. *Titi Livi ab urbe condita libri* (Berlin 1880–1911)

Wiegels, R. 'Livius per 55 und die Grundung von Valentia', *Chiron* 4 (1974) 153–76

'Iliturgi und der "deductor" Ti. Sempronius Gracchus', *Madrider Mitteilungen* 23 (1982) 152–211

Wilken, U. 'Ein Sosylos-Fragment in der Würzburger Papyrussamlung', *Hermes* 41 (1906) 103–41

'Zu Sosylos' *Hermes* 42 (1907) 510–12

Willems, P. *Le Sénat de la république romaine*, 2 vols. (Louvain 1878, 1883)

Wilsdorf, D. *Fasti Hispaniarum provinciarum* (Leipzig 1878)

Wilson, A. J. N. *Emigration from Italy in the republican age of Rome* (Manchester 1966)

Wiseman, T. P. 'Roman republican road building', *Papers of the British School at Rome* 38 (1970) 122–35

Index

Index

215

Index

Index

praetor urbanus, 66, 67, 68, 165
proskynesis, 60
provincia, meaning of, 5–10, 31, 35, 55–7,
  64–7, 68, 74, 75–7, 80, 93–4, 97–8, 99–100,
  104, 123–5, 128, 134–7, 152–3, 154–5,
  168–71, 175–80
publicani, 39, 57–8, 91, 115, 121, 161
Pyrenees, 4, 49, 83, 96, 100, 123, 179
Pyrrhus of Epirus, 152

quaestio de repetundis, 114, 137–40, 164, 165,
  168
quaestor, 117, 121–2
Quinctius (? pr. 143), 184, 189–91
Quinctius, L. Crispinus (pr. 186), 99–100, 108
Quinctius, T. Flamininus (cos. 198), 87

recuperatores, 114
redemptores, 82, 93
relations with native communities, 58–61, 64,
  73–4, 88, 97–8, 102, 108, 124
reports to the senate, 38, 48, 50, 51, 78–9, 81,
  89–90, 96–7, 98–9, 100, 108–9, 130–1
Rhode, 3, 17–18, 81
road-building, 166–7
Rosas, see Rhode
Rufius Festus, 193

Sabines, 152
Saguntum, 3, 21–9, 39–40, 46, 54–5, 58,
  63–4, 73–4
Sahara, 172
Salluienses, 164–5, 173
Samnites, 152
Santiponce, see Italica
Sardinia, 8–9, 19, 37, 38, 67, 69, 76, 178
Schulten, A., 91, 194–8
Schumpeter, J. A., 2
Schwartz, Ed., 194–7
Schweighaeuser, J., 189
Scilly Islands, 159
Scribonius, L. Libo (tr. pl. 149), 138–40
Sedetani, 53, 68, 85
Sedetanus, ager, 72
Segeda, 113, 126, 129, 132–4, 141, 153, 185
Segestica, 84
Segontia, 87
Segura, see Tader, river
Sempronius, C. Gracchus (tr. pl. 123 and 122),
  5, 114, 160, 163, 167, 168
Sempronius, Ti. Gracchus (cos. 238), 8
Sempronius, Ti. Gracchus (cos. 177 and 163),
  100–3, 105, 107–9, 112–24, 133–4, 141–2,
  160, 170–1
Sempronius, Ti. Gracchus (tr. pl. 133), 156
Sempronius, P. Longus (pr. 184), 100, 105
Sempronius, Ti. Longus (cos. 194), 71

Sempronius, C. Tuditanus (pr. 197), 75, 78–9,
  90, 181–2
senate, 31–5, 43, 48–9, 55–61, 62, 64–5, 69–71,
  74–5, 93–4, 95, 96–7, 104, 108, 109–12,
  119–20, 123–5, 130, 132–7, 140–55, 156,
  161–2, 164, 166–8, 175–80
Sergius, M'. (procos. late 2nd century), 166–7
Sergius, C. Plautus (pr. 200), 69
Sertorius, Q. (pr. 83), 163
Servilius, Cn. Caepio (cos. 169), 103, 106
Servilius, Q. Caepio (cos. 140), 127, 131,
  147–8, 184
Servilius, Q. Caepio (cos. 106), 158, 192
Servilius, Cn. Geminus (cos. 217), 37
Servilius, C. Glaucia (pr. 100), 169
Sexi, 18, 79
Sicily, 7–9, 39, 69, 76, 96, 115, 157, 178
silver mines, 34, 88, 91, 93, 117, 120–3, 161,
  163, 174, 195
Simon, H. 185–91, 194–8
Sophoniba, 52
Sosinestani, 164–5
Spanish imperialism, 176
Statellates, 151
Stephanus of Byzantium, 77
Stertinius, L. (procos. 199–6), 69, 71, 75, 76
stipendium, 54, 57–8, 72, 92, 115–16, 122–3,
  160–1
Strabo, 16, 18, 85, 119, 161, 163
Sucro, river, 18, 53
Suessetani, 42, 53, 85, 100
Sulpicius, C. Galus (cos. 166), 114
Sulpicius, Ser. Galba (cos. 144), 126, 136, 137,
  138–40, 151
Sulpicius, Ser. Galba (pr. ? 111), 157, 192–3
Sumner, G. V., 76–7, 78
supplementa, 98, 100, 103, 104
supplies for Spain, 38–9, 42–3, 57–8, 88, 93
Syphax, 39, 52

Tader, river, 41
Tagus, river, 12, 149
Tarraco, 34, 37, 39, 46, 48, 51, 52, 61, 63, 83,
  101, 165
Tarraconensis, provincia, 3, 165
Tarragona, see Tarraco
Tartessos, 17
Terentius, P. Afer, 5
Terentius, A. Varro (pr. 184), 100
Termantia, 16, 158
Termesos, 158
Teutones, 158
Titinius, M. Curvus (pr. 178), 103, 106, 111,
  114
Titthi, 124, 130, 133, 141–3, 195–8
Toledo, see Toletum
Toletum, 47, 97, 99

217

Index